Health Care Accounting

Third Edition

Steven M. Bragg

AccountingTools®

Published by AccountingTools, Inc., Centennial, Colorado.

For more information about AccountingTools® products, visit our Web site at www.accountingtools.com.

ISBN-13: 978-1-64221-103-0

Printed in the United States of America

Table of Contents

Preface

There are many types of businesses within the health care field, including hospitals, clinics, hospice care providers, laboratories, nursing homes, and continuing care retirement communities – totaling more than three-quarters of a million organizations. These entities have unique accounting requirements that set them apart from the standard accounting practices used in most industries. In *Health Care Accounting*, we address the unique aspects of the accounting in this field, with a particular emphasis on the financial reporting by for-profit, not-for-profit, and governmental organizations.

The book is divided into three parts. In Chapters 1 through 4, we cover the underpinnings of health care accounting, including such topics as the system of accounting, not-for-profit accounting, and governmental accounting. In Chapters 5 through 10, we address many elements of the balance sheet, including cash, receivables, investments, fixed assets, current liabilities, and debt liabilities. In Chapters 11 through 16, we discuss more specific accounting issues, including revenue recognition, payroll, split-interest agreements, affiliated organizations, and management accounting.

You can find the answers to many questions about health care accounting in the following chapters, including:

- Which accounts are included in the chart of accounts for a health care entity?
- What information is included in the financial statements of a not-for-profit health care organization?
- How are health care receivables valued?
- What types of intangible assets may be recorded by a health care business?
- What payment methods are used by third-party payors?
- How can conduit financing be used to channel funds to a hospital?
- What special revenue recognition rules apply to health care organizations?
- Which forms are needed to submit payroll-related information to the government?
- What is the accounting for split-interest agreements?
- What are the financial statement disclosure requirements pertaining specifically to health care entities?

Health Care Accounting is designed for professionals and students, who can use it as a reference tool for recording health care accounting transactions and generating financial statements.

Centennial, Colorado
April 2023

About the Author

Steven Bragg, CPA, has been the chief financial officer or controller of four companies, as well as a consulting manager at Ernst & Young. He received a master's degree in finance from Bentley College, an MBA from Babson College, and a Bachelor's degree in Economics from the University of Maine. He has been a two-time president of the Colorado Mountain Club, and is an avid alpine skier, mountain biker, and certified master diver. Mr. Bragg resides in Centennial, Colorado. He has written more than 250 books and courses, including *New Controller Guidebook*, *GAAP Guidebook*, and *Payroll Management*.

Steven maintains the accountingtools.com web site, which contains continuing professional education courses, the Accounting Best Practices podcast, and thousands of articles on accounting subjects.

Chapter 1
Overview of the Health Care Entity

Introduction

The health care industry is one of the largest industries in the United States. As of 2018, there were more than 780,000 health care companies in the country, employing more than 16.8 million people.[1] These entities derive most of their revenue from the provision of health care services, or from the oversight of organizations that provide this type of care. There are many types of organizations within the industry, including the following:

- Clinics
- Continuing care retirement communities
- Drug and alcohol rehabilitation centers
- Emergency care facilities
- Health care maintenance organizations
- Home health agencies
- Hospice care providers
- Hospitals
- Individual practice associations
- Individual practitioners
- Laboratories
- Medical group practices
- Nursing homes
- Surgery centers

Health care is one of the most-examined industries in the country, for two reasons. First, there is a massive amount of venture capital funding targeted at this area. And second, its high costs are negatively impacting the general population, since health care expenditures now account for nearly 18% of the country's gross domestic product[2]. In the first case, the amount of funding invested means that the financial reporting system must be sufficiently detailed that investors can be properly informed of the results being generated. In the second case, a detailed cost reporting system is needed to assure third-party payors, the general population, and the government that costs are being controlled. A third concern that is more internal in nature is that organizations in the health care industry (notably hospitals) are having difficulty staying solvent, and so must have accurate financial information in order to better manage their operations.

---

[1] Source: U. S. Census Bureau
[2] Source: Centers for Medicare and Medicaid Services

In this chapter and the following chapters, we discuss the nature of the accounting system that is needed to record and report on the financial position and financial results of health care entities.

Types of Health Care Organizations

Health care organizations are usually classified as investor-owned entities or not-for-profit, business-oriented entities. The characteristics of these two variations, as well as a non-business-oriented organization, are as follows:

- *Investor-owned entities*. As the name implies, an investor-owned health care entity is owned by investors and provides goods or services with the intent of earning a profit.
- *Not-for-profit, business-oriented entities*. As indicated by its name, a not-for-profit, business-oriented health care entity does not have any ownership interests, and sustains itself largely from the fees it charges for goods and services. This type of organization is usually exempt from federal income taxes, and may also receive contributions from third parties.
- *Not-for-profit, non-business-oriented entities*. When a health care entity is not business-oriented, it is accounted for as a not-for-profit entity. See the author's *Nonprofit Accounting* book for more information.

In addition, governmental health care entities operate as special-purpose governments that are only engaged in business-type activities. These entities record their activities in enterprise funds and issue financial reports that are structured for enterprise funds. These entities may be part of a larger entity, such as a university or general-purpose government.

North American Industry Classification System Codes

The most precise definition of the health care industry is stated within the North American Industry Classification System (NAICS), which is used to classify business establishments within all industries. NAICS aggregates health care businesses into the Health Care and Social Assistance sector, which is grouped within NAICS Code 62. The definition used by the NAICS to describe Code 62 is:

> The Health Care and Social Assistance sector comprises establishments providing health care and social assistance for individuals. The sector includes both health care and social assistance because it is sometimes difficult to distinguish between the boundaries of these two activities. The industries in this sector are arranged on a continuum starting with those establishments providing medical care exclusively, continuing with those providing health care and social assistance, and finally finishing with those providing only social assistance. The services provided by establishments in this sector are delivered by trained professionals. All industries in the sector share this commonality of process, namely, labor inputs of health practitioners or social workers with the requisite expertise. Many of the industries in the sector are defined based on the educational degree held by the practitioners included in the industry.

There are a number of sub-codes within Code 62 that further define the industry, as noted in the following table.

NAICS Code 62 Definitions

NAICS Code	Title
621	**Ambulatory Health Care Services**
6211	Offices of Physicians
6212	Offices of Dentists
6213	Offices of Other Health Care Practitioners (including chiropractors, optometrists, mental health practitioners, podiatrists, and physical, occupational and speech therapists)
6214	Outpatient Care Centers (including family planning centers, outpatient mental health and substance abuse centers, HMO medical centers, kidney dialysis centers, and freestanding ambulatory surgical and emergency centers)
6215	Medical and Diagnostic Laboratories
6216	Home Health Care Services
6219	Other Ambulatory Health Care Services (including ambulance services and blood and organ banks)
622	**Hospitals**
6221	General Medical and Surgical Hospitals
6222	Psychiatric and Substance Abuse Hospitals and Specialty Hospitals
6223	Specialty Hospitals
623	**Nursing and Residential Care Facilities**
6231	Nursing Care Facilities
6232	Residential Intellectual and Developmental Disability, Mental Health, and Substance Abuse Facilities
6233	Continuing Care Retirement Communities and Assisted Living Facilities for the Elderly
6239	Other Residential Care Facilities
624	**Social Assistance**
6241	Individual and Family Services
6242	Community Food and Housing, and Emergency and Other Relief Services
6243	Vocational Rehabilitation Services
6244	Child Day Care Services

The accounting topics discussed in this book apply to any of the businesses noted in NAICS Code 62.

Applicable Accounting

A significant part of the accounting that applies to health care entities mirrors the standard accounting practices of other industries. For example, the accounting for cash, inventory, and expenses are generally the same. However, there are some key

differences that are unique to this industry, which are stated in Topic 954, *Health Care Entities*, of the Accounting Standards Codification. The Codification is the central repository of all information concerning generally accepted accounting principles (GAAP), which governs the accounting for most organizations operating within the United States. Topic 954 adds recording and reporting requirements to GAAP that are specific to health care entities, such as the reporting of certain types of commitments and the manner in which certain types of revenue can be recognized. In the following chapters, we describe all GAAP topics that are relevant to the accounting function of a health care entity, while making particular note of accounting standards that are specifically targeted at this industry.

Financial Reporting Requirements

The financial reporting requirements for investor-owned entities and not-for-profit, business-oriented organizations are the same, except for instances in which the reporting clearly does not apply to the health care entity classification. For example, a not-for-profit health care entity would not report any shareholders' equity, since it has no shareholders. Similarly, a for-profit entity would not have any grounds for reporting contributions, since it should not receive any.

The financial statements that the two main types of health care entities should present are noted in the following table.

Types of Financial Statements Used by Health Care Entities

Investor-Owned Entities	Not-for-Profit, Business-Oriented Entities
Balance sheet	Balance sheet
Income statement	Statement of operations and changes in net assets
Statement of cash flows	Statement of cash flows
Statement of changes in equity	Statement of changes in net assets
Notes to the financial statements	Notes to the financial statements

A special-purpose government that is engaged in business type activities should issue the following financial statements and related information:

- Statement of net position (similar to a balance sheet)
- Statement of revenues, expenses, and changes in net position (similar to an income statement)
- Statement of cash flows
- Notes to the financial statements
- Required supplementary information

In the following chapters, we will delve into the reporting that must be issued by each of these types of health care entities.

The Structure of this Book

Health Care Accounting begins in Chapter 2 with a review of the underpinnings of a generic accounting system, which includes the baseline reporting system that would be employed by a for-profit business. Topics include double entry accounting, journal entries, the chart of accounts, ledgers, and the accrual basis of accounting. In Chapters 3 and 4, the book then branches into the differing reporting requirements for not-for-profit and governmental organizations. At this point, the accountant should have a reasonable understanding of how an accounting system functions and the nature of the reports that it generates.

We then move to a discussion of the assets and liabilities found in an organization's balance sheet. This discussion is found in Chapters 5 through 10. These chapters address such topics as bank reconciliations, the periodic and perpetual inventory systems, physical counts, and cost layering, as well as fixed asset classifications, depreciation, and asset derecognition. If an organization has a significant fixed asset base, it may need to account for asset retirement obligations, which are addressed in Chapter 8. The focus of discussion then changes to liabilities in Chapters 9 and 10. The topics covered include the basic accounting entries for payables and accrued liabilities, as well as debt accounting entries, the amortization schedule, municipal bond financing, and how to reconcile the debt account.

In Chapters 11 and 12, the accounting focus shifts to items impacting the reported profit or loss of a business – specifically, the recognition of revenue and the processing of payroll. There used to be a number of rules related to revenue recognition in the health care industry, but many of these rules have been replaced by Topic 606 of the Accounting Standards Codification, *Revenue from Contracts with Customers*. We lay out the new revenue recognition process in Chapter 11, while also making note of those few revenue rules specific to health care that still survive. Chapter 12 goes into great depth regarding how payroll is compiled, including gross pay calculations, payroll tax calculations and remittances, and income tax withholdings.

Chapters 13 through 15 address topics that are more specifically targeted at not-for-profit health care entities, as well as a collection of minor recording, presentation, and reporting topics. Chapter 13 covers split-interest agreements, in which funds are contributed under an arrangement where both the donor and the not-for-profit retain an interest in the underlying assets and liabilities. Chapter 14 covers affiliated organizations, involving the relationships between different not-for-profit organizations and how these relationships are reported in a set of financial statements. Chapter 15 covers a broad range of smaller topics, including the treatment of advertising expenses, agency funds, prepaid health services, and health care entity disclosures.

Finally, Chapter 16 covers several aspects of management accounting in a health care environment, with a particular emphasis on the mechanics of full costing.

Summary

The accounting discussion in the following chapters can be used by all health care organizations, except in those cases where rules are specifically associated with a particular type of health care entity, such as a continuing care retirement community. The reader may want to gain a more in-depth understanding of certain accounting topics than can be found in this book. If so, consider one of the author's other accounting books and courses, such as *Nonprofit Accounting*, *Governmental Accounting*, *Bookkeeping Guidebook*, *Closing the Books*, and *Fixed Asset Accounting*.

Chapter 2
The System of Accounting

Introduction

Before an accountant can engage in any health care accounting activities, it is first necessary to understand the basic underpinnings of accounting, as well as the general flow of accounting transactions. In this chapter, we describe the concept of an accounting framework and accounting principles, on which all accounting activities are based. We then give an overview of how accounting transactions are recorded and aggregated into financial statements, which involves the use of double entry accounting, journal entries, a chart of accounts, and ledgers. We conclude with examples of the financial statements that a for-profit health care entity can be expected to produce.

Financial Accounting Basics

This introductory section is intended to give an overview of financial accounting basics. Its orientation is toward recording financial information about an organization.

First, what do we mean by "financial" accounting? This refers to the recordation of information about money. Thus, we will talk about issuing an invoice to someone, as well as their payment of that invoice, but we will not address any change in the value of an organization's overall business, since the latter situation does not involve a specific transaction involving money.

A *transaction* is a business event that has a monetary impact, such as providing services to a patient or buying supplies from a vendor. In financial accounting, a transaction triggers the recording of information about the money involved in the event. For example, we would record in the accounting records such events (transactions) as:

- Incurring debt from a lender
- The receipt of an expense report from an employee
- Providing medical services to a patient
- Paying property taxes to the government
- Paying wages to employees

We record this information in *accounts*. An account is a separate, detailed record about a specific item, such as expenditures for office supplies, or accounts receivable, or accounts payable. There can be many accounts, of which the most common are:

- *Cash*. This is the current balance of cash held by an organization, usually in checking or savings accounts.
- *Accounts receivable*. These are sales on credit, which patients, residents, or third-party payors must pay for at a later date.
- *Inventory*. This is items held in stock, for eventual sale to customers – such as goods kept in a hospital's gift shop. Inventory may also refer to supplies, such as pharmaceuticals.
- *Fixed assets*. These are more expensive assets that the organization plans to use for multiple years.
- *Accounts payable*. These are liabilities payable to suppliers that have not yet been paid.
- *Accrued expenses*. These are liabilities for which the organization has not yet been billed, but for which it will eventually have to pay.
- *Debt*. This is cash loaned to the organization by another party.
- *Equity*. This is the ownership interest in the business, which is the founding capital and any subsequent profits that have been retained in the business. In a not-for-profit organization, equity is called *net assets*.
- *Revenue*. This is services provided to patients and residents (both on credit and in cash).
- *Administrative expenses*. These are a variety of expenses required to run a health care enterprise, such as salaries, rent, utilities, and office supplies.
- *Income taxes*. These are the taxes paid to the government on any income earned by the organization. A not-for-profit or governmental health care operation may not owe any income taxes.

How do we enter information about transactions into these accounts? There are two ways to do so:

- *Software module entries*. If accounting software is being used to record financial accounting transactions, there will probably be on-line forms to fill out for each of the major transactions, such as creating a patient or an invoice or recording a supplier invoice. Every time one of these forms is filled out, the software automatically populates the accounts.
- *Journal entries*. The accountant can access a journal entry form in the accounting software, or create a journal entry by hand. This is a more customized way to record accounting information.

The accounts are stored in the *general ledger*. This is the master set of all accounts, in which are stored all of the business transactions that have been entered into the accounts with journal entries or software module entries. There may be subsidiary ledgers in which are stored high-volume transactions, such as sales or purchases. Thus, the

general ledger is the go-to document for all of the detailed financial accounting information about a health care business.

To understand the detail for a particular account, such as the current amount of accounts receivable outstanding, access the general ledger for this information. In addition, most accounting software packages provide a number of reports that give better insights into the business than just reading through the accounts. In particular, there are aged accounts receivable and aged accounts payable reports that are useful for determining the current list of uncollected accounts receivable and unpaid accounts payable, respectively.

The general ledger is also the source document for the financial statements. There are several financial statements associated with an investor-owned health care entity, which are:

- *Income statement.* This report lists the revenues, expenses, and profit or loss of the business for a specific period of time.
- *Balance sheet.* This report lists the assets, liabilities, and equity of the business as of the report date.
- *Statement of cash flows.* This report lists the cash inflows and outflows generated by the business for a specific period of time.

In the preceding chapter, we noted that there are several variations on these financial statements if a health care entity operates as a business-oriented not-for-profit or as a government entity. We will cover these financial statement variations in the next two chapters.

In summary, we have shown that financial accounting involves the recording of business transactions in accounts, which in turn are summarized in the general ledger, which in turn is used to create financial statements. We will now walk through the building blocks of an accounting system, starting with the accounting frameworks from which accounting rules are derived.

Accounting Frameworks

The accounting profession operates under a set of guidelines for how business transactions are to be recorded and reported. There are a multitude of transactions that an organization might enter into, so the corresponding guidelines are also quite large. These guidelines can be subject to some interpretation, so there are standard-setting bodies that maintain and support the guidelines with official pronouncements.

Not every organization operates under the same set of guidelines. There may be different guidelines for different types of entities, and slight differences in guidelines by country. Each of these unique guidelines is referred to as an accounting framework. Once an organization adopts a certain accounting framework, it continues to record transactions and report financial results in accordance with the rules of that framework on a long-term basis. Doing so provides the users of its financial reports with a considerable amount of reporting continuity. Also, because an accounting framework provides a consistent set of rules, anyone reading the financial statements of multiple organizations that employ the same framework has a reasonable basis for comparison.

The most commonly-used accounting framework in the United States is GAAP, which is short for Generally Accepted Accounting Principles. GAAP is the most comprehensive accounting framework in the world, with an extensive set of detailed rules covering a massive range of accounting topics. GAAP also provides rules for how to handle accounting transactions in specific industries, such as health care.

GAAP is derived from the pronouncements of a series of government-sponsored accounting entities, of which the Financial Accounting Standards Board is the latest. The Securities and Exchange Commission also issues accounting pronouncements through its Staff Accounting Bulletins and other announcements that are applicable only to publicly-held companies, and which are considered to be part of GAAP.

International Financial Reporting Standards, or IFRS, is the accounting framework used in most other countries. GAAP is much more rules-based than IFRS, which focuses more on general principles than GAAP. This focus makes the IFRS body of work much smaller, cleaner, and easier to understand than GAAP.

There are several working groups that are gradually reducing the differences between the GAAP and IFRS accounting frameworks, so eventually there should be minor differences in the reported results of an organization if it switches between the two frameworks.

The accounting information in this book is based on the GAAP framework. At the higher level of discussion used in this book, there are few notable differences between GAAP and IFRS.

Accounting Principles

There are a number of accounting principles upon which the accounting frameworks are based. These principles have been derived from common usage, as well as from the documentary efforts of several standard-setting organizations. The principles are:

- *Accrual principle*. The concept that accounting transactions should be recorded in the accounting periods when they actually occur, rather than in the periods when there are cash flows associated with them. This is the foundation of the accrual basis of accounting (as described in a later section). It is important for the construction of financial statements that show what actually happened in an accounting period, rather than being artificially delayed or accelerated by the associated cash flows. For example, if an organization ignores the accrual principle, it records an expense only after paying for it, which might incorporate a lengthy delay caused by the payment terms for the associated supplier invoice.
- *Conservatism principle*. The concept that one should record expenses and liabilities as soon as possible, but record revenues and assets only when certain that they will occur. This introduces a conservative slant to the financial statements that may yield lower reported profits, since revenue and asset recognition may be delayed for some time. This principle tends to encourage the recordation of losses earlier, rather than later. The concept can be taken too far, where an organization persistently misstates its results to be worse than is realistically the case.
- *Consistency principle*. The concept that, once an organization adopts an accounting principle or method, it should continue to use the principle or method until a

demonstrably better one comes along. Not following the consistency principle means that an organization could continually jump between different accounting treatments of its transactions that make its long-term financial results extremely difficult to discern.

- *Cost principle.* The concept that an organization should only record its assets, liabilities, and equity investments at their original purchase costs. This principle is becoming less valid, as numerous accounting standards are heading in the direction of adjusting to the current fair value of many items.
- *Economic entity principle.* The concept that the transactions of an organization should be kept separate from those of its owners and other businesses. This prevents intermingling of assets and liabilities among multiple entities.
- *Full disclosure principle.* The concept that one should include in or alongside the financial statements of a business all of the information that may impact a reader's understanding of those financial statements. The accounting standards have greatly amplified upon this concept in specifying an enormous number of informational disclosures.
- *Going concern principle.* The concept that an organization will remain in operation for the foreseeable future. This means that a business would be justified in deferring the recognition of some expenses, such as depreciation, until later periods. Otherwise, it would have to recognize all expenses at once and not defer any of them.
- *Matching principle.* The concept that, when revenue is recorded, one should record all related expenses at the same time. Thus, an organization charges salaries to expense at the same time that it records revenue from the provision of services to patients by the people earning salaries. This is a cornerstone of the accrual basis of accounting.
- *Materiality principle.* The concept that one should record a transaction in the accounting records if not doing so might have altered the decision making process of someone reading the organization's financial statements. This is quite a vague concept that is difficult to quantify, which has led some of the more picayune accountants to record even the smallest transactions.
- *Monetary unit principle.* The concept that an organization should only record transactions that can be stated in terms of a unit of currency. Thus, it is easy enough to record the purchase of a fixed asset, since it was bought for a specific price, whereas the value of the quality control system of a hospital is not recorded. This concept keeps an organization from engaging in an excessive level of estimation in deriving the value of its assets and liabilities.
- *Reliability principle.* The concept that only those transactions that can be proven should be recorded. For example, a supplier invoice is solid evidence that an expense has been recorded. This concept is of prime interest to auditors, who are constantly in search of the evidence supporting transactions.
- *Revenue recognition principle.* The concept that one should only recognize revenue when a business has substantially completed the earnings process.

- *Time period principle*. The concept that a business should report the results of its operations over a standard period of time. This may qualify as the most glaringly obvious of all accounting principles, but is intended to create a standard set of comparable periods, which is useful for trend analysis.

It may not initially appear that accounting principles are of much use on a day-to-day basis. However, when there is a question about the proper treatment of a business transaction, it is sometimes useful to resolve the question by viewing the guidance in the relevant accounting framework in light of these accounting principles. Doing so may indicate that one solution more closely adheres to the general intent of the framework, and so is a better solution.

The Accounting Cycle

The accounting cycle is a sequential set of activities used to identify and record an entity's individual transactions. These transactions are then aggregated at the end of each reporting period into financial statements. The accounting cycle is essentially the core recordation activity that an accountant engages in, and is the basis upon which the financial statements are constructed. The following discussion breaks the accounting cycle into the treatment of individual transactions and then closing the books at the end of the accounting period. The accounting cycle for individual transactions is:

1. Identify the event causing an accounting transaction, such as buying pharmaceuticals or paying wages to employees.
2. Prepare the business document associated with the accounting transaction, such as a supplier invoice, patient invoice, or cash receipt.
3. Identify which accounts are affected by the business document.
4. Record in the appropriate accounts in the accounting database the amounts noted on the business document.

The preceding accounting cycle steps were associated with individual transactions. The following accounting cycle steps are only used at the end of the reporting period, and are associated with the aggregate amounts of the preceding transactions:

5. Prepare a preliminary trial balance, which itemizes the debit and credit totals for each account.
6. Add accrued items, record estimated reserves, and correct errors in the preliminary trial balance with adjusting entries. Examples are the recordation of an expense for supplier invoices that have not yet arrived, and accruing for unpaid wages earned.
7. Prepare an adjusted trial balance, which incorporates the preliminary trial balance and all adjusting entries. It may require several iterations before this report accurately reflects the results of operations of the organization.
8. Prepare financial statements from the adjusted trial balance.
9. Close the books for the reporting period.

In the following sections, we expand upon a number of the concepts just noted in the accounting cycle, including accounting transactions, journal entries, ledgers, and the trial balance.

Accounting Transactions

An accounting transaction is a business event having a monetary impact on the financial statements of a business. It is recorded in the accounting records of an organization. Examples of accounting transactions are:

- Sale of services in cash to a patient
- Sale of services on credit to a patient
- Receive cash in payment of an invoice owed by a patient
- Purchase fixed assets from a supplier
- Record the depreciation of a fixed asset over time
- Purchase consumable supplies from a supplier
- Invest in another business
- Borrow funds from a lender
- Issue a dividend to investors
- Sale of assets to a third party

Types of Transaction Cycles

A transaction cycle is an interlocking set of business transactions. Most business transactions can be aggregated into a relatively small number of transaction cycles related to the sale of goods and services, payments to suppliers, payments to employees, and payments to lenders. We explore the nature of these transaction cycles in the following bullet points:

- *Sales cycle.* A health care entity provides goods or services to a patient or resident, issues an invoice, and collects payment. This set of sequential, interrelated activities is known as the sales cycle, or revenue cycle.
- *Purchasing cycle.* A health care entity issues a purchase order to a supplier for goods, receives the goods, records an account payable, and pays the supplier. There are several ancillary activities, such as the use of petty cash or procurement cards for smaller purchases. This set of sequential, interrelated activities is known as the purchasing cycle, or expenditure cycle.
- *Payroll cycle.* A health care entity records the time of its employees, verifies hours and overtime worked, calculates gross pay, deducts taxes and other withholdings, and issues paychecks to employees. Other related activities include the payment of withheld income taxes to the government, as well as the issuance of annual W-2 forms to employees. This cluster of activities is known as the payroll cycle.
- *Financing cycle.* A health care entity borrows money from lenders, followed by a series of interest payments and repayments of the debt. Also, an investor-owned business issues stock to investors, in exchange for periodic dividend

payments and other payouts if the entity is dissolved. These clusters of transactions are more diverse than the preceding transaction cycles, but may involve substantially more money.

A key role of the accountant is to design an appropriate set of procedures, forms, and integrated controls for each of these transaction cycles, to mitigate the opportunities for fraud and ensure that transactions are processed in as reliable and consistent a manner as possible.

Source Documents

Source documents are the physical basis upon which business transactions are recorded. They usually contain the following information:

- A description of the transaction
- The date of the transaction
- A specific amount of money
- An authorizing signature (in some cases)

Examples of source documents and their related business transactions that appear in the financial records are:

- *Bank statement.* This contains a number of adjustments to an organization's book balance of cash on hand that it should reference to bring its records into alignment with those of a bank.
- *Credit card receipt.* This can be used as evidence for a disbursement of funds from petty cash.
- *Lockbox check images.* These images support the recordation of cash receipts from patients, residents, and third-party payors.
- *Supplier invoice.* This document supports the issuance of a cash, check, or electronic payment to a supplier. A supplier invoice also supports the recordation of an expense, inventory item, or fixed asset.
- *Time card.* This supports the issuance of a paycheck or electronic payment to an employee. If employee hours are being billed to patients, residents, or third-party payors, the time card also supports the creation of invoices to these parties.

Double Entry Accounting

Double entry accounting is a record keeping system under which every transaction is recorded in at least two accounts. There is no upper limit on the number of accounts used in a transaction, but the minimum is two accounts. There are two columns in each account, with debit entries on the left and credit entries on the right. In double entry accounting, the total of all debit entries must match the total of all credit entries. When this happens, a transaction is said to be *in balance*. If the totals do not agree,

the transaction is *out of balance*. An out of balance transaction must be corrected before financial statements can be created.

The definitions of a debit and credit are:

- A debit is an accounting entry that either increases an asset or expense account, or decreases a liability or equity account. It is positioned to the left in an accounting entry.
- A credit is an accounting entry that either increases a liability or equity account, or decreases an asset or expense account. It is positioned to the right in an accounting entry.

An account is a separate, detailed record associated with a specific asset, liability, equity, revenue, expense, gain, or loss. Examples of accounts are noted in the following exhibit.

Characteristics of Sample Accounts

Account Name	Account Type	Normal Account Balance
Cash	Asset	Debit
Accounts receivable	Asset	Debit
Inventory	Asset	Debit
Fixed assets	Asset	Debit
Accounts payable	Liability	Credit
Accrued liabilities	Liability	Credit
Notes payable	Liability	Credit
Common stock	Equity	Credit
Retained earnings	Equity	Credit
Revenue	Revenue	Credit
Compensation expense	Expense	Debit
Utilities expense	Expense	Debit
Travel and entertainment	Expense	Debit
Gain on sale of asset	Gain	Credit
Loss on sale of asset	Loss	Debit

The key point with double entry accounting is that a single transaction always triggers a recordation in *at least* two accounts, as assets and liabilities gradually flow through a business and are converted into revenues, expenses, gains, and losses. We expand upon this concept in the next section.

The Accounting Equation

The *accounting equation* is the basis upon which the double entry accounting system is constructed. In essence, the accounting equation is:

Assets = Liabilities + Shareholders' Equity

The assets in the accounting equation are the resources that an organization has available for its use, such as cash, accounts receivable, fixed assets, and inventory. The business pays for these resources by either incurring liabilities (which is the Liabilities part of the accounting equation) or by obtaining funding from investors (which is the Shareholders' Equity part of the equation). Thus, there can be resources with offsetting claims against those resources, either from creditors or investors.

The Liabilities part of the equation is usually comprised of accounts payable that are owed to suppliers, a variety of accrued liabilities, such as wages payable, and debt payable to lenders.

The Shareholders' Equity part of the equation is more complex than simply being the amount paid to the entity by its investors. It is actually their initial investment, plus any subsequent gains, minus any subsequent losses, minus any dividends or other withdrawals paid to the investors. This part of the equation is called *net assets* when a health care entity is organized as a not-for-profit.

This relationship between assets, liabilities, and shareholders' equity appears in the balance sheet, where the total of all assets always equals the sum of the liabilities and shareholders' equity sections.

The reason why the accounting equation is so important is that it is always true - and it forms the basis for all accounting transactions. At a general level, this means that whenever there is a recordable transaction, the choices for recording it all involve keeping the accounting equation in balance.

EXAMPLE

The Willows Retirement Community engages in the following series of transactions:

1. The Willows sells shares to an investor for $10,000. This increases the cash (asset) account as well as the capital (equity) account.
2. The Willows buys $4,000 of goods for its incidentals store from a supplier. This increases the inventory (asset) account as well as the payables (liability) account.
3. The Willows sells the inventory for $6,000. This decreases the inventory (asset) account and creates a cost of goods sold expense that appears as a decrease in the income (equity) account.
4. The sale of The Willows' inventory also creates a sale and offsetting receivable. This increases the receivables (asset) account by $6,000 and increases the income (equity) account by $6,000.
5. The Willows collects cash from the residents to which it sold the inventory. This increases the cash (asset) account by $6,000 and decreases the receivables (asset) account by $6,000.

These transactions appear in the following table.

Item	(Asset) Cash	(Asset) Receivables	(Asset) Inventory		(Liability) Payables	(Equity) Capital	(Equity) Income
(1)	$10,000			=		$10,000	
(2)			$4,000	=	$4,000		
(3)			-4,000	=			-$4,000
(4)		$6,000		=			6,000
(5)	6,000	-6,000		=			
Totals	$16,000	$0	$0	=	$4,000	$10,000	$2,000

In the example, note how every transaction is balanced within the accounting equation - either because there are changes on both sides of the equation, or because a transaction cancels itself out on one side of the equation (as was the case when the receivable was converted to cash).

The following exhibit shows how a number of typical accounting transactions are recorded within the framework of the accounting equation.

Sample Transactions

Transaction Type	Assets	Liabilities + Equity
Buy fixed assets on credit	Fixed assets increase	Accounts payable (liability) increases
Buy inventory on credit	Inventory increases	Accounts payable (liability) increases
Pay dividends	Cash decreases	Retained earnings (equity) decreases
Pay rent	Cash decreases	Income (equity) decreases
Pay supplier invoices	Cash decreases	Accounts payable (liability) decreases
Sell goods on credit (part 1)	Inventory decreases	Income (equity) decreases
Sell goods on credit (part 2)	Accounts receivable increases	Income (equity) increases
Sell services on credit	Accounts receivable increases	Income (equity) increases
Sell stock	Cash increases	Equity increases

Here are examples of each of the preceding transactions, where we show how they comply with the accounting equation:

- *Buy fixed assets on credit.* The Willows buys a machine on credit for $10,000. This increases the fixed assets (asset) account and increases the accounts payable (liability) account. Thus, the asset and liability sides of the transaction are equal.
- *Buy inventory on credit.* The Willows buys merchandise on credit for $5,000. This increases the inventory (asset) account and increases the accounts payable (liability) account. Thus, the asset and liability sides of the transaction are equal.

- *Pay dividends.* The Willows pays $25,000 in dividends. This reduces the cash (asset) account and reduces the retained earnings (equity) account. Thus, the asset and equity sides of the transaction are equal.
- *Pay rent.* The Willows pays $4,000 in rent. This reduces the cash (asset) account and reduces the accounts payable (liabilities) account. Thus, the asset and liability sides of the transaction are equal.
- *Pay supplier invoices.* The Willows pays $29,000 on existing supplier invoices. This reduces the cash (asset) account by $29,000 and reduces the accounts payable (liability) account. Thus, the asset and liability sides of the transaction are equal.
- *Sell goods on credit.* The Willows sells furniture to its residents for $55,000 on credit. This increases the accounts receivable (asset) account by $55,000, and increases the revenue (equity) account. Thus, the asset and equity sides of the transaction are equal.
- *Sell stock.* The Willows sells $120,000 of its shares to investors. This increases the cash account (asset) by $120,000, and increases the capital stock (equity) account. Thus, the asset and equity sides of the transaction are equal.

Journal Entries

A journal entry is a formalized method for recording a business transaction. It is recorded in the accounting records of an organization, usually in the general ledger, but sometimes in a subsidiary ledger that is then summarized and rolled forward into the general ledger (see the Ledger Concept section later in this chapter).

Journal entries are used in a double entry accounting system, where the intent is to record every business transaction in at least two places. For example, when an organization sells services for cash, this increases both the revenue account and the cash account. Or, if supplies are acquired on account, this increases both the accounts payable account and the supplies account.

The structure of a journal entry is:

- A header line may include a journal entry number and entry date.
- The first column includes the account number and account name into which the entry is recorded. This field is indented if it is for the account being credited.
- The second column contains the debit amount to be entered.
- The third column contains the credit amount to be entered.
- A footer line may also include a brief description of the reason for the entry.

Thus, the basic journal entry format is:

	Debit	Credit
Account name / number	$xx,xxx	
Account name / number		$xx,xxx

The structural rules of a journal entry are that there must be a minimum of two line items in the entry, and that the total amount entered in the debit column equals the total amount entered in the credit column.

A journal entry is usually printed and stored in a binder of accounting transactions, with backup materials attached that justify the entry. This information may be accessed by the organization's auditors as part of their annual audit activities.

There are several types of journal entries, including:

- *Adjusting entry*. An adjusting entry is used at month-end to alter the financial statements to bring them into compliance with the relevant accounting framework. For example, a hospital could accrue unpaid wages at month-end in order to recognize the wages expense in the current period.
- *Compound entry*. This is a journal entry that includes more than two lines of entries. It is frequently used to record complex transactions, or several transactions at once. For example, the journal entry to record a payroll usually contains many lines, since it involves the recordation of numerous tax liabilities and payroll deductions.
- *Reversing entry*. This is an adjusting entry that is reversed as of the beginning of the following period, usually because an expense was accrued in the preceding period and is no longer needed. Thus, a wage accrual in the preceding period is reversed in the next period, to be replaced by an actual payroll expenditure.

In general, journal entries are not used to record high-volume transactions, such as patient billings or supplier invoices. These transactions are handled through specialized software modules that present a standard on-line form to be filled out. Once the form is complete, the software automatically creates the accounting record.

The Accruals Concept

An accrual is a journal entry that is used to recognize revenues and expenses that have been earned or consumed, respectively, and for which the related source documents have not yet been received or generated. Accruals are needed to ensure that all revenue and expense elements are recognized within the correct reporting period, irrespective of the timing of related cash flows. Without accruals, the amount of revenue, expense, and profit or loss in a period will not necessarily reflect the actual level of economic activity within a business. Accruals are a key part of the closing process used to create

financial statements under the accrual basis of accounting; without accruals, financial statements would be considerably less accurate.

It is most efficient to initially record most accruals as reversing entries. This is a useful feature when an organization is expecting to issue an invoice to a patient or receive an invoice from a supplier in the following period. For example, an accountant may know that a supplier invoice for $20,000 will arrive a few days after the end of a month, but she wants to close the books as soon as possible. Accordingly, she records a $20,000 reversing entry to recognize the expense in the current month. In the next month, the accrual reverses, creating a negative $20,000 expense that is offset by the arrival and recordation of the supplier invoice.

Examples of accruals that an organization might record are:

- *Expense accrual for interest.* A local lender issues a loan to a health care entity and sends the borrower an invoice each month, detailing the amount of interest owed. The borrower can record the interest expense in advance of invoice receipt by recording accrued interest.
- *Expense accrual for wages.* An employer pays its employees once a month for the hours they have worked through the 26th day of the month. The employer can accrue all additional wages earned from the 27th through the last day of the month, to ensure that the full amount of the wage expense is recognized.
- *Sales accrual.* A hospital is compiling service charges for a major local employer, which it is contractually limited to do on a quarterly basis. In the meantime, the hospital can accrue revenue for the amount of services provided to date, even though the charges have not yet been billed.

If an organization records its transactions under the cash basis of accounting, it does not use accruals. Instead, the organization records transactions only when it either pays out or receives cash. See the later Cash Basis of Accounting section for an explanation of this concept.

The Chart of Accounts

The chart of accounts defines how accounting information is stored. A properly structured chart of accounts makes it much easier to accumulate and report on information, so the account structure is an area of interest to the accountant. In this section, we give an overview of the chart of accounts and the most common accounts used, and then address the account coding structures for a health care organization.

Related Podcast Episode: Episode 163 of the Accounting Best Practices Podcast discusses the chart of accounts. It is available at: **accountingtools.com/podcasts** or **iTunes**

The chart of accounts is a listing of all accounts used in the general ledger, usually sorted in order by account number. The accounts are typically numeric, but can also be alphabetic or alphanumeric. The account numbering system is used by the accounting software to aggregate information into an entity's financial statements.

Accounts are usually listed in order of their appearance in the financial statements, starting with the balance sheet and continuing with the income statement. Thus, the chart of accounts begins with cash, proceeds through liabilities and shareholders' equity, and then continues with accounts for revenues and then expenses. Many organizations structure their chart of accounts so that expense information is separately compiled by department; thus, the anesthesiology department, dialysis department, and emergency department could all have the same set of expense accounts.

A five-digit chart of accounts is used by organizations that want to track information at the departmental level. With a five-digit code, they can produce a separate income statement for each department. This format duplicates the account codes found in a three-digit chart of accounts, but then adds a two-digit code to the left, which identifies specific departments. The three-digit codes for expenses (and sometimes also revenues) are then duplicated for each department for which management wants to record information. A sample of the five-digit chart of accounts format follows, using the anesthesiology and emergency departments to show how expense account codes can be duplicated.

Sample Chart of Accounts

Account Number	Department	Description
00-010	xxx	General checking accounts
00-011	xxx	Payroll checking accounts
00-012	xxx	Other checking accounts
00-013	xxx	Cash on hand
00-014	xxx	Petty cash
00-020	xxx	Short-term investments
00-030	xxx	Accounts receivable
00-031	xxx	Settlements due from third-party payors
00-032	xxx	Allowance for doubtful accounts
00-033	xxx	Other short-term receivables
00-040	xxx	Prepaid expenses
00-050	xxx	Inventory
00-060	xxx	Long-term investments
00-100	xxx	Fixed assets – Buildings
00-110	xxx	Fixed assets – General practice furniture
00-120	xxx	Fixed assets – Information technology

Account Number	Department	Description
00-130	xxx	Fixed assets – Motor vehicles
00-140	xxx	Fixed assets – Research equipment
00-150	xxx	Fixed assets – Intangible assets
00-160	xxx	Accumulated depreciation
00-200	xxx	Accounts payable
00-210	xxx	Settlements due to third-party payors
00-300	xxx	Accrued payroll liability
00-310	xxx	Accrued vacation liability
00-320	xxx	Accrued expenses liability – other
00-330	xxx	Unremitted pension payments
00-340	xxx	Short-term notes payable
00-350	xxx	Other short-term liabilities
00-360	xxx	Long-term liabilities
00-400	xxx	Capital stock
00-410	xxx	Retained earnings
00-420	xxx	Net assets (for a not-for-profit entity)
10-500	Anesthesiology	Operating revenue – Services
20-500	Emergency	Operating revenue – Services
10-600	Anesthesiology	Salaries – Support staff
10-610	Anesthesiology	Salaries – Other
10-620	Anesthesiology	Payroll taxes
10-630	Anesthesiology	Employee benefits
10-640	Anesthesiology	Professional development
10-650	Anesthesiology	General and administrative expenses
10-660	Anesthesiology	Building and occupancy expenses
10-670	Anesthesiology	Vehicles and travel
10-680	Anesthesiology	Professional liability insurance
10-690	Anesthesiology	Bad debt expense
20-600	Emergency	Salaries – Support staff
20-610	Emergency	Salaries – Other
20-620	Emergency	Payroll taxes
20-630	Emergency	Employee benefits
20-640	Emergency	Professional development
20-650	Emergency	General and administrative expenses

Account Number	Department	Description
20-660	Emergency	Building and occupancy expenses
20-670	Emergency	Vehicles and travel
20-680	Emergency	Professional liability insurance
20-690	Emergency	Bad debt expense

The preceding sample chart of accounts duplicates accounts for each department listed. This is not necessarily the case in reality, since some departments have accounts for which they are the only probable users. Thus, some accounts can be avoided by flagging them as inactive in the accounting system. By doing so, they do not appear in the formal chart of accounts.

Major Journal Entries

The following journal entry examples are intended to provide an outline of the general structure of the more common entries encountered. It is impossible to provide a complete set of journal entries that address every variation on every situation, since there are thousands of possible entries.

In each of the following journal entries, we state the topic, the relevant debit and credit, and additional comments as needed.

Revenue journal entries:

- *Sales entry.* Debit accounts receivable and credit sales. If a sale is for cash, the debit is to the cash account instead of the accounts receivable account.
- *Allowance for doubtful accounts entry.* Debit bad debt expense and credit the allowance for doubtful accounts. When actual bad debts are identified, debit the allowance account and credit the accounts receivable account, thereby clearing out the associated invoice.

Expense journal entries:

- *Accounts payable entry.* Debit the asset or expense account to which a purchase relates and credit the accounts payable account. When an account payable is paid, debit accounts payable and credit the cash account.
- *Payroll entry.* Debit the wages expense and payroll tax expense accounts, and credit the cash account. There may be additional credits to account for deductions from benefit expense accounts, if employees have permitted deductions for benefits to be taken from their pay.
- *Accrued expense entry.* Debit the applicable expense and credit the accrued expenses liability account. This entry is usually reversed automatically in the following period.
- *Depreciation entry.* Debit depreciation expense and credit accumulated depreciation. These accounts may be categorized by type of fixed asset.

Asset entries:

- *Cash reconciliation entry*. This entry can take many forms, but there is usually a debit to the bank fees account to recognize changes made by the bank, with a credit to the cash account. There may also be a debit to office supplies expense for any check supplies purchased and paid for through the bank account.
- *Prepaid expense adjustment entry*. When recognizing prepaid expenses as expenses, debit the applicable expense account and credit the prepaid expense asset account.
- *Fixed asset addition entry*. Debit the applicable fixed asset account and credit accounts payable.
- *Fixed asset derecognition entry*. Debit accumulated depreciation and credit the applicable fixed asset account. There may also be a gain or loss on the asset derecognition.

Liability entries:

See the preceding accounts payable and accrued expense entries.

Equity entries:

- *Dividend declaration*. Debit the retained earnings account and credit the dividends payable account. Once dividends are paid, this is a debit to the dividends payable account and a credit to the cash account. This entry only applies to an investor-owned business.
- *Stock sale*. Debit the cash account and credit the common stock account. This entry only applies to an investor-owned business.

These journal entry examples are only intended to provide an overview of the general types and formats of accounting entries. There are many variations on the entries presented here that are used to deal with a broad range of business transactions. More detailed journal entries are provided in the following chapters.

The Ledger Concept

A *ledger* is a book or database in which double-entry accounting transactions are stored or summarized. A *subsidiary ledger* is a ledger designed for the storage of specific types of accounting transactions. If a subsidiary ledger is used, the information in it is then summarized and posted to an account in the *general ledger*, which in turn is used to construct the financial statements of an organization. The account in the general ledger where this summarized information is stored is called a *control account*. Most accounts in the general ledger are not control accounts; instead, transactions are recorded directly into them.

A subsidiary ledger can be set up to offload data storage for virtually any general ledger account. However, they are usually only created for areas in which there are high transaction volumes, which limits their use to a few areas. Examples of subsidiary ledgers are:

- Accounts receivable ledger
- Fixed assets ledger
- Inventory ledger
- Purchases ledger

> **Tip:** Subsidiary ledgers are used when there is a large amount of transaction information that would clutter up the general ledger. This situation typically arises in organizations with significant sales volume. Thus, there may be no need for subsidiary ledgers in a smaller health care entity, such as a single emergency care facility.

In order to research accounting information when a subsidiary ledger is used, drill down from the general ledger to the appropriate subsidiary ledger, where the detailed information is stored. Consequently, if one would prefer to conduct as much research as possible within the general ledger, use fewer subsidiary ledgers.

The following chart shows how the various data entry modules within an accounting system are used to create transactions which are recorded in either the general ledger or various subsidiary ledgers, and which are eventually aggregated to create the financial statements.

Transaction Flow in the Accounting System

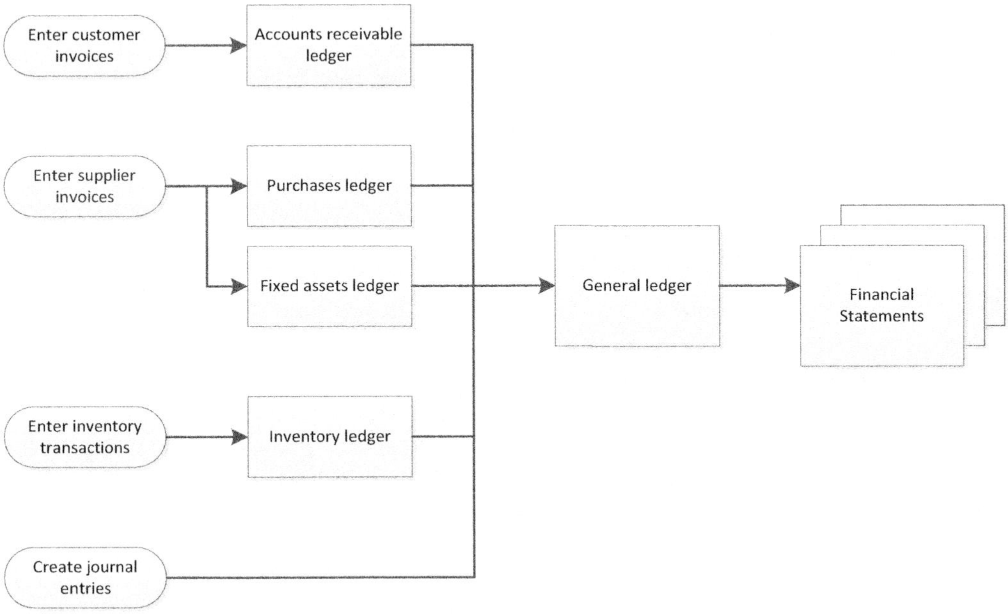

Part of the period-end closing process is to post the information in a subsidiary ledger to the general ledger. This is usually a manual step, so verify that all subsidiary ledgers have been appropriately completed and closed before posting their summarized totals to the general ledger. It can be quite a problem if the accountant forgets to post the totals from a subsidiary ledger to the general ledger, since that means the resulting financial statements may be missing a batch of crucial transactions.

Posting to the General Ledger

Posting refers to the aggregation of financial transactions from where they are stored in subsidiary ledgers, and transferring this information into the general ledger. Information in one of the subsidiary ledgers is aggregated at regular intervals, at which point a summary-level entry is made and posted in the general ledger. In a manual accounting environment, the aggregation may occur at fixed intervals, such as once a day or once a month. For example, if the source ledger were the accounts receivable ledger, the aggregated posting entry might include a debit to the accounts receivable account and a credit to the sales account. When posting this entry in the general ledger, a notation could be made in the description field, stating the date range to which the entry applies.

In a computerized accounting environment, posting to the general ledger may be unnoticeable. The software simply does so at regular intervals, or asks if the accountant wants to post, and then handles the underlying general ledger posting automatically. It is possible that no posting transaction even appears in the reports generated by the system.

Posting to the general ledger does not occur for lower-volume transactions, which are already recorded in the general ledger. For example, fixed asset purchases may be so infrequent that there is no need for a subsidiary ledger to house these transactions, so they are instead recorded directly in the general ledger.

General Ledger Overview

A general ledger is the master set of accounts in which is summarized all transactions occurring within an organization during a specific period of time. The general ledger contains all of the accounts currently being used in a chart of accounts, and is sorted by account number. Either individual transactions or summary-level postings from subsidiary ledgers are listed within each account number, and are sorted by transaction date. Each entry in the general ledger includes a reference number that states the source of the information. The source may be a subsidiary ledger, a journal entry, or a transaction entered directly into the general ledger.

The format of the general ledger varies somewhat, depending on the accounting software being used, but the basic set of information presented for an account within the general ledger is:

- *Transaction number*. The software assigns a unique number to each transaction, so that it can be more easily located in the accounting database if the accountant knows the transaction number.

- *Transaction date*. This is the date on which the transaction was entered into the accounting database.
- *Description*. This is a brief description that summarizes the reason for the entry.
- *Source*. Information may be forwarded to the general ledger from a variety of sources, so the report should state the source, in case there is a need to go back to the source to research the reason for the entry.
- *Debit and credit*. States the amount debited or credited to the account for a specific transaction.

The following sample of a general ledger report shows a possible format that could be used to present information for several transactions that are aggregated under a specific account number.

Sample General Ledger Presentation

Trans. No.	Trans. Date	Description	Source	Debit	Credit
Acct. 10400		**Acct: Accounts Receivable**		**Beginning balance**	**$127,500.00**
10473	3/22/xx	Patient invoice	ARL	93.99	
10474	3/23/xx	Patient invoice	ARL	47.80	
10475	3/24/xx	Credit memo	ARL		43.17
10476	3/25/xx	Patient invoice	ARL	65.25	
18903	3/26/xx	Cash receipt	CRJ		1,105.20
				Ending balance	**$126,558.67**

It is extremely easy to locate information pertinent to an accounting inquiry in the general ledger, which makes it the primary source of accounting information. For example:

- A manager reviews the balance sheet and notices that the amount of debt appears too high. The accountant looks up the debt account in the general ledger and sees that a loan was added at the end of the month.
- A manager reviews the income statement and sees that the bad debt expense for his department is very high. The accountant looks up the expense in the general ledger, drills down to the source journal entry, and sees that a new bad debt projection was the cause of the increase in bad debt expense.

As the examples show, the source of an inquiry is frequently the financial statements; when conducting an investigation, the accountant begins with the general ledger, and may drill down to source documents from there to ascertain the reason(s) for an issue.

The Trial Balance

The trial balance is a report run at the end of an accounting period. It is primarily used to ensure that the total of all debits equals the total of all credits, which means that there are no unbalanced journal entries in the accounting system that would make it impossible to generate accurate financial statements. Printing the trial balance to match debit and credit totals has fallen into disuse, since accounting software rejects the entry of unbalanced journal entries.

The trial balance can also be used to manually compile financial statements, though with the predominant use of computerized accounting systems that create the statements automatically, the report is rarely used for this purpose.

When the trial balance is first printed, it is called the *unadjusted trial balance*. Then, when the accountant corrects any errors found and makes adjustments to bring the financial statements into compliance with the accounting standards, the report is called the *adjusted trial balance*. Finally, after the period has been closed, the report is called the *post-closing trial balance*.

The Trial Balance Format

The initial trial balance report contains the following columns of information:

1. Account number
2. Account name
3. Ending debit balance (if any)
4. Ending credit balance (if any)

Each line item only contains the ending balance in an account, which comes from the general ledger. All accounts having an ending balance are listed in the trial balance; usually, the accounting software automatically blocks all accounts having a zero balance from appearing in the report, which reduces its length. A sample trial balance follows, which employs a compressed account numbering format of just four digits.

Sample Trial Balance

Account		Unadjusted Trial Balance	
Number	Account Description	Debit	Credit
1000	Cash	$60,000	
1500	Accounts receivable	180,000	
2000	Inventory	300,000	
3000	Fixed assets	210,000	
4000	Accounts payable		$90,000
4500	Accrued liabilities		50,000
4700	Notes payable		420,000
5000	Equity		350,000
6000	Revenue		400,000
7300	Salaries expense	490,000	
7400	Payroll tax expense	20,000	
7500	Rent expense	35,000	
7600	Other expenses	15,000	
	Totals	$1,310,000	$1,310,000

The adjusted version of a trial balance may combine the debit and credit columns into a single combined column, and add columns to show adjusting entries and a revised ending balance. An adjusting entry is a journal entry that is used at the end of an accounting period to adjust the balances in various general ledger accounts to meet the requirements of accounting standards. This format is useful for revealing the derivation of the line items in financial statements.

The following sample shows adjusting entries. It also combines the debit and credit totals into the second column, so that the summary balance for the total is (and should be) zero. Adjusting entries are added in the next column, yielding an adjusted trial balance in the far right column.

Sample Adjusted Trial Balance

Account Description	Unadjusted Trial Balance	Adjusting Entries	Adjusted Trial Balance
Cash	$60,000		$60,000
Accounts receivable	180,000	$50,000	230,000
Inventory	300,000		300,000
Fixed assets (net)	210,000		210,000
Accounts payable	-90,000		-90,000
Accrued liabilities	-50,000	-25,000	-75,000
Notes payable	-420,000		-420,000
Equity	-350,000		-350,000
Revenue	-400,000	-50,000	-450,000
Salaries expense	490,000	25,000	515,000
Payroll tax expense	20,000		20,000
Rent expense	35,000		35,000
Other expenses	15,000		15,000
Totals	$0	$0	$0

The Extended Trial Balance

An extended trial balance is a standard trial balance to which are added categories extending to the right, and in which are listed the account totals for the balance sheet and the income statement. Thus, all asset, liability, and equity accounts are stated in a balance sheet column, and all revenue, expense, gain, and loss accounts are stated in an income statement column.

The extended trial balance is useful for creating a visual representation of where each of the accounts in the standard trial balance goes in the financial statements, and may be useful for detecting anomalies in the trial balance that should be corrected. A sample of an extended trial balance is shown next. It uses the same trial balance information used to describe the adjusted trial balance format.

Sample Extended Trial Balance

	Unadjusted Trial Balance	Adjusting Entries	Adjusted Trial Balance	Balance Sheet	Income Statement
Cash	$60,000		$60,000	$60,000	
Accounts receivable	180,000	$50,000	230,000	230,000	
Inventory	300,000		300,000	300,000	
Fixed assets (net)	210,000		210,000	210,000	
Accounts payable	-90,000		-90,000	-90,000	
Accrued liabilities	-50,000	-25,000	-75,000	-75,000	
Notes payable	-420,000		-420,000	-420,000	
Equity	-350,000		-350,000	-350,000	
Retained earnings				-135,000	
Revenue	-400,000	-50,000	-450,000		-450,000
Salaries expense	490,000	25,000	515,000		515,000
Payroll tax expense	20,000		20,000		20,000
Rent expense	35,000		35,000		35,000
Other expenses	15,000		15,000		15,000
Totals	$0	$0	$0	$0	-$135,000

Any computerized accounting system automatically generates financial statements from the trial balance, so the extended trial balance is not a commonly generated report in computerized systems.

Note: The information in the balance sheet and income statement columns in an extended trial balance do not necessarily match the final presentation of these reports, because some of the line items may be aggregated for presentation purposes.

Accrual Basis of Accounting

The accrual basis of accounting is the concept of recording revenues when earned and expenses as incurred. This concept differs from the cash basis of accounting, under which revenues are recorded when cash is received, and expenses are recorded when cash is paid. For example, an organization operating under the accrual basis of accounting will record a sale as soon as service is provided to a patient, while a cash basis organization would instead wait to be paid before it records the sale. Similarly, an accrual basis organization will record an expense as incurred, while a cash basis company would instead wait to pay its supplier before recording the expense.

The accrual basis of accounting is advocated under both the GAAP and IFRS accounting frameworks. Both of these frameworks provide guidance regarding how to account for revenue and expense transactions in the absence of the cash receipts or

payments that would trigger the recordation of a transaction under the cash basis of accounting.

The accrual basis tends to provide more consistent recognition of revenues and expenses over time than the cash basis, and so is considered by investors and lenders to be the most valid accounting system for ascertaining the results of operations, financial position, and cash flows of an organization. In particular, it supports the matching principle, under which revenues and all related expenses are to be recorded within the same reporting period; by doing so, it should be possible to see the full extent of the profits and losses associated with specific business transactions within a single reporting period.

The accrual basis requires the use of estimated reserves in certain areas. For example, an organization should recognize an expense for estimated bad debts that have not yet been incurred. By doing so, all expenses related to a revenue transaction are recorded at the same time as the revenue, which results in an income statement that fully reflects the results of operations. These estimates may not be entirely accurate, and so can lead to materially inaccurate financial statements. Consequently, some care must be used when estimating reserves.

A significant failing of the accrual basis is that it can indicate the presence of profits, even though the associated cash inflows have not yet occurred. The result can be a supposedly profitable entity that is starved for cash, and which may therefore go bankrupt despite its reported level of profitability.

Cash Basis of Accounting

The cash basis of accounting is the practice of only recording revenue when cash is received, and recording expenses only when cash has been paid out. The cash basis is commonly used by individuals and small businesses, especially those with no inventory. A start-up company will frequently begin keeping its books under the cash basis and then switch to the accrual basis of accounting (see the preceding section) when it has grown to a sufficient size. The cash basis of accounting has the following advantages:

- *Taxation.* The method is commonly used to record financial results for tax purposes, since an organization can accelerate some payments in order to reduce its taxable profits, thereby deferring its tax liability.
- *Ease of use.* A person requires a reduced knowledge of accounting to keep records under the cash basis.

However, the cash basis of accounting also suffers from the following problems:

- *Accuracy.* The cash basis yields less accurate results than the accrual basis of accounting, since the timing of cash flows does not necessarily reflect the proper timing of changes in the financial condition of an organization.
- *Manipulation.* An organization can alter its reported results by not cashing received checks or altering the payment timing for its liabilities.

- *Lending*. Lenders do not feel that the cash basis generates overly accurate financial statements, and so may refuse to lend money to an organization reporting under the cash basis.
- *Audited financial statements*. Auditors will not approve financial statements that were compiled under the cash basis, so an organization will need to convert to the accrual basis if it wants to have audited financial statements.
- *Management reporting*. Since the results of cash basis financial statements can be inaccurate, management reports should not be issued that are based upon it.

In short, the numerous problems with the cash basis of accounting usually cause organizations to abandon it after they move beyond their initial startup phases.

The Financial Statements

The financial statements are used to present the results of operations, financial position, and cash flows of a health care entity. They are used by the owners, managers, and lenders of a business, and so may be perused by a large number of people. The accountant is responsible for the financial statements, since they essentially aggregate the results of all of the recordkeeping activities of the accounting department. The following sections describe the format of each component of the financial statements. The financial statements presented in this section are in the format used by an investor-owned enterprise. See the following two chapters for a discussion of the financial statements produced by not-for-profit and governmental entities operating in the health care field.

The Income Statement

The income statement is an integral part of an entity's financial statements, and contains the results of its operations during an accounting period, showing revenues and expenses and the resulting profit or loss. There are no specific requirements for the line items to include in the income statement. However, once a set of line items has been used, it is customary to continue using the same format in future income statements, thereby making the income statements easier to compare across a number of reporting periods.

The income statement should be presented using a classification based on the nature or function of expenses; the goal is to maximize the relevance and reliability of the presented information. If expenses are presented by their nature, the format looks similar to what appears in the following exhibit.

Sample Presentation by Nature of Items

Revenue		$xxx
Expenses		
Salaries expense	xxx	
Payroll taxes	xxx	
Employee benefits	xxx	
Depreciation expense	xxx	
Telephone expense	xxx	
Other expenses	xxx	
Total expenses		$xxx
Profit before tax		$xxx

Alternatively, if expenses are presented by their functional area, the format looks similar to the presentation in the following exhibit, where most expenses are aggregated at the department level.

Sample Presentation by Function of Items

Revenue	$xxx
Anesthesiology department	$xxx
Emergency department	xxx
General surgery department	xxx
Immunology department	xxx
Neurology department	xxx
Total expenses	$xxx
Profit before tax	$xxx

Of the two methods, presenting expenses by their nature is easier, since it requires no allocation of expenses between functional areas. Conversely, the functional area presentation may be more relevant to users of the information, who can more easily see where resources are being consumed.

A sample income statement for a for-profit health care entity appears next.

Ultra Healthcare, Inc.
Sample Income Statement

Revenue, net of contractual discounts	$2,864,000
Provision for uncompensated care	-1,266,000
Net revenue	1,598,000
Compensation and benefits	1,124,000
Operating expenses	253,000
Insurance expense	37,000
Selling, general and administrative expenses	38,000
Depreciation expense	57,000
Income from operations	89,000
Interest expense	-39,000
Income before taxes	50,000
Income tax expense	-19,000
Net income	$31,000

The Balance Sheet

A balance sheet (also known as a statement of financial position) presents information about an entity's assets, liabilities, and shareholders' equity, where the compiled result must match this formula:

Total assets = Total liabilities + Equity

The balance sheet reports the aggregate effect of transactions as of a specific date. The balance sheet is used to assess an entity's liquidity and ability to pay its debts.

There is no specific requirement for the line items to be included in the balance sheet – though, as was the case with the income statement, continue using the same line items in future periods, so that balance sheets can be more easily compared over time. The asset and liability line items are presented in order of how fast they can be liquidated (known as the *order of liquidity*), so that cash appears as the first asset, while the much more long-term fixed assets line item is stated further down the list of assets.

A sample balance sheet for a for-profit health care entity appears next.

Ultra Healthcare, Inc.
Sample Balance Sheet

Assets	
Current assets:	
Cash	$192,000
Trade and other accounts receivable, net	1,296,000
Parts and supplies inventory	34,000
Prepaids and other current assets	123,000
Total current assets	1,645,000
Non-current assets:	
Fixed assets, net	351,000
Other long-term assets	95,000
Total assets	$2,091,000
Liabilities and equity	
Current liabilities:	
Accounts payable	$63,000
Accrued liabilities	59,000
Current portion of long-term debt	24,000
Total current liabilities	146,000
Long-term debt obligations	1,417,000
Insurance reserves	249,000
Other long-term liabilities	55,000
Total liabilities	1,867,000
Equity	200,000
Retained earnings	24,000
Total equity	224,000
Total liabilities and equity	$2,091,000

The Statement of Cash Flows

The statement of cash flows contains information about the flows of cash into and out of a health care entity; in particular, it shows the extent of those activities that generate and use cash. The primary activities are:

- *Operating activities*. These are an entity's primary revenue-producing activities. Examples of operating activities are cash receipts from the sale of services, as well as amounts received or paid to settle lawsuits, payments to

employees and suppliers, cash payments to lenders for interest, contributions to charity, and the settlement of asset retirement obligations.

- *Investing activities.* These involve the acquisition and disposal of long-term assets. Examples of investing activities are cash receipts from the sale of property, the sale of the debt or equity instruments of other entities, the repayment of loans made to other entities, and proceeds from insurance settlements related to damaged fixed assets. Examples of cash payments that are investment activities include the acquisition of fixed assets, as well as the purchase of the debt or equity of other entities.
- *Financing activities.* These are the activities resulting in alterations to the amount of contributed equity and the entity's borrowings. Examples of financing activities include cash receipts from the sale of the entity's own equity instruments or from issuing debt, and cash payments to buy back shares, pay dividends, and pay off outstanding debt.

The statement of cash flows also incorporates the concept of cash and cash equivalents. A cash equivalent is a short-term, very liquid investment that is easily convertible into a known amount of cash, and which is so near its maturity that it presents an insignificant risk of a change in value because of changes in interest rates.

The *indirect method* is most commonly used to present the statement of cash flows. This presentation begins with net income or loss, with subsequent additions to or deductions from that amount for non-cash revenue and expense items, resulting in net income provided by operating activities. The format of the indirect method appears in the following example.

Ultra Healthcare, Inc.
Sample Statement of Cash Flows

Cash flows from operating activities	
Net income	$31,000
Adjustments to reconcile net income to net cash provided by (used in) operating activities:	
Depreciation	57,000
(Gain) loss on disposal of fixed assets	100
Dividends received	400
Deferred income taxes	8,600
Changes in operating assets and liabilities	
Trade and other accounts receivable	-38,000
Parts and supplies inventory	700
Prepaids and other current assets	-23,000
Accounts payable and accrued liabilities	50,900
Insurance reserves	-1,700
Net cash provided by (used in) operating activities	86,000
Cash flows from investing activities	
Purchases of available-for-sale securities	-3,000
Sales of available-for-sale securities	14,000
Purchased of fixed assets	-39,000
Net cash provided by (used in) investing activities	28,000
Cash flows from financing activities	
Borrowings under credit line	70,000
Repayment of term loan	-6,000
Other financing activities	3,500
Net cash provided by (used in) financing activities	67,500
Change in cash and cash equivalents	181,500
Cash and cash equivalents, beginning of period	10,500
Cash and cash equivalents, end of period	192,000

In previous sections of this chapter, we noted that the balance sheet and income statement can be derived from the trial balance. This is not the case for the statement of cash flows. Instead, the information in this report must be compiled from a number of line items in the balance sheet and income statement, as described in the following table. It is also possible to print a standardized version of this report from the organization's accounting software, but the result may be too generalized, and so will require some alterations before it adequately reflects actual cash flows.

Sample Sources of Information for the Statement of Cash Flows

Line Item	Derivation
Cash flows from operating activities	
Net income	From the net income line on the income statement
Adjustment for:	
Depreciation	From the corresponding line item in the income statement
Provision for losses on accounts receivable	From the change in the allowance for doubtful accounts in the period
Gain/loss on sale of fixed assets	From the gain/loss accounts in the income statement
Increase/decrease in trade receivables	Change in trade receivables during the period, from the balance sheet
Increase/decrease in inventories	Change in inventories during the period, from the balance sheet
Increase/decrease in trade payables	Change in trade payables during the period, from the balance sheet
Cash generated from operations	Summary of the preceding items in this section
Cash flows from investing activities	
Purchase of fixed assets	Itemized in the fixed asset accounts during the period
Proceeds from sale of fixed assets	Itemized in the fixed asset accounts during the period
Net cash used in investing activities	Summary of the preceding items in this section
Cash flows from financing activities	
Proceeds from issuance of common stock	Net increase in the common stock accounts during the period
Proceeds from issuance of long-term debt	Itemized in the long-term debt account during the period
Dividends paid	Itemized in the retained earnings account during the period
Net cash used in financing activities	Summary of the preceding items in this section
Net change in cash and cash equivalents	Summary of all preceding subtotals

Summary

The main focus of this chapter was to reveal how business transactions are recorded in the accounting database. The level of detail given was intended to provide the reader with a basic understanding of the process flow, where transactions are summarized into accounts. We also defined a number of key concepts, including accounts, journal entries, the chart of accounts, and ledgers. Finally, we noted how the various business transactions roll up into the general ledger, from which the trial balance and financial statements are derived. This entire process flow is the system of accounting that an accountant will use in a health care enterprise.

Chapter 3
Not-for-Profit Accounting and Reporting

Introduction

A great many health care entities are organized as not-for-profits. By gaining not-for-profit status from the Internal Revenue Service, an organization can avoid paying federal income taxes, and can instead plow these funds back into its core mission. According to the Financial Accounting Standards Board (which issues the accounting standards that govern not-for-profits), the key criteria that define a not-for-profit are:

- No ownership interests
- An operating purpose other than to earn a profit
- It receives significant contributions from third parties that do not expect a return

Conversely, an entity that cannot be considered a not-for-profit is one that is owned by investors, or which provides dividends or other economic benefits to its owners or members.

In this chapter, we explore the unique aspects of the accounting that a health care entity may be required to follow, also noting the different financial statements that must be reported. We are *only* making note of those accounting issues that relate most directly to not-for-profit accounting and reporting. There are many other accounting and reporting issues found in the remainder of this book that are broadly applicable to *all* types of health care entities. Please note that the discussions in the Investments, Split-Interest Agreements, and Affiliated Organizations chapters are from the perspective of a not-for-profit organization.

The Accounting Equation

In a for-profit organization, the basic underlying accounting structure is derived from the following formula, which (as noted in the preceding chapter) is called the accounting equation:

Assets = Liabilities + Stockholders' equity

However, there is no equity in a not-for-profit organization, since there are no stockholders to own shares in the business. Instead, the accounting equation is modified as follows:

Assets = Liabilities + Net assets

The Net Assets part of the equation contains the total amounts of two classifications of donated assets, which are:

- Net assets with donor restrictions
- Net assets without donor restrictions

We address the net assets topic in more detail in the next section.

Net Assets

We mentioned the net assets concept in the preceding Accounting Equation section. A net asset is the equivalent of retained earnings in the financial statements of a for-profit business. When contributing assets, a donor may impose restrictions on their use. The result is two types of net assets, which are classified as net assets with donor restrictions and net assets without donor restrictions. The accounting for these types of net assets varies, as noted in the following sub-sections.

Net Assets without Donor Restrictions

When a donor imposes no restriction on a contribution made to a not-for-profit, the not-for-profit records the contribution as an asset and as contribution revenue with no donor restrictions. These funds are used to pay for the general operations of the organization. The fundraising staff strongly encourages donors to make unrestricted donations, since these funds can be put to the broadest possible range of uses. Since this contribution revenue also creates a profit, the profit appears in the statement of financial position as an increase in net assets without donor restrictions.

Net Assets with Donor Restrictions

When a donor imposes a restriction on a contribution made to a not-for-profit, the not-for-profit records the contribution as contribution revenue with donor restrictions. Only the donor can change this designation; the organization's board of directors is not allowed to do so.

There may be a number of sub-accounts within the net assets with donor restrictions account, for those situations in which donors want to contribute to specific aspects of a project or to release funds for use over a period of time. For example, when a hospital is being built, donors may only want to contribute to certain departments. Or, donors may want their contributions to be spent evenly over the next five years. It is also possible that donors will require that an asset be held in perpetuity, usually allowing the not-for-profit to only spend any interest income derived from the funds.

Net Assets Summary

The following example shows various situations in which contributions fall into the two classifications.

EXAMPLE

Mr. Davis Templeton is a major contributor to Newton County Hospital. He is aware that Newton needs $25,000 for laptop computers for use by its interns. He therefore contributes $25,000 to Newton, under the provision that the funds will be used to buy laptops. This contribution increases both the cash account of Newton and the net assets with donor restrictions account by $25,000. Newton uses the money to acquire laptops. The result is a shift of $25,000 from the cash account to the fixed assets account, as well as a shift of $25,000 from the net assets with donor restrictions account to the net assets without donor restrictions account.

EXAMPLE

Mrs. Martha Anglesey is strongly supportive of indigent health care, and so contributes $500,000 to St. Luke Hospital, under the provision that only the interest on the contribution can be spent to pay for indigent health care. This contribution increases the hospital's net assets with donor restrictions account by $500,000.

The totals of each of these classifications are reported within the net assets section of the statement of financial position, along with a grand total for all net assets.

A final thought regarding net assets is that they do not refer to *assets*. An asset is an item of economic value that is expected to yield a benefit in future periods. A net asset is more like a separate project, for which a separate set of financial statements can be generated.

Types of Revenue

A not-for-profit health care entity may receive revenue from a number of sources, which may include the following general classifications:

- *Fee for services*. A not-for-profit may have operations similar to those of a for-profit enterprise, where it provides services in exchange for a fee. If so, the fee is treated as revenue, while the cost of the services provided are recognized as an operating expense. These fees are recognized during the period when services are provided. For example, a not-for-profit hospital charges patients a fee for services provided in its emergency room.
- *Donor contributions*. This is a payment made by a third party, where the third party does not expect to receive any compensation in exchange for the payment. A donor contribution may be unrestricted or restricted. The payment may be in cash, or in the form of some other asset, or by paying off a liability owed by a not-for-profit. Contributions received that have donor-imposed restrictions are reported as donor-restricted support that increases net assets with donor restrictions. When contributions have no donor-imposed restrictions, they are reported as support that increases net assets without donor restrictions. Donor-restricted contributions for which the conditions are met in the same reporting period can be reported as support within net assets without donor restrictions.

- *Fundraising proceeds.* A not-for-profit may engage in events that are designed to raise money for its general operations or for specific programs. Sample fundraising events are art shows, dinners, and periodic mailings. These activities may involve the transfer of some item of value back to a donor, such as art work, a dinner, or a trip. The value of these items of value is termed *exchange value*, which is dealt with in a later section.
- *Promises to give.* Donors may commit in writing to making payments to a not-for-profit, perhaps over several years. See the following Promises to Give section for more information.
- *Stock donations.* Donors may contribute some portion of their stock holdings to not-for-profits in order to take a tax deduction on the fair value of the stock. When this happens, the not-for-profit records the value of the stock received at its fair value on the date of receipt.
- *In-kind materials donations.* A donor may contribute assets other than cash. For example, foodstuffs or used cars may be donated. These donations are to be recorded at their fair values. The fair value of any inventory items contributed can be derived from published catalogs, vendors, appraisers, and so forth. The amount of effort that goes into the determination of fair value will likely depend on the extent of the donation; for example, a not-for-profit is more likely to engage the services of an appraiser if a facility is donated than if a bag of used clothes is received.
- *Items to be used in fundraising.* Donors may contribute such items as gift certificates, trips, and concert tickets to a not-for-profit, to be used as prizes in fundraising campaigns. These items are to be recorded as revenue at their fair values when received. Once these items are given away as part of a fundraising event, the not-for-profit can also recognize as revenue the difference between the fundraising total and the previously recorded revenue associated with the items used in the fundraising event.

Promises to Give

A donor may promise a not-for-profit to contribute money to it in the future. This promise is called a *pledge*. There are many types of pledges, such as ones that are to be fulfilled all at one time, in increments, and with or without restrictions. The accounting for a pledge depends upon the conditions attached to it. The variations are:

- *Unconditional pledge.* When a donor commits to a pledge without reservation, the not-for-profit receiving the funds records the pledge as revenue and an account receivable.
- *Conditional pledge.* When a donor commits to a pledge, but only when a condition is met, the not-for-profit does not record anything. Instead, it waits for the condition to be fulfilled and then records the pledge as revenue and an account receivable. If the probability that a condition will *not* be fulfilled is remote, the pledge can be treated as an unconditional pledge.

EXAMPLE

Mole Industries has a standing policy of matching all donations made by its employees to St. Luke Hospital. The offer of Mole Industries is a conditional pledge, since it is contingent upon donations being made by its employees. In May, Mole's employees contribute $500 to the hospital, so Mole pays St. Luke an additional $500. This matching amount can be recognized by St. Luke upon receipt.

EXAMPLE

The president of Mole Industries promises to give St. Luke an additional $10,000 donation if it provides him with its year-end financial statements. Since the probability that the hospital will withhold this information is remote, St. Luke could treat the promise as an unconditional one, and recognize the revenue and an offsetting receivable at once.

When in doubt, a not-for-profit should not record a pledge in the accounting records. Instead, wait for the situation to resolve itself, so that it can tell with certainty the circumstances under which a donor will make a contribution. In many cases, a simple notification of a forthcoming payment is not sufficient proof that a pledge exists. Instead, there should be a well-documented pledge that itemizes the amount to be paid and any conditions that must be fulfilled prior to payment.

If a pledge commitment is unconditional and legally enforceable, the not-for-profit is required to recognize the present value of the entire series of payments. Present value is the current worth of the cash to be received in the future with one or more payments, which has been discounted at a market rate of interest. The present value requirement is subject to the following variations:

- If the funds are to be received within one year, it is permissible to recognize the entire amount of the pledge, rather than just its present value.
- The estimated amount of cash flows can be used in the present value calculation, rather than the pledged amount. This allows management to be more conservative and recognize a lesser amount of revenue if it is uncertain about the total amount to be received or the timing of the receipt.

Tip: It is best to develop standardized pledge agreements for donors to sign, so that pledges can be recognized as revenue.

Exchange Value

Donors may agree to make a contribution to a not-for-profit in exchange for an item or service. For example, a person paying $100 might receive a book in exchange. The item or service given to a donor has an assigned exchange value. When a donor accepts this exchange, the value of the received item or service reduces the tax-deductible amount of the donor's contribution. For example, if a donor bids $50,000 at a

charity auction for a used vehicle that has a fair value of $30,000, the donor can only take a tax deduction of $20,000; this represents the net amount of contribution paid.

When a donor makes a contribution and does not accept any item or service in return, the donor can then use the entire amount of the contribution as a tax deduction.

The Allowance for Uncollectible Pledges

There tends to be a relatively large proportion of pledges made that are never paid by donors. This is because there is no incentive for donors to fulfill their pledges, and because not-for-profits are reluctant to pursue donors about late payments. Since such a large part of pledges receivable are never paid, it is necessary to use an allowance for uncollectible pledges. This account offsets the pledges receivable account, and contains management's best estimate of the proportion of outstanding receivables that will never be paid by donors. The result is a net receivables balance that should fairly reflect the amount of receivables that will actually be collected.

Overview of Government Grants

A major source of funds for a not-for-profit may be the government, which provides it with grants of various types. If so, it may be necessary to organize the recordation of accounting transactions by grant contract, so that incoming and outgoing funds can be traced to specific grants. For the larger grants, it may be necessary to create budgets for how funds are to be spent, and then trace actual expenditures back to the budget. Some governments want to see exactly how their funds were used, so the not-for-profit may also need to develop a unique report format for each grant, which is to be used when discussing fund usage with the applicable government representative.

In some instances, a not-for-profit may function as a general contractor. In this role, the not-for-profit takes in government grants and disburses it to other entities that perform the actual work. If so, the not-for-profit takes a portion of the grant in order to pay for its administrative costs in managing the disbursement of funds and how those funds are used. This situation typically arises when research is being conducted.

When a not-for-profit subsists on government grants, the tracking and reporting of grant-related funds is likely to be the central responsibility of the accounting department – to the point where the accounting staff can be considered key to obtaining and retaining government grants. If so, it may be necessary to assign some of the accounting staff to specific government contracts, so that they can closely monitor activity. These personnel are specialists, and are not involved in the more general functional activities of the department.

Grant Accounting

A government grant is essentially a contribution, in that the funds are not to be repaid. However, the grant concept differs from a contribution in that the grant is tied to the provision of goods or services by the not-for-profit, usually in relation to a specific program.

Grants may be paid in advance; if so, the related funds are booked into net asset with donor restriction accounts. When funds are spent against these grants, an equivalent amount of funds are released from the applicable net asset accounts. Thus, the amount released matches the amount spent. Alternatively, a not-for-profit may spend the funds first and then apply for a drawdown of a matching amount from the applicable grant.

Whenever possible, costs should be designated as direct costs; this means that they are directly related to a specific activity, and so would not be incurred if the related activity did not exist. For example, the salaries of technical staff, project supplies, project publications, computer costs, travel costs, and specialized services can usually be treated as direct costs when they can be linked to a specific program. However, the salaries of administrative staff are usually *not* treated as a direct cost, except when a project or activity explicitly requires and budgets for administrative services and individuals can be specifically identified with the project or activity.

A not-for-profit is typically allowed to charge an additional amount of expense against a grant, called the *indirect rate*. The indirect rate is an overhead charge. The compilation of the indirect rate is based on one of two formulas allowed by the federal government. The first is called the *simplified allocation method*, and is described as follows in Circular 122 of the Office of Management and Budget:

> The allocation of indirect costs may be accomplished by (i) separating the organization's total costs for the base period as either direct or indirect, and (ii) dividing the total allowable indirect costs (net of applicable credits) by an equitable distribution base. The result of this process is an indirect cost rate which is used to distribute indirect costs to individual awards. The rate should be expressed as the percentage which the total amount of allowable indirect costs bears to the base selected.

The preceding description of the simplified allocation method refers to indirect costs, which are costs not directly associated with a specific activity or program. The "equitable distribution base" noted in the description is usually considered to be the total amount of direct costs charged to a program. Direct costs are most commonly the salaries of those people working on a program.

EXAMPLE

Cancer Resolution has total indirect costs of $3,500,000 and total direct costs of $15,900,000. Direct costs are considered an equitable distribution base. Accordingly, the indirect cost rate is derived by dividing total indirect costs into total direct costs, for an allocation rate of 22%.

Cancer Resolution has obtained $1,000,000 of funding from the federal government to engage in research regarding cancer of the pancreas. Seven researchers will work full-time on this project, at a cost of $750,000. The $750,000 is the total direct cost associated with the project, and is considered the base upon which indirect costs will be allocated to the project. The entity's indirect cost rate is 22%, so the direct cost figure is multiplied by 22% to arrive at an indirect cost allocation of $165,000.

A considerably more complex approach is the *multiple allocation base method*, which is described in the same publication as follows:

> Aggregate indirect costs are accumulated into separate cost groupings. Each grouping is then allocated individually to benefitting functions by means of a base which best measures the relative benefits. Each grouping constitutes a pool of expenses that are of like character in terms of functions they benefit and in terms of the allocation base which best measures the relative benefits provided to each function. The indirect cost pools are defined as follows:
>
> - *Depreciation and use allowances.* The portion of the costs of the organization's buildings, capital improvements to land and buildings, and equipment.
> - *Interest.* Interest on debt associated with certain buildings, equipment and capital improvements.
> - *Operation and maintenance expenses.* Those costs that have been incurred for the administration, operation, maintenance, preservation, and protection of the organization's physical plant. They include expenses normally incurred for such items as: janitorial and utility services; repairs and ordinary or normal alterations of buildings, furniture and equipment; care of grounds; maintenance and operation of buildings and other plant facilities; security; earthquake and disaster preparedness; environmental safety; hazardous waste disposal; property, liability and other insurance relating to property; space and capital leasing; facility planning and management; and, central receiving. The operation and maintenance expenses category shall also include its allocable share of fringe benefit costs, depreciation and use allowances, and interest costs.
> - *General and administrative expenses.* Those costs that have been incurred for the overall general executive and administrative offices of the organization and other expenses of a general nature which do not relate solely to any major function of the organization. This category shall also include its allocable share of fringe benefit costs, operation and maintenance expense, depreciation and use allowances, and interest costs. Examples of this category include central offices, such as the director's office, the office of finance, business services, budget and planning, personnel, safety and risk management, general counsel, management information systems, and library costs.

Given the increased level of accounting difficulty associated with the multiple allocation base method, one should be knowledgeable about when its use can be avoided. The key factors to consider are:

- *One major function.* When a not-for-profit has just one major function that may encompass several projects, use the simplified allocation method.
- *Minimal funding.* When the level of federal awards to a not-for-profit is relatively small, use the simplified allocation method.
- *Differing levels of benefit.* When a not-for-profit's indirect costs benefit its major functions in the same degree, use the simplified allocation method.

If any of these issues are *not* the case, use the multiple allocation base method instead.

There are situations where a not-for-profit may want to use an indirect cost rate that is not derived precisely from either of the two preceding methods. If so, it can submit an allocation plan to the federal agency from which it obtains the largest proportion of its government grants. If approved, the result is an official indirect cost rate that can be applied to most grants originating from federal agencies, and sometimes also from state and local agencies.

Income from Government Grants

There are situations in which government funds result in the generation of additional revenue. For example, there may not be an immediate need for all of the funds in a grant, so they are parked in an interest-bearing investment account. Alternatively, the funds may result in a profit-making endeavor that generates its own cash flow. In either case, how is this additional income to be handled in the accounting records? There are several possibilities:

- Add the additional income to the amount of the government grant, thereby resulting in more cash being made available for the applicable program.
- Use the cash to fund the other parts of the applicable program that are not being paid for by a government grant, thereby reducing the fundraising burden of the not-for-profit.
- Subtract the extra income from the expenses associated with the applicable program, thereby reducing the amount of expenses, and allowing for additional expenditures.

The contract associated with a grant will typically state which of these alternatives can be used.

Required Not-for-Profit Financial Statements

The financial reporting package for a not-for-profit is comprised of a statement of financial position, a statement of activities, and a statement of cash flows. We address issues related to the specific financial statements in this reporting package in the following sub-sections.

Statement of Financial Position

A not-for-profit entity needs to report the state of its assets and liabilities as of the end of each reporting period, as well as provide an indication of its ability to meet its financial obligations. In a for-profit business, the financial statement used to report this information is the balance sheet. A not-for-profit entity reports similar information in the *statement of financial position*. The main difference between a balance sheet and a not-for-profit's statement of financial position is that the balance sheet contains a shareholders' equity section, which is replaced by a net assets section in the statement of financial position. A sample statement of financial position for a health care entity appears in the following exhibit.

St. Bernard Hospital
Statement of Financial Position

Assets	
Current assets:	
Cash and cash equivalents	$426,000
Short-term investments	37,000
Patient accounts receivable, net of estimated uncollectibles of $173,000	630,000
Due from others, current portion	69,000
Inventories of supplies	135,000
Prepaid expenses and other current assets	61,000
Total current assets	1,358,000
Assets whose use is limited by donors or grantors for:	
Future facility development	11,000
Pledges receivable	30,000
By Board of Trustees	843,000
Total assets whose use is limited	884,000
Investments	1,873,000
Fixed assets, net of $1,917,000 of accumulated depreciation	2,885,000
Total assets	$7,000,000
Liabilities and net assets	
Current liabilities:	
Accounts payable and accrued liabilities	$637,000
Medical claims reserve	95,000
Deferred revenue	120,000
Total current liabilities	852,000
Estimated malpractice costs	481,000
Net pension liability	1,389,000
Other long-term liabilities	371,000
Total liabilities	3,093,000
Net assets:	
Unrestricted	3,275,000
Restricted	632,000
Total net assets	3,907,000
Total liabilities and net assets	$7,000,000

Statement of Activities

The primary intent of a not-for-profit is (as the name implies) something other than earning a profit. Consequently, a not-for-profit does not issue an income statement, as

does a for-profit business. Instead, a not-for-profit issues an alternative called a *statement of activities* or *statement of operations*. This statement quantifies the revenue and expenses of a not-for-profit for a reporting period. Despite the implication that a not-for-profit is not supposed to earn a profit, it may need to generate substantial profits in order to guard against shortfalls in donor funding or unexpected increases in expenses. Consequently, the results appearing in the statement of activities are closely perused by the managers of a not-for-profit, to see if the business is generating sufficient profits to guard against future financial difficulties.

The following reporting requirements are only mandated for a not-for-profit, business-oriented health care entity:

- *Functional classifications*. Expenses are generally grouped for reporting purposes by function. The two most common classifications are health services and general and administrative. More detailed functional distinctions can also be used, such as physician services, research, and teaching.
- *Reconciliation*. The ending net assets figure in the statement of activities should tie back to the information in the statement of financial position. This is the beginning amount of net assets, net of any changes in net assets during the reporting period.
- *Performance indicator*. The statement of operations must include a performance indicator, showing the results of operations. This line item must be presented in a statement with the total changes in unrestricted net assets. Examples of titles that can be used for the performance indicator are:
    - Earned income
    - Performance earnings
    - Revenues and gains over expenses and losses
    - Revenues over expenses
- *Additional line items*. The following line items must be included in the statement of activities separately from the performance indicator:
    - *Equity transfers*. All equity transfers with entities that control the reporting entity, are controlled by it, or are under common control.
    - *Inherent contributions*. Any contributions resulting from a voluntary transfer of assets or the performance of services in exchange for either no assets or assets of substantially lower value.
    - *Investment gains*. Any investment gains that increase unrestricted net assets back to a required amount from which there had previously been losses.
    - *Investment losses*. Any investment losses that reduce the assets of a donor-restricted endowment fund below a required amount.
    - *Mandated separate reporting*. Any items that are required to be reported separately, such as discontinued operations.
    - *Owner transactions*. Any transactions with the owners of the entity.
    - *Released contributions*. Any contributions that have been released from donor restrictions that relate to long-lived assets.

- *Restricted contributions*. The receipt of any restricted contributions.
- *Restricted returns*. Any investment returns that have been restricted by donors or applicable laws.
- *Unrealized income*. Any items that are reported in or reclassified from other comprehensive income.

A sample statement of activities for a health care entity appears in the following exhibit.

St. Bernadette Hospital
Statement of Activities

Operating revenues	
Patient service revenue before provision for bad debts	$5,193,000
Provision for bad debts	-86,000
Net patient service revenue	5,107,000
Other revenue	631,000
Investment income	61,000
Net assets released from restrictions used for operations	11,000
Total operating revenues	5,810,000
Operating expenses	
Salaries, wages and benefits	2,207,000
Purchased services	2,193,000
Supplies and other	947,000
Interest	33,000
Depreciation	262,000
Total operating expenses	5,642,000
Income from operations	168,000
Non-operating revenues and expenses:	
Net realized gains on investments	42,000
Excess of revenues over expenses	210,000
Net assets released from restrictions used for purchases of fixed assets	9,000
Increase in unrestricted net assets	219,000
Changes in restricted net assets	
Gifts, grants and bequests	17,000
Net assets released from restrictions used for purchases of fixed assets	-9,000
Net assets released from restrictions used for operations	-11,000
Decrease in restricted net assets	-3,000
Increase in net assets	216,000
Net assets at beginning of year	3,755,000
Net assets at end of year	$3,971,000

Statement of Cash Flows

As was the case in the preceding chapter for a for-profit entity, a not-for-profit entity must also produce a statement of cash flows. We refer the reader back to the System of Accounting chapter for a full discussion of the contents of this report. A sample statement of cash flows for a health care entity appears in the following exhibit.

St. Bartholomew
Statement of Cash Flows

Operating activities	
Change in net assets	-$301,000
Adjustments to reconcile change in net assets to net cash and cash equivalents provided by operating activities:	
Depreciation	260,000
Provision for bad debts	86,000
Net realized losses on investments	61,000
Restricted contributions and investment income received	-11,000
Gains on equity investments	-26,000
Change in assets and liabilities:	
Patient accounts receivable	-128,000
Inventories of supplies	-48,000
Pledges receivable	8,000
Accounts payable	53,000
Medical claims reserve	20,000
Deferred revenue	-73,000
Estimated malpractice costs	-3,000
Other long-term liabilities	2,000
Net cash and cash equivalents provided by operating activities	-100,000
Investing activities	
Purchases of fixed assets	-174,000
Purchases of investment securities	-1,421,000
Sales of investment securities	1,258,000
Other investing activities	-6,000
Net cash and cash equivalents used in investing activities	-343,000
Financing activities	
Proceeds from restricted contributions and investment income received	11,000
Proceeds from long-term borrowings	406,000
Other financing activities	2,000
Net cash and cash equivalents used in financing activities	419,000
Change in cash and cash equivalents	-24,000
Cash and cash equivalents at beginning of year	579,000
Cash and cash equivalents at end of year	$555,000

Summary

In this chapter, we touched upon just those topics in the not-for-profit accounting area that are most likely to pertain to a not-for-profit health care entity, with a particular emphasis on net assets and financial statement presentation. Not-for-profit accounting is a broad topic, encompassing many areas that are not found in for-profit organizations. For a more complete treatment of this topic, see the latest edition of the author's *Nonprofit Accounting* book.

Chapter 4
Governmental Accounting and Reporting

Introduction

Some health care entities are owned or administered by governments. As such, these entities are subject to governmental accounting standards, which differ in some respects from the accounting used by for-profit and not-for-profit entities. In this chapter, we explore the unique aspects of governmental accounting that a health care entity may be required to follow, also noting the different financial statements that must be reported. We are *only* making note of those accounting issues that relate most directly to governmental accounting and reporting. There are many other accounting and reporting issues found in the remainder of this book that are broadly applicable to *all* types of health care entities.

Fund Accounting Systems

A *fund* is an accounting entity with a self-balancing set of accounts that is used to record financial resources and liabilities, as well as operating activities, and which is segregated in order to carry on certain activities or attain targeted objectives. Funds are used by governments because governments need to maintain tight control over their resources, and funds are designed to monitor resource inflows and outflows, with particular attention to the remaining amount of funds available. By segregating resources into multiple funds, a government can more closely monitor resource usage, thereby minimizing the risk of overspending or of spending in areas not authorized by a government budget.

There are many types of funds, but we will concentrate on just one fund, which is the *enterprise fund*. These funds are used to account for any activity for which external users are charged a fee for goods and services, even when the government subsidizes a portion of the activity's costs. Thus, a government-owned health care entity is most likely to be accounted for with an enterprise fund.

EXAMPLE

Helix City's municipal hospital is governed by an annual operating budget in which fees are set at a level sufficient to fully recover all budgeted costs, as well as the depreciation on related assets. Since the costs of the hospital operations are recovered with fees, the related accounting should be for an enterprise fund.

Basis of Accounting and Measurement Focus

The enterprise fund operates in a manner similar to what is found in a for-profit organization, where the accrual basis of accounting is the default type of accounting. This approach differs from what is found in many other government funds, where the modified accrual basis of accounting is the norm. We will not explain the modified accrual basis here, since it is not relevant to the operation of an enterprise fund. However, we will reiterate that under the accrual basis of accounting, the occurrence of a business event triggers the recognition of most transactions, irrespective of the underlying movement of cash.

Governmental accounting involves a concept not found in other types of organizations, which is the measurement focus. The measurement focus governs *what* transactions will be recorded. An enterprise fund employs the *economic resources measurement focus*. This approach focuses on whether a fund is economically better off because of transactions occurring within the fiscal period being reported. Thus, when a transaction improves the economic position of the fund, the transaction is recorded as revenue or a gain. Conversely, when a transaction reduces the economic position of the fund, the transaction is recorded as an expense or a loss. The time period addressed by the economic resources measurement focus extends beyond the short-term, so an enterprise fund will include long-term assets and liabilities on its balance sheet. This approach is quite similar to what is used by commercial organizations.

The economic measurement focus might seem quite logical (which it is). We only make note of it because most government funds *do not* use it. Instead, they use the current financial resources measurement focus, where the focus of a fund is on current financial resources, which means assets that can be converted into cash and liabilities that will be paid for with that cash. Stated differently, the balance sheets of most government funds do not include long-term assets or any assets that will not be converted into cash in order to settle current liabilities. Similarly, these balance sheets will not contain any long-term liabilities, since they do not require the use of current financial resources for their settlement. The current financial resources measurement focus is only used in governmental accounting.

Fund Contents

Each enterprise fund must include a set of self-balancing accounts that addresses the needs for which the fund was created. The accounts included in a fund should address all of the following:

- Assets
- Liabilities
- Net assets (instead of equity)
- Revenues
- Expenses
- Transfers (between funds)

Budgetary Reporting

Governments use budgeting as one of their key financial planning and control tools. Ideally, every government should prepare an annual budget for each of its enterprise funds. The governments of states and larger municipalities require their various departments and agencies to submit budget requests, which are then used by the applicable legislative body as the basis for appropriation bills or ordinances. These appropriations state the maximum expenditures allowed for the budget year. The government cannot exceed these expenditure levels, unless the legislative body subsequently amends its appropriation bill to accommodate more expenditures.

A budget is structured to be either fixed or flexible. A fixed budget contains fixed dollar amounts for all stated line items. This document is based on a single activity level for the government entity to which it is related. A flexible budget contains formulas that will alter the stated amount of a line item, depending on the related activity level.

Most government budgets are fixed, on the assumption that revenue levels are relatively fixed. The control system that underlies these budgets is targeted at keeping expenditure levels from surpassing projected revenue levels. An enterprise fund is more likely to have a flexible budget associated with it, since this type of fund tends to have a variable revenue level, depending on the amount of demand for the fund's goods and services. Since revenues fluctuate, the expenditure budget must be flexible enough to change in accordance with revenue levels. Budgetary control is achieved by comparing actual expense levels to the expense amounts indicated in the budget, once the effects of revenue changes on the budgeted expenses have been considered.

Interfund Activity

Interfund activity between an enterprise fund and other government funds should be classified in the following manner:

- *Reciprocal interfund activity*. This type of activity involves the transfer of funds that are expected to be paid back. Such a loan should be reported as an inter-fund receivable by the lending fund and as an inter-fund payable by the borrowing fund. In situations where repayment is not expected within a reasonable time frame, reduce the amount not expected to be paid as a transfer from the lending fund to the receiving fund. An alternative situation is when there is a sale and purchase of goods and services between funds at prices approximating the market rate. These transactions should be reported by the selling fund as revenue and as an expense or expenditure by the purchasing fund. Any of these amounts that are unpaid are recorded as interfund receivables by the seller and as interfund payables by the purchaser.
- *Non-reciprocal interfund activity*. A non-reciprocal interfund transfer occurs when there is a one-way flow of assets between funds (that is, there is no repayment requirement). This type of transfer is to be reported as other financing uses by the fund issuing the transfer and as other financing sources by the receiving fund. There may also be interfund reimbursements, where a

fund responsible for an expenditure or expense transfers a payment to the fund that initially paid for the item in question.

Asset Transfers

When a capital asset is transferred within the same reporting entity, the receiving fund should continue to report the asset's original cost and the related amount of accumulated depreciation. Thus, the accumulated depreciation for a capital asset follows the asset, no matter where it goes within a government entity.

When a capital asset is shifted to an entirely different entity, the asset is removed from the accounting records of the entity that is losing the asset and added to the records of the entity that is gaining the asset.

EXAMPLE

The town of North Aldan is shifting the ownership of a medical clinic to the town of South Aldan. North Aldan's accountant should write off the clinic's book value in the period of the transfer, recording an expense in the amount of the clinic's book value.

Presentation Issues

A government has a reasonable amount of leeway in structuring the financial statements of its enterprise funds. Nonetheless, it should adhere to some presentation standards, so that its financials are comparable to those of similar entities run by other governments, while also being comparable from period to period. In general, the following principles should be followed in structuring financial statements:

- Report enterprise fund revenues by major sources and distinguish them as being operating and non-operating.
- Classify enterprise fund expenses in the same manner as those of similar business organizations or activities, and distinguish them as being operating and non-operating.
- Report contributions and transfers separately after non-operating revenues and expenses in an enterprise fund's statement of revenues, expenses, and changes in fund net position.

Reporting Net Position

The *net position* is the difference between all other elements in a statement of financial position (the balance sheet), so it is a summarization of other line items. Net position should be displayed in three components on the statement, as follows:

- *Net investment in capital assets*. Includes capital assets (net of accumulated depreciation), less the outstanding balances of bonds, mortgages, notes, and other borrowings associated with the acquisition or construction of capital

assets. If there is no debt associated with the capital assets, consider classifying this line item as "investment in capital assets" to avoid misleading readers.

Note: If debt is issued to refund existing debt that is related to capital assets, the replacement debt is also considered to be capital-related.

- *Restricted.* Report a restricted net position component when there are externally-imposed constraints placed on the net position, such as by creditors, grantors, contributors, or laws. It may be necessary to display the restricted component of net position in two components, which are expendable and non-expendable. A non-expendable net position must be reported when amounts are to be retained in perpetuity. The restricted component represents restricted assets that have been reduced by any liabilities related to those assets. A liability is considered to be related to an asset when the asset is a direct result of the liability being incurred, or if the liability will be liquidated along with the asset with which it is paired.
- *Unrestricted.* The unrestricted component of net position is the residual amount remaining that was not included in the calculation of the net investment in capital assets or the restricted components of net position.

Note: There may be internal constraints, where resources have been committed to specific activities. These commitments cannot be classified as restricted, since they can be removed or altered.

EXAMPLE

A municipal hospital's intern training center has received a $2 million bequest from someone who once benefited from its services. According to the terms of the bequest, the principal amount must be maintained, while any investment earnings can be used to pay for additional intern training. As of year-end, the fair value of this endowment has declined to $1.9 million. The restricted non-expendable net position should state the reported amount of $1.9 million. If the market recovers, allowing the $2 million principal amount to be regained, the restricted non-expendable net position would be reported as $2 million. If the market is unusually robust and the principal amount exceeds $2 million, the excess amount over $2 million would be reported as a restricted expendable net position.

Required Enterprise Fund Financial Statements

The financial reporting package for an enterprise fund is comprised of a statement of net position, a statement of revenues, expenses, and changes in fund net position, and a statement of cash flows. We address issues related to the specific financial statements in this reporting package in the following sub-sections.

Statement of Net Position

The statement of net position presents the financial position of an enterprise fund. The following rules apply to the classification and reporting of information within this statement:

- *Current and long-term differentiation.* Differentiate between the line items for current and long-term assets and liabilities.
- *Offsetting.* Do not offset assets and liabilities except when there is a right of offset.
- *Net position.* Break the net position into three parts, which are the net investment in capital assets, restricted, and unrestricted.
- *Receivable deductions.* When unearned discounts, finance charges, and interest have been added to the face amount of receivables, state these amounts in aggregate as a deduction from the receivables with which they are paired.
- *Allowances.* When there is an asset valuation allowance for expected losses, deduct it on the statement of net position from the asset(s) with which it is paired.
- *Asset restrictions.* When there are restrictions on the use of assets that alter their normal availability, report these assets separately as restricted assets.

A sample statement of net position for a health care entity appears in the following exhibit.

Central Hospital District
Statement of Net Position

Assets	
Current assets:	
Cash and cash equivalents	$545,000
Investments	1,201,000
Patient accounts receivable, net of estimated uncollectibles of $36,000	2,241,000
Inventories	142,000
Other current assets	56,000
Total current assets	4,185,000
Noncurrent assets	
Assets whose use is limited:	
Investments under self-insurance trust agreements	47,000
Restricted assets, net of current portion:	
Under indenture agreements	21,000
Under indenture – project funds	52,000
Capital assets, net	3,666,000
Other assets	29,000
Total assets	$8,000,000
Liabilities	
Current liabilities:	
Accounts payable and accrued expenses	$81,000
Accrued compensation and payroll taxes	141,000
Estimated third-party payor settlements	35,000
Current installments of long-term debt	10,000
Other current liabilities	32,000
Total current liabilities	299,000
Net pension liability	159,000
Long-term debt	625,000
Total liabilities	1,083,000
Net position	
Net investment in capital assets	3,041,000
Restricted for debt service	75,000
Unrestricted	3,801,000
Total net position	$8,000,000

Statement of Revenues, Expenses, and Changes in Fund Net Position

The statement of revenues, expenses, and changes in fund net position is the operating statement for an enterprise fund. The following rules apply to the classification and reporting of information within this statement:

- *Revenue*. Report revenues by major source, net of discounts and allowances. Also, distinguish between operating and non-operating revenues.
- *Expenses*. Distinguish between operating and non-operating expenses.
- *Non-operating revenues and expenses*. Report non-operating revenues and expenses after operating income.
- *Subtotals*. Present a separate subtotal for operating revenues, operating expenses, and operating income.

> **Tip:** Create a policy that defines operating revenues and expenses and use it consistently over time to ensure consistent classification of revenue and expense transactions.

The statement of revenues, expenses, and changes in fund net position should follow the general format that appears in the following exhibit.

Sample Statement of Revenues, Expenses, and Changes in Fund Net Position

Operating revenues (multiple line items)
Total operating revenues
Operating expenses (multiple line items)
Total operating expenses
Operating income (loss)
Non-operating revenues and expenses (multiple line items)
Income before other revenues, expenses, gains, losses, and transfers
Capital contributions, additions to permanent and term endowments, special and extraordinary items (multiple line items) and transfers
Increase (decrease) in net position
Net position – beginning of period
Net position – end of period

A sample statement of revenues, expenses, and changes in fund net position for a health care entity appears in the following exhibit.

Western Hospital District
Statement of Revenues, Expenses, and Changes in Fund Net Position

Operating revenue:	
Net patient service revenue	$1,807,000
Other operating revenues	45,000
Total operating revenue	1,852,000
Operating expenses:	
Salaries and wages	842,000
Employee benefits	158,000
Professional fees	44,000
Supplies	220,000
Purchased services	108,000
Facilities	73,000
Depreciation	98,000
Other expenses	69,000
Total operating expenses	1,612,000
Operating income	240,000
Non-operating losses	7,000
Income before capital contributions and grants	233,000
Capital contributions and grants	4,000
Increase in net position	237,000
Net position at the beginning of the year	1,694,000
Net position at the end of the year	$1,931,000

Statement of Cash Flows

A statement of cash flows should be included in the financial statement package for an enterprise fund. The information in the statement is broken into four main classifications, which are cash flows from operating activities, cash flows from noncapital financing activities, cash flows from capital and related financing activities, and cash flows from investing activities. These classifications are discussed next.

Cash Flows from Operating Activities

One of the main classifications in a statement of cash flows is cash flows from operating activities. The results listed within this classification typically result from providing services and producing and delivering goods. It can also be a catchall classification that includes results that do not readily fall into any of the other classifications (which are covered in the following bullet points). As a general rule, results

included in cash flows from operating activities are those involving transactions and other events that are included in the determination of operating income. The cash inflows and outflows usually broken out within this classification are as follows:

Cash inflows from operating activities

- Cash received from the sale of goods or services, including the collection of receivables
- Cash received from the provision of interfund services
- Cash received from grants for specific activities that the granting entity considers to be operating activities
- Cash received from interfund reimbursements
- All other cash receipts not relating to the other reporting classifications

Cash outflows from operating activities

- Cash paid to buy materials for the provision of goods and services, including the payment of supplier invoices for such materials
- Cash paid to suppliers for other types of goods and services
- Cash paid to employees in exchange for their services
- Cash paid as grants to other entities for activities that the grantor considers to be operating activities
- Cash paid for taxes, fines, and other fees or penalties
- Cash paid for interfund services used
- All other cash payments not relating to the other reporting classifications

Additional line items can be added if the resulting detail is considered useful.

Cash Flows from Noncapital Financing Activities

The second classification used in the statement of cash flows is cash flows from noncapital financing activities. The line items within this classification include the borrowing of money for any activity that does not include the acquisition, construction, or improvement of capital assets, as well as the repayment of these borrowings. Also, any proceeds from borrowings that are not clearly associated with capital assets are stated here. The cash inflows and outflows usually broken out within this classification are as follows:

Cash inflows from noncapital financing activities

- Cash received from the issuance of bonds, notes, and other borrowings not clearly associated with capital asset activities
- Cash received from grants or subsidies, not including any cash specifically restricted for capital uses and those designated for activities that are classified as operating activities by the granting entity

- Cash received from other funds, not including any cash specifically attributable to capital asset activities, interfund services provided, or interfund reimbursements
- Cash received from tax collections for the enterprise and which are not restricted for capital asset activities

Cash outflows from noncapital financing activities

- Cash paid to reduce borrowings that were not intended for capital asset activities
- Cash paid to reduce the interest obligation to lenders on borrowings not associated with capital asset activities
- Cash paid as grants or subsidies to other entities, except in relation to activities considered to be operating activities by the grantor
- Cash paid to other funds, except in relation to the usage of interfund services

Cash Flows from Capital and Related Financing Activities

The third classification used in the statement of cash flows is cash flows from capital and related financing activities. The line items within this classification primarily address the acquisition and disposition of capital assets. The cash inflows and outflows usually broken out within this classification are as follows:

Cash inflows from capital and related financing activities

- Cash received from the issuance of bonds, mortgages, notes and other borrowings clearly associated with the acquisition, construction, or improvement of capital assets
- Cash received from capital grants
- Cash received from contributions made by other funds or other entities in order to defray the cost of acquiring, constructing, or improving capital assets
- Cash received from the sale of capital assets
- Cash received from insurance on capital assets that have been destroyed or stolen
- Cash received from taxes or special assessments levied specifically to finance capital asset activities

Cash outflows from capital and related financing activities

- Cash paid to acquire, construct, or improve capital assets
- Repayments of amounts borrowed to acquire, construct, or improve capital assets
- Other trade credit payments to suppliers related to capital asset activities
- Cash paid for the interest associated with capital asset activities

There can be some confusion in deciding whether to classify a cash flow as capital financing or non-capital financing in nature. The following rules can be used to make the determination:

- *Relationship to capital assets*. Debt that is not clearly attributable to the construction, acquisition, or improvement of capital assets should be classified as noncapital debt. Also, the debt proceeds and all subsequent principal and interest payments are considered noncapital financing.
- *Subsequent sale of assets*. When principal and interest payments are being made on debt that was originally used to acquire, construct or improve a capital asset, and that asset has since been disposed of in some way, continue to classify the payments as capital and related financing.
- *Debt refunding*. When debt is being recalled and then reissued, the proceeds of a debt issuance that is intended to refund capital debt is classified as a cash inflow within the capital and related financing category. Also, payments made to recall the original capital debt are classified as a cash outflow in the same category. Further, all subsequent principal and interest payments made against the refunding debt are classified as cash outflows in the capital and related financing category.

Cash Flows from Investing Activities

The fourth classification used in the statement of cash flows is cash flows from investing activities. The line items within this classification primarily address the issuance and collection of loans, as well as the acquisition and disposal of debt or equity securities. The cash inflows and outflows usually broken out within this classification are as follows:

Cash inflows from investing activities

- Cash received from collecting payments on loans made by the governmental enterprise, as well as from the sale of the debt instruments of other entities that had been purchased by the enterprise
- Cash received from the sale of equity securities
- Cash received from interest and dividends
- Cash received from the withdrawal of funds from investment pools

Cash outflows from investing activities

- Cash paid to acquire the debt instruments of other entities
- Cash paid to acquire equity securities
- Cash paid as deposits into investment pools

A statement of cash flows for a health care entity appears in the following exhibit.

Eastern Hospital District
Statement of Cash Flows

Operating activities	
Receipts from third-party payors and patients	$1,782,000
Payments to vendors	-610,000
Other receipts	98,000
Payments to employees	-936,000
Claims and self-insurance payments	-42,000
Net cash provided by operating activities	292,000
Noncapital financing activities	
Contributions and grant receipts	8,000
Contribution payments	-10,000
Net cash used in noncapital financial activities	-2,000
Capital and related financing activities	
Acquisition and construction of capital assets	-84,000
Principal payments on long-term debt	-9,000
Interest payments on long-term debt	-44,000
Net cash used in capital and related financing activities	-137,000
Investing activities	
Proceeds from sales, maturities, or repayment of investments	705,000
Cost of investments acquired	-792,000
Investment income received	35,000
Net cash used in investing activities	-52,000
Net change in cash and cash equivalents	101,000
Cash and cash equivalents at beginning of year	449,000
Cash and cash equivalents at end of year	550,000

Reconciliation of operating income to net cash provided by operating activities	
Operating income	$196,000
Adjustments to reconcile operating income to net cash provided by operating activities:	
Depreciation	101,000
Provision for doubtful accounts	417,000
Loss on disposal of capital assets	1,000
Changes in operating assets and liabilities:	
Patient accounts receivable	-462,000
Other current assets and inventories	3,000
Other assets	-10,000
Accounts payable and accrued expenses	-4,000
Accrued compensation and payroll taxes	25,000
Estimated third-party payor settlements	21,000
Other current liabilities	-6,000
Other liabilities	9,000
Estimated claims liabilities	1,000
Net cash provided by operating activities	$292,000

Summary

In this chapter, we touched upon just those topics in the governmental accounting area that are most likely to pertain to a government-owned health care entity, focusing entirely on enterprise funds. Governmental accounting is a broad topic, encompassing many types of funds and accounting issues that are not found in other organizations. For a more complete treatment of this topic, see the latest edition of the author's *Governmental Accounting* book.

Chapter 5
Cash and Receivable Accounting

Introduction

A health care enterprise has significant cash requirements, and so needs to maintain tight control over its cash. This means having a solid system in place for receiving and recording cash, as well as for shifting checks and cash into its bank accounts. In this chapter, we address the processing of several types of incoming payment, as well as the mechanics of the bank reconciliation. A bank reconciliation involves the comparison of a bank's record of the transactions passing through a company bank account to those recorded by the organization, to identify and adjust for any differences between the two. This can be a major issue, since *not* reconciling the books for several months introduces the very real prospect that the cash balance an accountant thinks he has does not resemble the actual balance.

Related Podcast Episodes: Episodes 41 and 137 of the Accounting Best Practices Podcast discuss remote deposit capture and a lean system for cash receipts, respectively. They are available at: **accountingtools.com/podcasts** or **iTunes**

Some types of health care entities (especially hospitals) will collect significantly less than their full rates, either due to contractual arrangements with third-party payors or because patients cannot pay. In this chapter, we also cover the proper accounting for these receivable shortfalls.

Check Receipts

The primary form of payment to many health care entities remains the check. The basic process flow for the handling of received checks involves the receipt, recordation, and depositing of checks by different people, where there are controls in place to monitor the checks at each transfer from one person to the next. This process is designed to mitigate the risk of loss, but does so at the price of being extremely inefficient.

The processing of check receipts involves the transfer of incoming payments from the mailroom to the accountant, then to a bank courier, and finally to a person who reconciles received to deposited cash. The following steps show the basic transaction flow:

1. *Record incoming checks*. The mailroom staff opens incoming mail, records all checks received, and stamps checks "for deposit only," before forwarding payments to the accountant. This step is a control point, designed to keep a

second record of check receipts in case the accountant attempts to abscond with any funds.

2. *Transfer checks*. The mailroom uses a locked pouch to transfer checks to the accountant, along with a copy of their record of checks received.
3. *Apply checks*. The accountant records the received checks, either directly to sales or as reductions of specific accounts receivable. The amount of the checks recorded by the accountant should match the amount of the checks recorded by the mailroom staff.
4. *Deposit checks*. The accountant creates a deposit slip for the checks. A courier takes the deposit to the bank, where a bank teller tallies the deposit and issues a receipt.
5. *Match to bank receipt*. The accountant matches the organization's record of checks transferred to the bank to the bank's record of the amount received. This step is a control point that can detect checks removed from the deposit by the courier, or a recordation difference between the accountant and the bank teller.
6. *Conduct bank reconciliation*. At month-end, reconcile the bank's record of check and cash transactions to the organization's record. This is not part of the daily check receipts process flow, but is closely related to it.

The check receipts process is laced with controls, since a business wants to ensure that no payments are lost or stolen. This means that payments are recorded at each step of the process and reconciled to the information recorded in the preceding step, which slows down the entire transaction. Errors are most likely to arise because check totals were incorrectly recorded during one processing step, requiring a reconciliation at the next processing step. Thus, the system of controls is itself causing errors that must be reviewed and corrected.

Check Receipt Improvements

There are several excellent techniques available that can truncate most or a portion of the check receipts process. These techniques are noted in the remainder of this section.

The Bank Lockbox

The cash receipts process and related controls can be vastly reduced by having patients, residents, or third-party payors (depending on the situation) send their payments to a bank lockbox. Under this approach, the bank manages the mailbox address to which payments are sent, so that the health care entity is taken out of the business of handling checks. Instead, the bank deposits all checks received, and posts scanned images of all receipts on its website. The accountant then accesses the check images on this secure site, which are used to record the payments. This approach has the added advantage of posting cash to the organization's bank account somewhat sooner, so that it can take advantage of additional interest income on its invested funds. The cash receipts process flow when a lockbox is used is compressed to the following steps:

1. The bank processes receipts that arrive at the lockbox. This involves depositing payments into the organization's bank account, as well as storing digital images of checks and remittances on-line.
2. The accountant accesses the bank's website each day to view the images of scanned payments from the preceding day. The accountant uses this information to apply the payments to open accounts receivable.
3. The accountant reconciles the applied amount of cash to the amount reported by the bank.

It is possible to expand upon the lockbox concept by opening a *lockbox network*. The larger banks offer lockboxes throughout the country that are linked to a single bank account, so that customers can be instructed to send payments to the lockbox located closest to them, thereby reducing the amount of mail float. The lockbox network is especially useful for large regional or national health care organizations that cater to many customers throughout a large geographic region. Conversely, a business with a smaller regional presence may find that a single lockbox is sufficient for its needs.

The downside of the bank lockbox is a combination of fixed monthly fees and per-receipt fees charged by the bank, which makes this alternative cost-effective only for medium to larger-size organizations that receive large numbers of checks. If this method does not appear to be cost-effective, then consider the later discussion of remote deposit capture, which may be available for free, and which can accelerate the speed with which cash becomes available to earn interest.

The use of a lockbox is the key enhancement of the cash receipts process, since the only person directly involved in check receipts is now the accountant; the activities of the mailroom staff, courier, and bank teller are eliminated. If a lockbox is implemented, there is no need for remote deposit capture, which is discussed next.

Remote Deposit Capture

A remote deposit capture system involves the use of a check scanner and bank-provided scanning software that creates an electronic image of each check to be deposited. The accountant then sends the scanned check information in an electronic message to the bank, rather than making a physical deposit. The bank accepts the deposit information directly into its database, posts the related funds to the organization's account, and assigns funds availability based on a predetermined schedule.

Remote deposit capture requires slightly more time by the accountant to prepare a deposit (by scanning checks) than by the traditional approach of preparing a deposit slip. However, it completely eliminates the time required to make a physical deposit at the bank, as well as the control point of matching the bank's receipt to the deposit slip.

Tip: Remote deposit capture has the side benefit of allowing an organization to do business with a bank that is not located nearby. Thus, a health care firm can search among a larger group of banks for the best pricing deal.

> **Tip:** Some banks require a monthly scanner rental fee. Consider shifting to a bank that offers the scanning equipment for free, or attempt to negotiate a lower rental charge.

Remote deposit capture will require the inclusion of new steps in the check processing work flow, which are:

1. Derive the batch total for all checks to be scanned.
2. Scan all checks in the batch.
3. Match the scanned total to the batch total and adjust as necessary.
4. Transmit the batch to the bank.
5. Print and retain a deposit slip.

There may also need to be an additional step to retain the scanned checks for a short time to ensure that they have been accepted by the bank, after which they should be shredded or perforated with a "deposited" stamp. The check destruction or mutilation is required to ensure that they are not inadvertently deposited again.

Cash Receipts

Cash is the most fungible of all assets, and therefore the one most likely to be stolen. Because of the high risk of theft, the receipt and subsequent handling of cash is choked with controls. The following steps show only the most basic cash receipts processing steps, but should convey the point that cash receipts is *not* an efficient process. We also note that cash payments are quite uncommon in the health care industry, except for walk-in patients at clinics.

1. *Accept and record cash.* If a patient pays in cash, record the payment in a cash register. If there is no cash register (as may be the case in a low-volume sales environment), the clerk instead fills out a two-part receipt, gives a copy to the patient, and retains the other copy.
2. *Match receipts to cash.* Compare the amount of cash received to either the cash register receipt total or the total of all receipt copies, and investigate any differences. Complete a reconciliation form for any differences found.
3. *Aggregate and post receipt information.* Summarize the information in the cash register and post this information to the general ledger as a sale and cash receipt. If the cash register is linked to the organization's accounting system and is tracking individual sales, then sales are being recorded automatically. If clerks are manually completing receipts, summarize the information in the receipts and record the sales in the general ledger.
4. *Deposit cash.* Prepare a bank deposit slip, retain a copy, and enclose the original slip along with all cash in a locked container for transport to the bank. After counting the cash, the bank issues a receipt stating the amount it has received.

5. *Match to deposit slip.* Compare the copy of the deposit slip to the bank receipt, and investigate any differences. A variation is to compare the cash receipts journal to the bank receipt.

As was the case with handling check payments, errors are most likely to arise when cash is counted before being passed to the next person in the process flow. Again, this means that the control system itself is causing errors.

Credit Card Receipts

Credit card receipts are an important source of cash in many health care entities, especially in clinics and emergency care facilities. There are several ways to process these receipts. In order to show the most complete process flow, we are assuming that the most complex version of credit card payments is in use, where card information is written down and then manually entered into an on-line form. The steps are:

1. *Collect information.* Record not only the information needed for the credit card payment, but also the contact information for the patient, in case it is necessary to verify or replace credit card information.
2. *Enter card information.* Access the credit card processing site on the Internet and enter the credit card information through an on-line form. When the information is accepted, print a receipt and staple it to the sales receipt. If the payment is not accepted, contact the patient to verify or replace the card information.
3. *Record the sale.* Enter the receipt into the accounting system as a sale. Then stamp the receipt as having been recorded.
4. *Issue receipt to patient.* Give the patient a receipt, which acts as a control, so that patients can independently verify the amount charged.
5. *Verify the transaction.* Before filing receipts for credit card transactions, verify that the cash related to them has been posted to the organization's bank account, and that they were posted to the accounting system.
6. *File documents.* File the organization's copy of the sales receipt, as well as the attached credit card processing receipt, in the accounting records by patient name.

When credit card information is being manually entered, the error rate is extremely high. The problem is caused by a combination of taking down credit card information incorrectly and/or incorrectly inputting the information into the on-line form. The error rate is much lower when a credit card is swiped to obtain card information.

The full process flow described for the on-line entry of credit card information can be reduced with any of the on-line apps now available for smart phones and tablet computers. These apps allow for the creation of a transaction on a portable computing device by typing in or swiping credit card information, processing payment with an integrated on-line form, and sending an e-mail receipt to the patient.

This combination of a fully integrated payment processing and receipt issuance platform allows for the elimination of many steps in the traditional credit card

processing transaction. In essence, payment information is both collected and confirmed in one step, leaving only a final step to record the transaction.

The Bank Reconciliation

It is extremely important to complete a bank reconciliation for every account that contains a significant amount of cash. This is needed to obtain an understanding of the types and timing of cash flows and the unrecorded transactions that can arise, as well as to ensure that the organization's cash balance information is correct.

A likely outcome of the reconciliation process will be several adjustments to an entity's recorded cash balance. It is unlikely that the organization's ending cash balance and the bank's ending cash balance will be identical, since there are probably multiple payments and deposits in transit at all times, as well as bank service fees, penalties, and not sufficient funds deposits that the entity's accountant has not yet recorded.

The essential process flow for a bank reconciliation is to start with the bank's ending cash balance (known as the *bank balance*), add to it any deposits in transit from the business to the bank, subtract any checks that have not yet cleared the bank, and either add or deduct any other reconciling items. Then find the organization's ending cash balance and deduct from it any bank service fees, not sufficient funds (NSF) checks and penalties, and add to it any interest earned. At the end of this process, the adjusted bank balance should equal the entity's ending adjusted cash balance.

The following bank reconciliation procedure assumes that the bank reconciliation is being created in an accounting software package, which makes the reconciliation process easier:

1. Enter the bank reconciliation software module. A listing of uncleared checks and uncleared deposits will appear.
2. Check off in the bank reconciliation module all checks that are listed on the bank statement as having cleared the bank.
3. Check off in the bank reconciliation module all deposits that are listed on the bank statement as having cleared the bank.
4. Enter as expenses all bank charges appearing on the bank statement, and which have not already been recorded in the organization's records.
5. Enter the ending balance on the bank statement. If the book and bank balances match, then post all changes recorded in the bank reconciliation and close the module. If the balances do *not* match, then continue reviewing the bank reconciliation for additional reconciling items. Look for the following items:
    - Checks recorded in the bank records at a different amount from what is recorded in the organization's records.
    - Deposits recorded in the bank records at a different amount from what is recorded in the organization's records.
    - Checks recorded in the bank records that are not recorded at all in the organization's records.

- Deposits recorded in the bank records that are not recorded at all in the organization's records.
- Inbound wire transfers from which a processing fee has been extracted.

EXAMPLE

Suture Medical is closing its books for the month ended April 30. Suture's accountant must prepare a bank reconciliation based on the following issues:

1. The bank statement contains an ending bank balance of $320,000.
2. The bank statement contains a $200 check printing charge for new checks that Suture ordered.
3. The bank statement contains a $150 service charge for operating the bank account.
4. The bank rejected a deposit of $500 due to not sufficient funds, and charges Suture a $10 fee associated with the rejection.
5. The bank statement contains interest income of $30.
6. Suture issued $80,000 of checks that have not yet cleared the bank.
7. Suture deposited $25,000 of checks at month-end that were not deposited in time to appear on the bank statement.

The accountant creates the following reconciliation:

		Item #	Adjustment to Books
Bank balance	$320,000	1	
- Check printing charge	-200	2	Debit expense, credit cash
- Service charge	-150	3	Debit expense, credit cash
- NSF fee	-10	4	Debit expense, credit cash
- NSF deposit rejected	-500	4	Debit receivable, credit cash
+ Interest income	+30	5	Debit cash, credit interest income
- Uncleared checks	-80,000	6	None
+ Deposits in transit	+25,000	7	None
= Book balance	$264,170		

When the bank reconciliation process is complete, print a report through the accounting software that shows the bank and book balances, the identified differences between the two (most likely to be uncleared checks), and any remaining unreconciled difference. Retain a copy of this report for each month, since the outside auditors will want to see them as part of the year-end audit.

The format of the report will vary by software package; a simplistic layout follows.

Sample Bank Reconciliation Statement

For the month ended March 31, 20x3		
Bank balance	$850,000	
Less: Checks outstanding	-225,000	See detail
Add: Deposits in transit	+100,000	See detail
+/- Other adjustments	0	
Book balance	$725,000	
Unreconciled difference	$0	

The standard approach to bank reconciliations is to complete them for all accounts shortly after the end of each month, since the reconciliations are derived from the bank statements that are issued after month-end.

The Not Sufficient Funds Concept

In the last section, we noted how to deal with not sufficient funds checks. What are they? The not sufficient funds (NSF) designation is a condition where a bank does not honor a check, because the checking account on which it was drawn does not contain sufficient funds.

For example, Mr. Jones writes a check to Mr. Smith for $500, which Mr. Smith deposits. Upon presentation of the check, Mr. Jones' bank refuses to honor it on the grounds that there is only $300 in his checking account. This is a not sufficient funds check.

The recipient of an NSF check may be charged a processing fee by the bank at which it deposited the check. The entity that issues an NSF check is always charged a significant fee by the bank where its checking account is located.

A not sufficient funds check is a reconciling item on a bank reconciliation. If a check is deposited, the assumption is that it has cleared the bank, whereas a not sufficient funds check has *not* cleared the bank, thereby reducing the on-hand cash balance.

Bank Reconciliation Problems

There are several problems that continually arise as part of a bank reconciliation. They are:

- *Uncleared checks that continue to not be presented.* There will be a residual number of checks that either are not presented to the bank for payment for a long time, or which are never presented for payment. In the short term, treat them in the same manner as any other uncleared checks - just keep them in the uncleared checks listing in the accounting software, so they will be an ongoing reconciling item. In the long term, contact the payee to see if they ever received the check; it will likely be necessary to void the old check and issue them a new one.

- *Checks clear the bank after having been voided.* As just noted, if a check remains uncleared for a long time, the old check will likely be voided and replaced with a new check. But what if the payee then cashes the original check? If it was voided with the bank, the bank should reject the check when it is presented. If the accountant did *not* void it with the bank, then record the check again in the accounting records, which will reduce the cash balance. If the payee has not yet cashed the replacement check, void it with the bank at once to avoid a double payment. Otherwise, it will be necessary to pursue repayment of the second check by the payee.
- *Deposited checks are returned.* There are cases where the bank will refuse to deposit a check, usually because it is drawn on a bank account located in another country. In this case, reverse the original entry related to that deposit, which will reduce the cash balance.

The Daily Bank Reconciliation

The procedure for the monthly bank reconciliation that was just outlined is the standard approach – in terms of its timing. An alternative is to conduct a *daily* bank reconciliation, which is based on the daily transactions posted by a bank on its website. By completing a daily reconciliation, it is possible to immediately identify unrecorded incoming cash. In addition, any unusual or unauthorized transactions impacting a cash account can be investigated at once. For example, if a third party fraudulently removes cash from an account with an ACH debit, the accountant can immediately institute a debit block to keep any additional debits from impacting the remaining cash.

The procedure to be followed for a daily bank reconciliation is essentially the same as the one just noted for a monthly reconciliation. We recommend completing it at the beginning of each work day, which makes it easier to contact the bank to discuss and take corrective action regarding any anomalies found. Also, completing this chore early makes it easier to reliably check off the department work list, before other issues take up the remaining time available.

> **Tip:** Completing a daily bank reconciliation makes it easier to close the books and issue reliable financial statements, since there are unlikely to be many reconciling items left to investigate by the end of the reporting period.

Billings

Health care billings can be quite complex, which introduces the risk of preparing incorrect invoices. There are several ways in which this can occur. For example, physicians may not document a procedure correctly, so that the wrong procedure is billed. Or, the person coding information into an invoice does not correctly interpret the information submitted by the medical staff. Another possibility is that the wrong code is used to classify a billed item. For example, a third-party payor may require that all billings sent to it contain a classification code from the latest version of the World Health Organization's ICD list (which is short for the International Statistical

Classification of Diseases and Related Health Problems). Including sub-classifications, the ICD contains more than 16,000 codes, so a billing clerk could easily enter the wrong ICD code.

Given the risk of incorrect billings, this is an excellent place in which to implement comprehensive controls. For example, controls could address the level of documentation submitted for billing, the coding applied to invoices, verification of who is to be billed, and verification of contact information.

When a third-party payor receives an invoice from a health care provider, an accounting clerk reviews the document and assigns a payment code to an invoice. The amount paid can vary significantly, depending on the payment code associated with the invoice. It behooves the health care provider to regularly examine the payment codes being assigned to its invoices, to see if they are appropriate. When there are discrepancies, the accounting staff will need to present its case for why a different payment code with a higher reimbursement rate should be used.

Third-Party Payor Payment Methods

Third-party payors may use a broad array of payment methods. To deal with these different types of payment methods, a health care entity will need to create a range of billing and revenue recognition procedures. The following list provides an overview of the payment methods that may be used:

- *Fee for service*. Payments are based on the specific services provided to patients. The amounts paid may be based on a standard rate schedule or at a discount from the health care entity's full pricing.
- *Per diem*. Payments are based on a flat rate per day of inpatient care, irrespective of the level of service provided.
- *Per case*. Payments are based on the discharge category to which a patient is assigned.
- *Episodic*. Payments are based on a predetermined amount for services provided during an episode of care, such as a certain number of days. The payments are linked to the type of patient condition or the treatment being provided.
- *Capitation*. Payments are a fixed amount per period, made at the beginning of the month, in exchange for a commitment to provide service for the month. Payment is made even if the patient never appears.
- *Risk-based*. Payments involve a sharing of risk, where the provider agrees to provide certain services in exchange for a negotiated price. The intent is to improve quality and control costs.

Valuation of Receivables

The amounts that a health care provider receives from third-party payors will likely be less than its established rates. Instead, the amounts actually received will probably be based on one of the following:

- A contractual agreement with a third-party payor. For example, an agreement with a Blue Cross plan sets prices.
- Legislation or regulation, such as established rates to be paid for workers' compensation claims.
- A provider policy, such as discounts given to members of the medical staff.

The health care provider should make a reasonable estimate of the amount of each receivable in the period when services are rendered.

The following additional issues can apply to the recognition and reporting of receivables by a health care entity:

- *Contractual adjustments and discounts*. The health care entity shall recognize its best estimate of the contractual adjustments and discounts associated with receivables in the period when the services are provided, even though the actual amounts may not be known until a later date.
- *Loans and advances*. Any loans or advances given to a related entity are to be recorded as receivables, as long as repayment is reasonably assured.
- *Non-payment by related entities*. When a related entity is not going to pay a receivable, the write-off of the receivable can be treated as an equity transfer, where the health care entity holding the receivable reduces its net assets and the non-paying entity increases its net assets.
- *Subsequent adjustments*. Reserves for contractual adjustments, discounts, and doubtful accounts should be adjusted over time to match the most recent best estimates, so that receivables are recorded at their net realizable value. Reserves are discussed in the next section.

Calculating and Recording Bad Debts

As noted in the preceding section, the full amount of an invoice may not be paid. Or, a patient, resident, or third-party payor does not pay at all. If so, the accountant must write off these invoices as bad debts. There are two ways to do so, which are covered in this section under the headings of the direct write-off method and the allowance for doubtful accounts.

Direct Write-Off Method

The direct write-off method is the practice of charging bad debts to expense in the period when individual invoices have been clearly identified as bad debts. The specific activity needed to write off an account receivable under this method is to create a credit memo for the payor in question, which exactly offsets the amount of the bad

debt. Creating the credit memo will require a debit to a bad debt expense account and a credit to the accounts receivable account.

The method does not involve a reduction in the amount of recorded revenue, only an increase of the bad debt expense. For example, a hospital records revenue of $10,000, doing so with a debit to the accounts receivable account and a credit to the sales account. After two months, the payor is only able to pay $8,000 of the open balance, so $2,000 must be written off. The needed entry calls for a $2,000 credit to the accounts receivable account and an offsetting debit to the bad debt expense account. Thus, the revenue amount remains the same, the remaining receivable is eliminated, and an expense is created in the amount of the bad debt.

The direct write off approach violates the matching principle, under which all costs related to revenue are charged to expense in the same period in which revenue is recognized, so that the financial results of an entity reveal the entire extent of a revenue-generating transaction in a single accounting period.

The direct write off method delays the recognition of expenses related to a revenue-generating transaction, and so is considered an excessively aggressive accounting method, since it delays some expense recognition, making a business appear more profitable in the short term than it really is. For example, an organization may recognize $1 million in sales in one period, and then wait three or four months to collect all of the related accounts receivable before finally charging some items off to the bad debt expense. This creates a lengthy delay between revenue recognition and the recognition of expenses that are directly related to that revenue. Thus, the profit in the initial month is overstated, while profit is understated in the month when the bad debts are finally charged to expense.

The direct write off method can be considered a reasonable accounting method if the amount that is written off is an immaterial amount, since doing so has a minimal impact on an entity's reported financial results.

Allowance for Doubtful Accounts

The allowance for doubtful accounts is a reduction of the total amount of accounts receivable appearing on an organization's balance sheet. This allowance represents management's best estimate of the amount of accounts receivable that will not be paid in the future by patient, residents, and third-party payors.

If an organization is using the accrual basis of accounting, it should record an allowance for doubtful accounts, since this approach provides an estimate of future bad debts that improves the accuracy of the financial statements. Also, by recording the allowance at the same time it records a sale, a health care entity is properly matching the projected bad debt expense against the related sale in the same period, which provides a more accurate view of the true profitability of a sale.

For example, a hospital records $10,000,000 of revenue that relates to several hundred patients, and projects (based on historical experience) that it will incur 15% of this amount as bad debts, though it does not know exactly where the shortfalls will occur. It records the 15% of projected bad debts as a $1,500,000 debit to the bad debt expense account and a $1,500,000 credit to the allowance for doubtful accounts. The bad debt expense is charged to expense right away, and the allowance for doubtful

accounts becomes a reserve account that offsets the account receivable of $10,000,000 (for a net receivable outstanding of $8,500,000).

Later, several direct-pay patients default on payments totaling $40,000. Accordingly, the hospital credits the accounts receivable account by $40,000 to reduce the amount of outstanding accounts receivable, and debits the allowance for doubtful accounts by $40,000. This entry reduces the balance in the allowance account to $1,460,000. The entry does not impact earnings in the current period.

Estimation of Bad Debts

It is rarely possible to make a precise estimation of the amount of receivables that will never be paid. However, it *is* possible to make a reasonable guess, usually based on historical experience. For example, an accountant could apply the historical bad debt percentage to the grand total accounts receivable balance at the end of a reporting period. A more precise method is to assign a greater probability of nonpayment to those receivables that have not been paid within the normal collection period. For example, the bad debt rate could be 10% for those receivables more than 60 days old but less than 90 days old, while the bad debt rate could be 25% for receivables more than 90 days old. The latter approach is more in-depth, and so tends to provide a more accurate estimate of bad debts than simply applying a single historical percentage to the grand total ending receivable balance.

Contractual Adjustments

When there are contractual arrangements with third-party payors, a health care entity is agreeing to receive less than its full rates. In these situations, the accountant can record a reserve at the time of a sale that is similar to the allowance for doubtful accounts, except that it is an allowance for contractual adjustments. The amount of this allowance should be based on the underlying contractual arrangements. However, the amount eventually paid could still differ from the amount stated in the agreement, perhaps due to a dispute between the parties in regard to the need for a procedure. Consequently, the accountant will need to monitor the amounts actually paid to see if they match the amounts recorded in the allowance. If not, it will be necessary to make ongoing adjustments to the allowance to bring it into alignment with the amount that will actually be paid by the payors.

Summary

In this chapter, we have described the basic process flows for different types of cash receipts. Any cash processing within an organization is bound to be inefficient, given the number of controls involved. This inefficiency can be reduced by using one or more lockboxes, so that cash and checks never appear within a business – they arrive at the entity's bank, and stay there.

The bank reconciliation is an important insurance policy for the accountant who does not have large cash balances to work with, and so needs to know the exact amount of available cash every day. Even in an organization with massive cash balances and

minimal investing activities, it still makes sense to use bank reconciliations to identify and record expenses that might otherwise pile up for many months and eventually result in a fairly large adjusting entry.

The proper valuation of receivables can be a major problem for some health care organizations. There may be a need to establish allowances for bad debts and contractual adjustments that offset receivables, so that the net receivable appearing on the balance sheet constitutes management's best guess as to the amount of receivables that will actually be collected.

Chapter 6
Inventory Accounting

Introduction

In many industries, the investment in inventory is so large that it becomes the focus of a great deal of management attention. The situation differs somewhat in the health care industry, where some organizations will rarely stock any inventory, while others will maintain significant amounts of quite expensive inventory items. The focus of this chapter is on the latter group of organizations, where inventory represents a significant investment.

In this chapter, we discuss the periodic and perpetual inventory systems, which form the basis for reliable inventory accounting processes. We make note of the process flows in these systems, as well as the circumstances in which each one is most applicable.

Once an inventory system has been created, the next decision is what type of cost layering to adopt; this is a method for determining which tranche of costs is charged to expense when an inventory item is sold. The accountant must decide upon a methodology for determining which cost layering system to follow, and then employ that system consistently when compiling financial statements. In this chapter, we describe the concept of cost layering, the types of cost layering systems, and how they function. In cases where it is necessary to estimate the ending inventory balance, we provide two calculations for doing so.

Related Podcast Episodes: Episodes 56, 186, 192, 200, and 225 of the Accounting Best Practices Podcast discuss inventory record accuracy, inventory variances, cycle counting, the revised lower of cost or market rule, and the reserve for obsolete inventory, respectively. These episodes are available at: **accountingtools.com/podcasts** or **iTunes**

The Periodic Inventory System

The minimum inventory accounting system is the periodic system. It is impossible to devise an ending inventory valuation without having a functioning periodic inventory system in place. The system is dependent upon just two activities, which are:

- Compiling the cost of all inventory-related purchases during the reporting period; and
- Conducting a physical count of the ending inventory.

The compilation of inventory-related purchases is quite easy in any accounting system, and is only dependent upon recording targeted purchases in an inventory purchases account as the offsetting debit to each accounts payable transaction.

Since physical inventory counts are time-consuming, few organizations do them more than once a quarter or year. In the meantime, the inventory asset account continues to show the cost of the inventory that was recorded as of the last physical inventory count; the balance is not adjusted until there is another physical count or an ending valuation is estimated. The longer it takes to conduct a replacement physical inventory count, the longer the time period in which errors and inventory losses of various kinds can pile up undetected. As a result, there is an increasing risk of overstating ending inventory and understating the cost of sales over time. Given this problem, we recommend frequent physical counts.

To operate a periodic inventory system, follow these steps:

1. Compile all inventory purchases during the reporting period in a separate account.
2. At the end of the period, conduct a physical count to derive the ending inventory valuation.
3. Calculate the cost of sales for the period, using the following formula:

   Beginning inventory + Purchases = Cost of goods available for sale

   Cost of goods available for sale – Ending inventory = Cost of sales

4. Complete the following entry to zero out the balance in the purchases account, adjust the inventory account to match the ending physical count, and record the cost of sales:

	Debit	Credit
Cost of sales	xxx	
Purchases		xxx
Inventory		xxx

EXAMPLE

St. Peter Hospital has beginning inventory of $10,000, has paid $17,000 for purchases, and its physical inventory count reveals an ending inventory cost of $8,000. The calculation of its cost of sales is:

$10,000 Beginning inventory + $17,000 Purchases - $8,000 Ending inventory

= $19,000 Cost of sales

St. Peter's controller records the following journal entry to document this calculation:

	Debit	Credit
Cost of sales	19,000	
Purchases		17,000
Inventory		2,000

The periodic inventory system is most useful for smaller businesses that maintain minimal amounts of inventory. For them, a physical inventory count is easy to complete, and they can estimate cost of sales figures for interim periods. However, there are several problems with the system, which are:

- *Inaccuracy in the absence of a count.* The system does not yield any information about the cost of sales or ending inventory balances during interim periods when there has been no physical inventory count.
- *Subsequent catch-up adjustments.* The accountant must estimate the cost of sales during interim periods, which will likely result in a significant adjustment to the actual cost of sales whenever the organization eventually completes a physical inventory count.
- *Spoiled or missing adjustments.* There is no way to adjust for spoiled or missing inventory during interim periods, so there tends to be a significant (and expensive) adjustment for these issues when a physical inventory count is eventually completed.

A more up-to-date and accurate alternative to the periodic inventory system is the perpetual inventory system, which is described in the next section.

The Perpetual Inventory System

Under the perpetual inventory system, an entity continually updates its inventory records to account for additions to and subtractions from inventory for such activities as received inventory items and goods sold from stock. Thus, a perpetual inventory system has the advantages of both providing up-to-date inventory balance information and requiring a reduced level of physical inventory counts. However, the calculated inventory levels derived by a perpetual inventory system may gradually diverge from actual inventory levels, due to unrecorded transactions or theft, so it is necessary to periodically compare book balances to actual on-hand quantities. The following example shows how a perpetual system functions.

EXAMPLE

This example contains several journal entries used to account for transactions in a perpetual inventory system. The controller of St. Xystus Hospital records a purchase of $1,500 of merchandise that is stored in inventory:

	Debit	Credit
Inventory	1,500	
Accounts payable		1,500

The controller records $250 of inbound freight cost associated with the delivery of the merchandise:

	Debit	Credit
Inventory	250	
Accounts payable		250

The controller records the sale of inventory for $2,000, for which the associated inventory cost is $800:

	Debit	Credit
Accounts receivable	2,000	
Revenue		2,000
Cost of sales	800	
Inventory		800

The controller records a downward inventory adjustment of $300, caused by inventory theft, and detected during an inventory count:

	Debit	Credit
Inventory shrinkage expense	300	
Inventory		300

The net effect of these entries, assuming a zero beginning balance, is an ending inventory balance of $650.

The downside of using a perpetual inventory system is a massive increase in the number of inventory-related transactions that must be recorded. This burden may require the addition of clerks to record transactions, or the use of bar code scanning, portable data entry terminals, or other labor-saving devices.

The initial comparison of a perpetual system's recorded inventory valuation to the physical count will likely reveal a significant disparity. This variance will be caused

by a number of transactions not being recorded or recorded incorrectly. If the causes of these variances are tracked down and corrected (usually with procedural changes and training updates), the perpetual system will eventually become quite reliable. However, if an organization has a small and low-cost inventory that rarely experiences much turnover, it is possible that the increased reliability of a perpetual system will not be worth its added cost. If so, the periodic inventory system may be the more applicable system.

The Physical Inventory Count

A physical inventory count provides the unit totals that form the basis for the ending inventory valuation, and can also be used to update inventory unit count records. A physical count is most necessary when inventory record accuracy levels are quite low, but can be avoided when there is an effective system of cycle counts in place. Cycle counting involves the daily counting of small amounts of inventory, so that all parts of the inventory investment can be examined on a regular basis.

Use the following steps when administering a physical inventory count. The steps are intended for use in a storeroom, since this environment is most easily controlled during a count.

<u>Prior to the count</u>:

1. *Tags*. Order a sufficient number of sequentially numbered count tags for the count. These should be two-part tags, and include line items for the product name, product identification number, quantity, and location. Also consider adding space for the counter's initials. There may be a punch hole in the top center, which can be used to tie the count tag to an inventory item. A sample count tag follows.
2. *Part numbers*. Identify all inventory items that do not have a legible part number and properly identify them prior to the count.
3. *Pre-counts*. Where possible, count items in advance, seal them in containers, and mark the quantities on the outside of the containers.
4. *Management area*. Set up management areas within the storeroom where counters are to assemble for instructions, as well as to collect and return all reports and forms needed for the count.
5. *Segregation*. Move all items not to be counted out of the counting area, or identify them with "Do not count" tags.
6. *Cutoff*. Segregate all received inventory items if they arrive after the cutoff date for the physical inventory count. Doing so ensures that only items properly logged into the inventory system will be counted.
7. *Finalize data entry*. Have the storeroom staff complete all manual data entry of inventory transactions by the close of business before the count is scheduled to begin.

Sample Inventory Count Tag

Counting activities:

1. *Train teams*. Instruct the counting teams regarding counting procedures and issue them count tags that are numerically sequential. Keep track of which team has been issued a set of tags.
2. *Count inventory*. Each counting team must count the inventory in the area assigned to it, fill out the count information on an inventory tag, and tape a tag to each inventory item, retaining the copy of each tag. One person should count inventory, while a second person writes down the information on tags. When a count team is done, it turns in its copies of the tags, as well as any unused tags.
3. *Track tags*. A person responsible for tags verifies that all used and unused tags have been received and accounts for any missing tags.
4. *Data entry*. Enter all tags into a database or spreadsheet and summarize the quantities by part number and location.

5. *Comparison.* If the organization uses a perpetual inventory system, compare the count totals to the inventory records. Investigate any variances by recounting the inventory.
6. *Reporting.* Print a final report that summarizes the unit quantities of all counted inventory items.
7. *Review the process.* Examine the entire physical count process, identify areas in which it could be improved, and write down these issues for consideration as part of the next physical count.
8. *Subsequent counts.* Create a list of the largest variances noted during the physical inventory count and return to these items for ongoing cycle counts. It is entirely possible that a counting error caused the variances, and will require correction.

Inventory Cost Layering Overview

The typical inventory asset is comprised of many identical items that may have been acquired during different time periods. In each of these time periods, it is likely that the costs incurred varied somewhat from those incurred in other time periods. The result is a mish-mash of inventory items that all look the same, but which have different costs associated with them. How is the accountant to decide which costs to assign to goods when they are sold? A possible solution is the cost layering concept. Under cost layering, we assume that different tranches of costs have been incurred to acquire certain clusters of inventory. The following example illustrates the concept.

EXAMPLE

St. Dominic Hospital acquires embroidered shirts from a contract manufacturer, for sale through its gift shop. Over the past three months, the hospital made the following purchases of these shirts from the manufacturer:

Date	Quantity	Price/each
1/05/X3	320	$9.00
1/29/X3	85	9.25
2/15/X3	170	9.60
3/09/X3	135	9.60

Since the first two purchases were made at different prices, the units in each of these purchases can be considered a separate cost layer. Since the last two purchases were made at the same price, they can be aggregated into the same cost layer, or they may be treated as separate cost layers.

Depending on the cost layering system that the hospital chooses to use, it can assume that the cost of an embroidered shirt that is charged to the cost of sales may come from the first of these cost layers (the first in, first out system), from the last of the cost layers (the last in, first out system) or from an average of these costs (the weighted-average system).

Several methods for calculating the cost of inventory that employ the cost layering concept are shown in this chapter. Of the methods presented, only the first in, first out method and the weighted average method have gained worldwide recognition. The last in, first out method cannot realistically be justified based on the actual flow of inventory, and is only used in the United States under the sanction of the Internal Revenue Service; it is specifically banned under international financial reporting standards.

The First in, First Out Method

The first in, first out (FIFO) method of inventory valuation operates under the assumption that the first goods purchased are also the first goods sold. In most organizations, this accounting assumption closely matches the actual flow of goods, and so is considered the most theoretically correct inventory valuation method.

Under the FIFO method, the earliest goods purchased are the first ones removed from the inventory account. This results in the remaining items in inventory being accounted for at the most recently incurred costs, so that the inventory asset recorded on the balance sheet contains costs quite close to the most recent costs that could be obtained in the marketplace. Conversely, this method also results in older historical costs being matched against current revenues and recorded in the cost of sales, so the gross margin does not necessarily reflect a proper matching of revenues and costs.

EXAMPLE

St. Raymond Hospital decides to use the FIFO method for the month of January. During that month, it records the following transactions:

	Quantity Change	Actual Unit Cost	Actual Total Cost
Beginning inventory (layer 1)	+100	$9.00	$900
Sale	-75		
Purchase (layer 2)	+150	9.20	1,380
Sale	-100		
Purchase (layer 3)	+50	9.30	465
Ending inventory	= 125		$2,745

The cost of sales in units is calculated as:

100 Beginning inventory + 200 Purchased – 125 Ending inventory = 175 Units

The hospital's accountant uses the information in the preceding table to calculate the cost of sales for January, as well as the cost of the inventory balance as of the end of January. The calculations appear in the following table.

	Units	Unit Cost	Total Cost
Cost of sales			
FIFO layer 1	100	$9.00	$900
FIFO layer 2	75	9.20	690
Total cost of sales	175		$1,590
Ending inventory			
FIFO layer 2	75	9.20	$690
FIFO layer 3	50	9.30	465
Total ending inventory	125		$1,155

Thus, the first FIFO layer, which was the beginning inventory layer, is completely used up during the month, as well as half of Layer 2, leaving half of Layer 2 and all of Layer 3 to be the sole components of the ending inventory.

Note that the $1,590 cost of sales and $1,155 ending inventory equals the $2,745 combined total of beginning inventory and purchases during the month.

From a database management perspective, the FIFO method results in the smallest number of cost layers to track, since the oldest layers are constantly being eliminated.

The Last in, First Out Method

The last in, first out (LIFO) method operates under the assumption that the last item of inventory purchased is the first one sold. Picture a shelf where a clerk adds items from the front, and clerks also take their selections from the front; the remaining items of inventory that are located further from the front of the shelf are rarely picked, and so remain on the shelf – that is a LIFO scenario.

The trouble with the LIFO scenario is that it is rarely encountered in practice. If an organization were to use the process flow embodied by LIFO, a significant part of its inventory would be very old, and likely obsolete or spoiled. Nonetheless, a health care entity does not actually have to experience the LIFO process flow in order to use the method to calculate its inventory valuation.

The reason why organizations use LIFO is the assumption that the cost of inventory increases over time, which is reasonable in inflationary periods. If one were to use LIFO in such a situation, the cost of the most recently acquired inventory would always be higher than the cost of earlier purchases, so the ending inventory balance would be valued at earlier costs, while the most recent costs appear in the cost of sales. By shifting high-cost inventory into the cost of sales, an organization can reduce its reported level of profitability and thereby defer its recognition of income taxes (which may not apply in the case of a not-for-profit organization).

EXAMPLE

St. Donatus Hospital decides to use the LIFO method for the month of March. The following table shows the various purchasing transactions for the hospital's inventory purchases. The quantity purchased on March 1 actually reflects the inventory beginning balance.

Date Purchased	Quantity Purchased	Cost per Unit	Units Sold	Cost of Layer #1	Cost of Layer #2	Total Cost
March 1	150	$9.10	95	(55 × $9.10)		$501
March 7	100	9.35	110	(45 × $9.10)		410
March 11	200	9.50	180	(45 × $9.10)	(20 × $9.50)	600
March 17	125	9.40	125	(45 × $9.10)	(20 × $9.50)	600
March 25	80	9.60	120	(25 × $9.10)		228

The following bullet points describe the transactions noted in the preceding table:

- *March 1*. The hospital has a beginning inventory balance of 150 units, and sells 95 of these units between March 1 and March 7. This leaves one inventory layer of 55 units at a cost of $9.10 each.
- *March 7*. The hospital buys 100 additional units on March 7, and sells 110 units between March 7 and March 11. Under LIFO, we assume that the latest purchase was sold first, so there is still just one inventory layer, which has now been reduced to 45 units.
- *March 11*. The hospital buys 200 additional units on March 11, and sells 180 units between March 11 and March 17, which creates a new inventory layer that is comprised of 20 units at a cost of $9.50. This new layer appears in the table in the "Cost of Layer #2" column.
- *March 17*. The hospital buys 125 additional units on March 17, and sells 125 units between March 17 and March 25, so there is no change in the inventory layers.
- *March 25*. The hospital buys 80 additional units on March 25, and sells 120 units between March 25 and the end of the month. Sales exceed purchases during this period, so the second inventory layer is eliminated, as well as part of the first layer. The result is an ending inventory balance of $228, which is derived from 25 units of ending inventory, multiplied by the $9.10 cost in the first layer that existed at the beginning of the month.

Before implementing the LIFO system, consider the following points:

- *Consistent usage*. The Internal Revenue Service states that a business using LIFO for its tax reporting must also use LIFO for its financial reporting. Thus, an organization wanting to defer tax recognition through early expense recognition must show those same low profit numbers to the outside users of its financial statements. This may not be a problem in a privately-held business that does not release its financial results to outsiders.
- *Covenant compliance*. When LIFO has been used for a long period of time and materials prices have increased during that period, the reported inventory

asset may be so low that an organization has trouble meeting the terms of its loan covenants that require a certain amount of current assets.

- *Layering*. Since the LIFO system is intended to use the most recent layers of inventory, one may never access earlier layers, which can result in an administrative problem if there are many layers to document.
- *Profit fluctuations*. If early layers contain inventory costs that depart substantially from current market prices, an organization could experience sharp changes in its profitability if those layers are ever accessed.

In summary, LIFO is only useful for deferring income tax payments in periods of cost inflation. It does not reflect the actual flow of inventory in most situations, and may even yield unusual financial results that differ markedly from reality.

The Weighted Average Method

When using the weighted average method, divide the cost of goods available for sale by the number of units available for sale, which yields the weighted-average cost per unit. In this calculation, the cost of goods available for sale is the sum of beginning inventory and net purchases. This weighted-average figure is then used to assign a cost to both ending inventory and the cost of sales.

The singular advantage of the weighted average method is the complete absence of any inventory layers, which avoids the record keeping problems encountered with either the FIFO or LIFO methods described earlier.

EXAMPLE

The controller of St. Severian Hospital elects to use the weighted-average method for the month of May. During that month, the hospital records the following transactions:

	Quantity Change	Actual Unit Cost	Actual Total Cost
Beginning inventory	+150	$9.10	$1,365
Sale	-125		
Purchase	+200	9.70	1,940
Sale	-150		
Purchase	+100	9.90	990
Ending inventory	= 175		$4,295

The actual total cost of all purchased or beginning inventory units in the preceding table is $4,295. The total of all purchased or beginning inventory units is 450 (150 beginning inventory + 300 purchased). The weighted average cost per unit is therefore $9.54 ($4,295 ÷ 450 units).

The ending inventory valuation is $1,670 (175 units × $9.54 weighted average cost), while the cost of sales valuation is $2,624 (275 units × $9.54 weighted average cost). The sum of these

two amounts (less a rounding error) equals the $4,295 total actual cost of all purchases and beginning inventory.

In the preceding example, if St. Severian used a perpetual inventory system to record its inventory transactions, it would have to recompute the weighted average after every purchase. The following exhibit uses the same information in the preceding example to show the recomputations.

Weighted-Average Calculations Under the Perpetual Inventory System

	Units on Hand	Purchases	Cost of Sales	Inventory Total Cost	Inventory Moving Average Unit Cost
Beginning inventory	150	$--	$--	$1,365	$9.10
Sale (125 units @ $9.10)	25	--	1,138	227	9.10
Purchase (200 units @ $9.70)	225	1,940	--	2,167	9.63
Sale (150 units @ $9.63)	75	--	1,445	722	9.63
Purchase (100 units @ $9.90)	175	990	--	1,712	9.78
Total			$2,583		

Note that the cost of sales of $2,583 and the ending inventory balance of $1,712 equal $4,295, which matches the total of the costs in the original example. Thus, the totals are the same, but the moving weighted average calculation results in slight differences in the apportionment of costs between the cost of sales and ending inventory.

Estimating Ending Inventory

The accountant cannot always expect a physical inventory count at the end of each month. Instead, it may be necessary to devise an estimate of the ending inventory balance, so that the cost of sales can be derived. The *gross profit method* is the most generic method used to estimate the amount of ending inventory. Follow these steps to estimate ending inventory using the gross profit method:

1. Add together the cost of beginning inventory and the cost of purchases during the period to arrive at the cost of goods available for sale.
2. Multiply (1 - expected gross profit percentage) by sales during the period to arrive at the estimated cost of sales.
3. Subtract the estimated cost of sales (step 2) from the cost of goods available for sale (step 1) to arrive at the ending inventory.

EXAMPLE

The St. Salvator Hospital is calculating its month-end inventory for March. Its beginning inventory was $175,000 and its purchases during the month were $225,000. Thus, its cost of goods available for sale is:

$175,000 beginning inventory + $225,000 purchases

= $400,000 cost of goods available for sale

The hospital's gross margin percentage related to the sale of inventory for all of the past 12 months was 35%, which is considered a reliable long-term margin. Its sales during March were $500,000. Thus, its estimated cost of sales is:

(1 - 35%) × $500,000 = $325,000 cost of sales

By subtracting the estimated cost of sales from the cost of goods available for sale, the hospital arrives at an estimated ending inventory balance of $75,000.

There are several issues with the gross profit method that make it unreliable as a long-term method for determining the value of inventory, which are:

- *Historical basis*. The gross profit percentage is a key component of the calculation, but the percentage is based on a health care entity's historical experience. If the current situation yields a different percentage (as may be caused by a special sale at reduced prices), the gross profit percentage used in the calculation will be incorrect.
- *Inventory losses*. The calculation assumes that the long-term rate of losses due to theft, spoilage, and other causes is included in the historical gross profit percentage. If not, or if these losses have not previously been recognized, the calculation likely will result in an inaccurate estimated ending inventory (and probably one that is too high).

In short, this method is most useful for a small number of consecutive accounting periods, after which the estimated ending balance should be updated with a physical inventory count.

Summary

The size of the inventory investment can drive the accountant's decisions regarding how inventory is to be accounted for. When there is little inventory on hand, a periodic inventory system may prove to be sufficient. Conversely, a large inventory investment, and especially one where the organization relies upon an exact knowledge of which items are in stock, will strongly favor use of the perpetual inventory system.

The cost layering method adopted may be driven by the capabilities of the entity's accounting system. If a certain type of cost layering is supported by the software, then it may be most efficient to use that method, irrespective of the benefits that could be gleaned from using a different method.

Chapter 7
Fixed Asset Accounting

Introduction

A health care entity may have a substantial investment in buildings and equipment. When this is the case, the accountant must create classifications for the assets, decide which expenditures should be recorded as assets, and depreciate them over time. This chapter delves into the types of asset classifications, the capitalization limit, the concept of base units, different types of depreciation, and other issues relating to the proper accounting for fixed assets.

Related Podcast Episodes: Episodes 139 and 196 of the Accounting Best Practices Podcast discuss a lean system for fixed asset accounting and counting, respectively. They are available at: **accountingtools.com/podcasts** or **iTunes**

What are Fixed Assets?

Fixed assets are items that generate economic benefits over a long period of time. Because of the long period of usefulness of a fixed asset, it is not justifiable to charge its entire cost to expense when incurred. Instead, the matching principle comes into play. Under the matching principle, an organization should recognize both the benefits and expenses associated with a transaction (or, in this case, an asset) at the same time. To do so, we convert an expenditure into an asset and use depreciation to gradually charge it to expense.

By designating an expenditure as a fixed asset, we are shifting the expenditure away from the income statement, where expenditures normally go, and instead place it in the balance sheet. As we gradually reduce its recorded cost through depreciation, the expenditure flows from the balance sheet to the income statement. Thus, the main difference between a normal expenditure and a fixed asset is that the fixed asset is charged to expense over a longer period of time.

The process of identifying fixed assets, recording them as assets, and depreciating them is time-consuming, so it is customary to build some limitations into the process that will route most expenditures directly to expense. One such limitation is to charge an expenditure to expense immediately unless it has a useful life of at least one year. Another limitation is to only recognize an expenditure as a fixed asset if it exceeds a certain dollar amount, known as the *capitalization limit*. These limits keep the vast majority of expenditures from being classified as fixed assets, which reduces the work of the accountant.

EXAMPLE

The Autumn Breeze Nursing Home incurs expenditures for three items and the accountant must decide whether they should be classified as fixed assets. The nursing home's capitalization limit is $2,500. The expenditures are:

- It buys a very used plow to clear snow from the parking lot for $3,000. The accountant expects that the plow only has six months of useful life left, after which it should be scrapped. Since the useful life is so short, the accountant elects to charge the expenditure to expense immediately.
- It buys a laptop computer for $1,500, which has a useful life of three years. This expenditure is less than the capitalization limit, so it is charged to expense.
- It constructs a new overhead cover for a set of parking spaces for $200,000, which has a useful life of 20 years. Since this expenditure has a useful life of longer than one year and a cost greater than the capitalization limit, the accountant records it as a fixed asset and will depreciate it over its 20-year useful life.

An alternative treatment of the $3,000 plow in the preceding example would be to record it in the Other Assets account in the balance sheet and charge the cost to expense over six months. This is a reasonable alternative for expenditures that have useful lives of greater than one accounting period, but less than one year. It is a less time-consuming alternative for the accountant, who does not have to create a fixed asset record or engage in any depreciation calculations.

Types of Fixed Assets

Fixed assets comprise a significant part of the asset base of many health care entities, such as hospitals and nursing homes. The following classifications are commonly used to categorize fixed asset purchases:

- Buildings and improvements
- Construction in progress
- Fixed and movable equipment
- Land
- Land improvements
- Leased property and equipment
- Leasehold improvements

The names of the preceding classifications are generally sufficient to clarify the types of assets that should be recorded within them. A few, however, require further clarification. The land improvements classification includes any expenditures that add functionality to a parcel of land, such as irrigation systems, fencing, and landscaping. The leasehold improvements classification includes any improvements to leased space that are made by the tenant and typically include office space, air conditioning, telephone wiring, and related permanent fixtures. The buildings and improvements

classification may contain the bulk of a health care entity's assets, since it includes buildings, garages, storage facilities, heating and cooling facilities, and so forth.

EXAMPLE

The president of American Nursing Providers wants to construct a new company headquarters in an especially parched area of the Nevada desert. American purchases land for $3 million, updates the land with irrigation systems for $400,000 and constructs an office tower for $10 million. It then purchases furniture and equipment for $300,000. The company aggregates these purchases into the following fixed asset classifications:

Expenditure Item	Classification	Useful Life	Depreciation Method
Building - $10 million	Buildings and improvements	30 years	Straight line
Furniture and equipment - $300,000	Fixed and movable equipment	7 years	Straight line
Irrigation - $400,000	Land improvements	15 years	Straight line
Land - $3 million	Land	Indeterminate	None

A larger health care entity, such as a hospital, may have a large number of assets, and so may find that the preceding classifications are too broad for its needs. If so, it is quite acceptable to refine the classifications. For example, the fixed and movable equipment classification could be sub-divided into:

- *Fixed equipment.* Includes the equipment affixed to a building, such as generators, pumps, and boilers.
- *Major movable equipment.* Includes higher-cost equipment that can be readily moved between locations, such as operating tables and radiology equipment. These assets are regularly inventoried.
- *Minor equipment.* Includes lower-cost equipment that can be readily moved between locations, such as surgical instruments. These assets may not be regularly inventoried.

If an expenditure qualifies as a fixed asset, it must be recorded within an account classification. Account classifications are used to aggregate fixed assets into groups, so that the same depreciation methods and useful lives can be applied to them.

A health entity may also record intangible assets, which result from the acquisition of other entities or from outright purchases. Examples of intangible assets are:

Health plans

- Customer relationships, such as with employer groups
- Favorable leases
- Goodwill
- Licenses

- Noncompete agreements
- Provider networks
- Software
- Trade names
- Trademarks

Hospitals and related health care facilities

- Certificates of need
- Favorable leases
- Goodwill
- Licenses
- Managed care contracts

Physician practices

- Favorable leases
- Goodwill
- Managed care contracts
- Medical charts
- Noncompete agreements

A continuing-care retirement community may incur costs to acquire continuing-care contracts. These costs can be capitalized if they have been incurred to originate a contract, the costs are essential to contract acquisition, and the costs are incurred through the date of occupancy but not for more than one year from the date when construction is complete. These costs can include the following:

- *Compensation and benefits*. Includes that portion of employee pay and benefits relating to initial contract acquisitions.
- *Contract processing*. Includes the costs of evaluating the finances of a prospective resident, examining guarantees and collateral, contract negotiation, processing contract documents, and closing transactions.
- *Solicitations*. Includes the costs of soliciting potential initial residents, such as models, brochures, tours, and sales salaries.

The following costs cannot be capitalized into an asset for the acquisition of continuing care contracts:

- Administration
- Advertising
- Depreciation
- Interest
- Rent
- Any other costs related to occupancy or equipment

The asset created for the acquisition of continuing care contracts should be amortized on a straight-line basis over the shorter of the contract term or the average expected remaining lives of the residents covered by the contract.

Accounting for Fixed Assets

There are several key points in the life of a fixed asset that require recognition in the accounting records; these are the initial recordation of the asset, the recognition of depreciation, and the eventual derecognition of the asset. There may also be cases in which the value of an asset is impaired. We describe these general concepts in the following bullet points:

- *Initial recognition.* There are a number of factors to consider when initially recording a fixed asset, such as the base unit, which costs to include, and when to stop capitalizing costs.
- *Depreciation.* The cost of a fixed asset is gradually charged to expense over time, using depreciation. There are a variety of depreciation methods available, which are described in later sections.
- *Impairment.* There are numerous circumstances under which an asset's recorded value is considered to be impaired. If so, the value of the asset is written down on the books of the health care entity.
- *Derecognition.* When an asset comes to the end of its useful life, the organization will likely sell or otherwise dispose of it. At this time, remove it from the accounting records, as well as record a gain or loss (if any) on the final disposal transaction.

The Capitalization Limit

One of the most important decisions to be made in the initial recognition of a fixed asset is what minimum cost level to use, below which an expenditure is recorded as an expense in the period incurred, rather than as a fixed asset. This capitalization limit, which is frequently abbreviated as the *cap limit*, is usually driven by the following factors:

- *Asset tracking.* If an expenditure is recorded as a fixed asset, the fixed asset tracking system may impose a significant amount of control over the newly-recorded fixed asset. This can be good, if the accountant needs to know where an asset is at any time. Conversely, there is not usually a tracking system in place for an expenditure that is charged to expense, since the assumption is that such items are consumed at once and so require no subsequent tracking.
- *Fixed asset volume.* The number of expenditures that will be recorded as fixed assets will increase dramatically as the cap limit is lowered. For example, there may only be one fixed asset if the cap limit is $100,000, 50 assets if the cap limit is $10,000, and 500 assets if the cap limit is $1,000. Analyze historical expenditures to estimate a cap limit that will prevent the accountant from being deluged with additional fixed asset records.

- *Profit pressure.* Senior management may have a strong interest in reporting the highest possible profit levels right now, which means that they want a very low cap limit that shifts as many expenditures as possible into capitalized assets. Since this pressure can result in a vast number of very low-cost fixed assets, this issue can create a significant work load for the accountant.
- *Record keeping.* The accountant can spend an excessive amount of time tracking fixed assets, formulating depreciation and eliminating fixed assets from the records once they have been disposed of. This can be quite a burden if there are a large number of assets.
- *Tax requirements.* Some government entities require a business to report fixed assets, so that they can charge a personal property tax that is calculated from the reported fixed asset levels. Clearly, a high cap limit will reduce the number of reported fixed assets, and therefore the tax paid. However, government entities may require a minimum cap limit in order to protect their tax revenues.

From an efficiency or tax liability perspective, a high cap limit is always best, since it greatly reduces the work of the accountant and results in lower personal property taxes. From a profitability or asset tracking perspective, the reverse situation is the most favorable, with a very low cap limit. These conflicting objectives call for some discussion within the management team about the most appropriate cap limit – it should not simply be imposed on the organization by the accountant.

The Base Unit

There is no specific guidance in the accounting standards about the unit of measure for a fixed asset. This unit of measure, or *base unit*, is essentially an organization's definition of what constitutes a fixed asset. This definition can be formalized into a policy, so that it is applied consistently over time. Here are several issues to consider when creating a definition of a base unit:

- *Aggregation.* Should individually insignificant items be aggregated into a fixed asset, such as a group of tables or chairs? This increases the administrative burden, but does delay recognition of the expense associated with the items.
- *Component replacement.* Is it likely that large components of an asset will be replaced during its useful life? If so, designate the smaller units as the most appropriate base unit to track in the accounting records. This decision may be influenced by the probability of these smaller components actually being replaced over time. For example, the roof of a building could be designated as a separate asset, since it may be replaced several times over the life of the building.
- *Identification.* Can an asset that has been designated as a base unit be physically identified? If not, it will be impossible to track the asset, so it should not

be designated as a base unit. This is a common problem in a larger health care entity that may have dozens of identical tables, chairs, and other furniture.

- *Tax treatment*. Is there a tax advantage in separately accounting for the components of a major asset? This may be the case where the useful life of a component is shorter than that of a major asset of which it is a part, so that it can be depreciated quicker.
- *Useful life*. The useful lives of the components of a base unit should be similar, so that the entire unit can be eliminated or replaced at approximately the same time.

EXAMPLE

Oklahoma Hospitals owns a number of hospitals throughout the center of the United States. It maintains office buildings in areas that are subject to major hailstorms, which commonly result in hail damage to the roofs of the buildings. On average, hail damage will require the replacement of a roof every ten years, while the rest of each structure is estimated to be viable for at least 50 years. Given these differences, it makes sense for this hospital chain to designate the roofs as separate base units.

The Initial Measurement of a Fixed Asset

Initially record a fixed asset at the historical cost of acquiring it, which includes the costs to bring it to the condition and location necessary for its intended use. These activities include the following:

- Physical construction of the asset
- Demolition of any preexisting structures
- Renovating a preexisting structure to alter it for use by the buyer
- Administrative and technical activities during preconstruction, such as designing the asset and obtaining permits
- Administrative and technical work after construction commences, such as litigation, labor disputes, and technical problems

---

EXAMPLE

A nursing home decides to add an additional air conditioning unit to its main office, which involves the creation of a concrete pad for the unit, stringing electrical cabling to it, linking it to the building's air conditioning vents, and obtaining an electrical permit. All of the following costs can be included in the fixed asset cost of the unit:

Air conditioning unit price	$120,000
Concrete pad	3,000
Wiring and ducts	5,000
Electrical permit	200
Total	$128,200

A health care entity may receive donations of fixed assets. These donations are recorded at their fair value as of the date of donation. This recorded fair value then becomes the cost basis for the asset. Donated assets are depreciated in the normal manner, as described in the following sections.

The Purpose of Depreciation

The purpose of depreciation is to charge to expense a portion of an asset that relates to the revenue generated by that asset. This is called the matching principle, where revenues and expenses both appear in the income statement in the same reporting period, which gives the best view of how well a health care entity has performed in a given accounting period. The trouble with this matching concept is that there is usually only a tenuous connection between the generation of revenue and a specific asset.

To get around this linkage problem, we usually assume a steady rate of depreciation over the useful life of each asset, so that we approximate a linkage between the recognition of revenues and expenses. This approximation threatens our credulity even more when an organization uses accelerated depreciation, since the main reason for using it is to defer taxes (and not to better match revenues and expenses).

If we were not to use depreciation at all, we would be forced to charge all assets to expense as soon as we buy them. This would result in large losses in the months when this purchase transaction occurs, followed by unusually high profitability in those periods when the corresponding amount of revenue is recognized, with no offsetting expense. Thus, an organization that does not use depreciation will have front-loaded expenses and extremely variable financial results.

Depreciation Concepts

There are three factors to consider in the calculation of depreciation, which are as follows:

- *Useful life*. This is the time period over which it is expected that an asset will be productive, or the amount of activity expected to be generated by it. Past its useful life, it is no longer cost-effective to continue operating the asset, so the organization would dispose of it or stop using it. Depreciation is recognized over the useful life of an asset.

Tip: Rather than recording a different useful life for every asset, it is easier to assign each asset to an asset class, where every asset in that asset class has the same useful life. This approach may not work for very high-cost assets, where a greater degree of precision may be needed.

Tip: When evaluating whether the designated useful life of a fixed asset is reasonable, consider that social, economic, and scientific advances within the health care industry can render assets obsolete within a relatively short period of time.

- *Salvage value.* When a health care entity eventually disposes of an asset, it may be able to sell the asset for some reduced amount, which is the salvage value. Depreciation is calculated based on the asset cost, less any estimated salvage value. If salvage value is expected to be quite small, it is generally ignored for the purpose of calculating depreciation.

EXAMPLE

St. Quadratus Hospital buys an employee shuttle van for $75,000 and estimates that its salvage value will be $15,000 in five years, when it plans to dispose of the asset. This means that the hospital will depreciate $60,000 of the asset cost over five years, leaving $15,000 of the cost remaining at the end of that time. The hospital's accountant expects to then sell the asset for $15,000, which will eliminate the asset from its accounting records.

- *Depreciation method.* Depreciation expense can be calculated using an accelerated depreciation method, or evenly over the useful life of the asset. The advantage of using an accelerated method is that an organization can recognize more depreciation early in the life of a fixed asset, which defers some income tax expense recognition to a later period. The advantage of using a steady depreciation rate is the ease of calculation. Examples of accelerated depreciation methods are the double declining balance and sum-of-the-years' digits methods. The primary method for steady depreciation is the straight-line method.

The *mid-month convention* states that, no matter when a fixed asset is purchased in a month, it is assumed to have been purchased in the middle of the month for depreciation purposes. Thus, if a fixed asset was purchased on January 5th, assume that it was bought on January 15th; or, if it was acquired on January 28, still assume that it was bought on January 15th. By doing so, it is easier to calculate a standard half-month of depreciation for the first month of ownership.

If the decision is made to use the mid-month convention, this also means that it will be necessary to record a half-month of depreciation for the *last* month of the asset's useful life. By doing so, the two half-month depreciation calculations equal one full month of depreciation.

Many organizations prefer to use full-month depreciation in the first month of ownership, irrespective of the actual date of purchase within the month, so that they can slightly accelerate their recognition of depreciation, which in turn reduces their taxable income in the near term.

Accelerated Depreciation

Accelerated depreciation is the depreciation of fixed assets at a very fast rate early in their useful lives. The primary reason for using accelerated depreciation is to reduce the reported amount of taxable income over the first few years of an asset's life, so that an organization pays a smaller amount of income taxes during those early years. Later on, when most of the depreciation will have already been recognized, the effect reverses, so there will be less depreciation available to shelter taxable income. The result is that more income taxes are paid in later years. Thus, the net effect of accelerated depreciation is the deferral of income taxes to later time periods.

Note: Many health care entities are structured as not-for-profit organizations, and so will not pay income taxes, making the use of accelerated depreciation irrelevant. However, they may own or be associated with for-profit entities that *do* pay income taxes, and where accelerated depreciation will therefore be a useful tool.

A secondary reason for using accelerated depreciation is that it may actually reflect the usage pattern of the underlying assets, where they experience heavy usage early in their useful lives.

There are several calculations available for accelerated depreciation, such as the double declining balance method and the sum of the years' digits method. We will describe these methods in the following sub-sections.

All of the depreciation methods end up recognizing the same amount of depreciation, which is the cost of the fixed asset less any expected salvage value. The only difference between the various methods is the speed with which depreciation is recognized.

Accelerated depreciation requires additional depreciation calculations and record keeping, so some organizations avoid it for that reason (though fixed asset software can readily overcome this issue).

Sum-of-the-Years' Digits Method

The sum of the years' digits (SYD) method is used to calculate depreciation on an accelerated basis. Use the following formula to calculate it:

$$\text{Depreciation percentage} = \frac{\text{Number of estimated years of life as of beginning of the year}}{\text{Sum of the years' digits}}$$

The following exhibit contains examples of the sum of the years' digits noted in the denominator of the preceding formula.

Sample Sum of the Years' Digits Calculation

Total Depreciation Period	Initial Sum of the Years' Digits	Calculation
2 years	3	1 + 2
3 years	6	1 + 2 + 3
4 years	10	1 + 2 + 3 + 4
5 years	15	1 + 2 + 3 + 4 + 5

The concept is illustrated in the following example.

EXAMPLE

Executive Surgery Associates buys a surgical table for $10,000. The table has no estimated salvage value and a useful life of five years. Executive calculates the annual sum of the years' digits depreciation for this machine as:

Year	Number of estimated years of life as of beginning of the year	SYD Calculation	Depreciation Percentage	Annual Depreciation
1	5	5/15	33.33%	$3,333
2	4	4/15	26.67%	2,667
3	3	3/15	20.00%	2,000
4	2	2/15	13.33%	1,333
5	1	1/15	6.67%	667
To-tals	15		100.00%	$10,000

Double-Declining Balance Method

The double declining balance (DDB) method is a form of accelerated depreciation. To calculate the double-declining balance depreciation rate, divide the number of years of useful life of an asset into 100 percent, and multiply the result by two. The formula is:

$$(100\% \div \text{Years of useful life}) \times 2$$

The DDB calculation proceeds until the asset's salvage value is reached, after which depreciation ends.

EXAMPLE

Executive Surgery Associates purchases a respiratory ventilator for $50,000. It has an estimated salvage value of $5,000 and a useful life of five years. The calculation of the double declining balance depreciation rate is:

$$(100\% \div \text{Years of useful life}) \times 2 = 40\%$$

By applying the 40% rate, Executive arrives at the following table of depreciation charges per year:

Year	Book Value at Beginning of Year	Depreciation Percentage	DDB Depreciation	Book Value Net of Depreciation
1	$50,000	40%	$20,000	$30,000
2	30,000	40%	12,000	18,000
3	18,000	40%	7,200	10,800
4	10,800	40%	4,320	6,480
5	6,480	40%	1,480	5,000
Total			$45,000	

Note that the depreciation in the fifth and final year is only for $1,480, rather than the $3,240 that would be indicated by the 40% depreciation rate. The reason for the smaller depreciation charge is that Executive stops any further depreciation once the remaining book value declines to the amount of the estimated salvage value.

A variation on the double-declining balance method is the 150% method, which substitutes 1.5 for the 2.0 figure used in the calculation. The 150% method does not result in as rapid a rate of depreciation as the double declining method, though the pace of depreciation is still accelerated.

Straight-Line Method

If a health care entity elects not to use accelerated depreciation, it can instead use the straight-line method, where it depreciates an asset at the same standard rate throughout its useful life. Under the straight-line method of depreciation, recognize depreciation expense evenly over the estimated useful life of an asset. The straight-line calculation steps are:

1. Subtract the estimated salvage value of the asset from the amount at which it is recorded on the books.
2. Determine the estimated useful life of the asset. It is easiest to use a standard useful life for each class of assets.
3. Divide the estimated useful life (in years) into 1 to arrive at the straight-line depreciation rate.
4. Multiply the depreciation rate by the asset cost (less salvage value).

EXAMPLE

Executive Surgery Associates buys surgical lights for $6,000. The lights have an estimated salvage value of $1,000 and a useful life of five years. Executive calculates the annual straight-line depreciation for the lights as:

1. Purchase cost of $6,000 – Estimated salvage value of $1,000 = Depreciable asset cost of $5,000
2. 1 ÷ 5-Year useful life = 20% Depreciation rate per year
3. 20% Depreciation rate × $5,000 Depreciable asset cost = $1,000 Annual depreciation

---

The Depreciation of Land

Nearly all fixed assets have a useful life, after which they no longer contribute to the operations of an organization or they stop generating revenue. During this useful life, they are depreciated, which reduces their cost to what they are supposed to be worth at the end of their useful lives. Land, however, has no definitive useful life, so there is no way to depreciate it.

The Depreciation of Land Improvements

Land improvements are enhancements to a plot of land to make it more usable. If these improvements have a useful life, depreciate them. If there is no way to estimate a useful life, do not depreciate the cost of the improvements.

If land is being prepared for its intended purpose, include these costs in the cost of the land asset. They are not depreciated. Examples of such costs are:

- Demolishing an existing building
- Clearing and leveling the land

If functionality is being added to the land and the expenditures have a useful life, record them in a separate Land Improvements account. Examples of land improvements are:

- Drainage and irrigation systems
- Fencing
- Landscaping
- Parking lots and walkways

A special item is the ongoing cost of landscaping. This is a period cost, not a fixed asset, and so should be charged to expense as incurred.

EXAMPLE

Medical Record Processing Corporation (MRP) buys a parcel of land for $1,000,000. Since it is a purchase of land, MRP cannot depreciate the cost. MRP then razes a building that was located on the property at a cost of $25,000, fills in the old foundation for $5,000 and levels the land for $50,000. All of these costs are to prepare the land for its intended purpose, so they are all added to the cost of the land. MRP cannot depreciate these costs.

MRP intends to use the land as a parking lot for its corporate headquarters, so it spends $350,000 to create a parking lot. It estimates that these improvements have a useful life of 10 years. It should record this cost in the Land Improvements account and depreciate it over 10 years.

Depreciation Accounting Entries

The basic depreciation entry is to debit the depreciation expense account (which appears in the income statement) and credit the accumulated depreciation account (which appears in the balance sheet as a contra account that reduces the amount of fixed assets). Over time, the accumulated depreciation balance will continue to increase as more depreciation is added to it, until such time as it equals the original cost of the asset. At that time, stop recording any depreciation expense, since the cost of the asset has now been reduced to zero.

The journal entry for depreciation can be a simple two-line entry designed to accommodate all types of fixed assets, or it may be subdivided into separate entries for each type of fixed asset.

EXAMPLE

St. Bartholomew Hospital calculates that it should have $25,000 of depreciation expense in the current month. The entry is:

	Debit	Credit
Depreciation expense	25,000	
Accumulated depreciation		25,000

In the following month, the accountant decides to show a higher level of precision at the expense account level, and instead elects to apportion the $25,000 of depreciation among different expense accounts, so that each class of asset has a separate depreciation charge. The entry is:

	Debit	Credit
Depreciation expense – Buildings and improvements	4,000	
Depreciation expense – Fixed and movable equipment	8,000	
Depreciation expense – Land improvements	6,000	
Depreciation expense – Leasehold improvements	7,000	
Accumulated depreciation		25,000

Accumulated Depreciation

When an asset is sold or otherwise disposed of, remove all related accumulated depreciation from the accounting records at the same time. Otherwise, an unusually large amount of accumulated depreciation will build up on the balance sheet.

EXAMPLE

Bright Smile Dentistry has $1,000,000 of fixed assets, for which it has charged $380,000 of accumulated depreciation. This results in the following presentation on Bright's balance sheet:

Fixed assets	$1,000,000
Less: Accumulated depreciation	(380,000)
Net fixed assets	$620,000

Bright then sells equipment for $80,000 that had an original cost of $140,000, and for which it had already recorded accumulated depreciation of $50,000. It records the sale with this journal entry:

	Debit	Credit
Cash	80,000	
Accumulated depreciation	50,000	
Loss on asset sale	10,000	
Fixed assets		140,000

As a result of this entry, Bright's balance sheet presentation of fixed assets has changed, so that fixed assets before accumulated depreciation have declined to $860,000 and accumulated depreciation has declined to $330,000. The new presentation is:

Fixed assets	$860,000
Less: Accumulated depreciation	(330,000)
Net fixed assets	$530,000

The amount of net fixed assets declined by $90,000 as a result of the asset sale, which is the sum of the $80,000 cash proceeds and the $10,000 loss resulting from the asset sale.

Asset Impairment

Some health care entities have massive investments in long-term assets. They may find that the value of these assets have become impaired when their carrying amount exceeds their fair value. *Carrying amount* is the original cost of an asset, minus all accumulated depreciation and impairment charges (as described in this section). There are a number of circumstances that can indicate possible asset impairment for a health care entity, such as:

- Asset usage has declined. For example, MRI business has been lost to a competing facility.
- Patient volumes have significantly declined, perhaps due to a reduction in the local population.
- Market conditions have negatively impacted cash flows. For example, Medicaid reimbursement rates may have been reduced for the services that a facility provides.
- The entity has lost a major contract with a third-party payor.
- A not-for-profit entity has lost its federal tax exemption, which will likely choke off its flow of inbound contributions.

A particular asset impairment concern for a health care entity arises when it supports a service or facility that does not generate positive cash flows, but which it is committed to support, because it is central to the mission of the organization.

An impairment loss is recognized on a fixed asset when its carrying amount is not recoverable and exceeds its fair value. The carrying amount of an asset is not recoverable if it exceeds the sum of the undiscounted cash flows expected to result from the use of the asset over its remaining useful life and the final disposition of the asset. These cash flow estimates should incorporate assumptions that are reasonable in relation to the assumptions the health care entity uses for its budgets, forecasts, and so forth. If there are a range of possible cash flow outcomes, consider using a probability-weighted cash flow analysis.

The amount of an impairment loss is the difference between an asset's carrying amount and its fair value. Once this loss is recognized, it reduces the carrying amount of the asset, so it may be necessary to alter the amount of periodic depreciation being charged against the asset to adjust for this lower carrying amount (otherwise, an excessively large depreciation expense will be incurred over the remaining useful life of the asset).

Asset Derecognition

An asset is derecognized upon its disposal, or when no future economic benefits can be expected from its use or disposal. Derecognition can arise from a variety of events, such as an asset's sale, scrapping, or donation. The net effect of asset derecognition is to remove an asset and its associated accumulated depreciation from the balance sheet, as well as to recognize any related gain or loss. The gain or loss on derecognition is calculated as the net disposal proceeds, minus the asset's carrying amount.

The asset disposal form is used to formalize the disposition of assets. Ideally, the purchasing department should be involved in disposals, since it presumably has the most experience in obtaining the best prices for goods. Consequently, a large part of the form is set aside for the use of the purchasing staff, which describes how the asset is disposed of and the amount of funds (if any) received. There is space to state billing information, in case the buyer is to be billed. There is also a separate section containing a checklist of activities that the accountant must complete. A sample of the form is presented next.

Sample Asset Disposal Form

Asset Disposal Form

Asset Tag Number	Asset Serial Number	Current Location

Asset Description

Reason for Disposal

- ☐ No longer usable
- ☐ Past recommended life span
- ☐ Being replaced
- ☐ Being traded in
- ☐ Lost or stolen*
- ☐ Other ____________________

* Contact building security to file a police report

Department Manager Approval Signature

For Use by Purchasing Department

Type of Disposition

- ☐ Sold ($____________)
- ☐ Donated
- ☐ Scrapped
- ☐ Other ____________________

If buyer is to be invoiced, state billing information:

Buyer billing information

Purchasing Manager Approval Signature	Disposal Date

For Use by Accounting Department

Accounting Actions Completed

☐ Asset removed from general ledger	Initials	Date
☐ Asset removed from equipment register	Initials	Date
☐ Buyer billed for sale amount	Initials	Date
☐ Cash receipt recorded	Initials	Date

Abandoned and Idle Assets

If a health care entity abandons an asset, consider the asset to be disposed of and account for it as such (even if it remains on the premises). However, if the asset is only temporarily idle, do not consider it to be abandoned and continue to depreciate it in a normal manner. If an asset has been abandoned, reduce its carrying amount down

to any remaining salvage value on the date when the decision is made to abandon the asset.

Some fixed assets will be idle from time to time. There is no specific consideration of idle assets in the accounting standards, so continue to depreciate these assets in the normal manner. However, if an asset is idle, this may indicate that its useful life is shorter than the amount currently used to calculate its depreciation. This may call for a re-evaluation of its useful life.

Asset Disposal Accounting

There are two scenarios under which a business may dispose of a fixed asset. The first situation arises when a fixed asset is being eliminated without receiving any payment in return. This is a common situation when a fixed asset is being scrapped because it is obsolete or no longer in use and there is no resale market for it. In this case, reverse any accumulated depreciation and reverse the original asset cost. If the asset is fully depreciated, that is the extent of the entry.

EXAMPLE

Cardiac Surgery Associates buys a used surgical chair for $10,000 and recognizes $1,000 of depreciation per year over the following ten years. At that time, the chair is not only fully depreciated, but also ready for the scrap heap. Cardiac gives away the chair for free and records the following entry.

	Debit	Credit
Accumulated depreciation	10,000	
Equipment asset		10,000

A variation on this situation is to write off a fixed asset that has not yet been completely depreciated. In this case, write off the remaining undepreciated amount of the asset to a loss account.

EXAMPLE

To use the same example, Cardiac gives away the surgical chair after eight years, when it has not yet depreciated $2,000 of the asset's original $10,000 cost. In this case, Cardiac records the following entry:

	Debit	Credit
Loss on asset disposal	2,000	
Accumulated depreciation	8,000	
Equipment asset		10,000

Another scenario arises when an asset is sold, so that the organization receives cash in exchange for the fixed asset being sold. Depending upon the price paid and the remaining amount of depreciation that has not yet been charged to expense, this can result in either a gain or a loss on sale of the asset.

EXAMPLE

Cardiac Surgery Associates still disposes of its $10,000 used surgical chair, but does so after seven years and sells it for $3,500 in cash. In this case, it has already recorded $7,000 of depreciation expense. The entry is:

	Debit	Credit
Cash	3,500	
Accumulated depreciation	7,000	
Gain on asset disposal		500
Equipment asset		10,000

What if Cardiac had sold the surgical chair for $2,500 instead of $3,500? Then there would be a loss of $500 on the sale. The entry would be:

	Debit	Credit
Cash	2,500	
Accumulated depreciation	7,000	
Loss on asset disposal	500	
Equipment asset		10,000

The "loss on asset disposal" or "gain on asset disposal" accounts noted in the preceding sample entries are called *disposal accounts*. They may be combined into a single account or used separately to store gains and losses resulting from the disposal of fixed assets.

Summary

From the perspective of the accountant, the tracking of fixed assets can be quite time-consuming. Consequently, we recommend setting a relatively high capitalization limit in order to charge most purchases to expense at once, rather than recording them as fixed assets.

Depreciation is one of the central concerns of the accountant, since the broad range of available methods can result in significant differences in the amount of depreciation expense recorded in each period. Generally, adopt the straight-line depreciation method to minimize the amount of depreciation calculations, unless the usage rate of the assets involved more closely matches a different depreciation method.

Chapter 8
Asset Retirement and Environmental Remediation Obligations

Introduction

An asset retirement obligation (ARO) is a liability associated with the retirement of a fixed asset, such as a legal requirement to return a site to its previous condition. Many health care entities operate older facilities that were constructed many years ago, prior to the more stringent building codes of recent times. When these facilities are eventually shut down, an entity may find that it is liable for substantial asset retirement costs or (worse yet) environmental remediation costs, which can be much greater. A facility shutdown may result in notable expenditures to deal with asbestos, underground storage tanks, hazardous chemicals, and similar issues.

This chapter addresses the circumstances under which these obligations may be present, as well as the related accounting. An example near the end of the chapter illustrates many of the concepts noted in the following sections.

Overview of Asset Retirement Obligations

A health care entity usually incurs an ARO due to a legal obligation. It may also incur an ARO if the firm promises a third party (even the public at large) that it will engage in ARO activities; the circumstances of this promise will drive the determination of whether there is an actual liability. This liability may exist even if there has been no formal action against the business. When making the determination of liability, base the evaluation on current laws, not on projections of what laws there may be in the future, when the asset retirement occurs.

EXAMPLE

Arduous Research Labs (ARL) operates a radioactive pellet facility, for use in treating prostate cancer, and is required by law to bring the property back to its original condition when the plant is eventually decertified. The lab has come under some pressure by various environmental organizations to take the remediation one step further and create a public park on the premises. Because of the significant negative publicity generated by these groups, the lab issues a press release in which it commits to create the park. There is no legal requirement for the firm to incur this additional expense, so ARL's legal counsel should evaluate the facts to determine if there is a legal obligation.

A health care entity should recognize the fair value of an ARO when it incurs the liability, and if it can make a reasonable estimate of the fair value of the ARO.

EXAMPLE

Arduous Research Labs has completed the construction of a radioactive pellet formulation facility, but has not yet taken delivery of any radioactive materials or undergone certification tests. It will incur an ARO for decontamination, but since it has not yet begun operations, it has not begun to contaminate, and therefore should not yet record an ARO liability.

If a fair value is not initially obtainable, recognize the ARO at a later date, when the fair value becomes available. If a health care entity acquires a fixed asset to which an ARO is attached, recognize a liability for the ARO as of the fixed asset acquisition date.

If there is not sufficient information available to reasonably estimate the fair value of an ARO, it may be possible to use an expected present value technique that assigns probabilities to cash flows, thereby creating an estimate of the fair value of the ARO. Use an expected present value technique under either of the following scenarios:

- Other parties have specified the settlement date and method of settlement, so that the only uncertainty is whether the obligation will be enforced.
- There is information available from which to estimate the range of possible settlement dates and possible methods of settlement, as well as the probabilities associated with them.

Examples of the sources from which to obtain the information needed for the preceding estimation requirements are past practice within the business, industry practice, the stated intentions of management, or the estimated useful life of the asset (which indicates a likely ARO settlement date at the end of the useful life).

If there is an unambiguous requirement that causes an ARO, but there is a low likelihood of a performance requirement, a liability must still be recognized. When a low probability of performance is incorporated into the expected present value calculation for the ARO liability, this will likely reduce the amount of the ARO to be recognized. Even if there has been a history of non-enforcement of prior AROs for which there was an unambiguous obligation, do not defer the recognition of a liability.

The Initial Measurement of an Asset Retirement Obligation

In most cases, the only way to determine the fair value of an ARO is to use an expected present value technique. When constructing an expected present value of future cash flows, incorporate the following points into the calculation:

- *Discount rate.* Use a credit-adjusted risk-free rate to discount cash flows to their present value. Thus, the credit standing of a business may impact the discount rate used.
- *Probability distribution.* When calculating the expected present value of an ARO, and there are only two possible outcomes, assign a 50 percent probability to each one until there is additional information that alters the initial

probability distribution. Otherwise, spread the probability across the full set of possible scenarios.

EXAMPLE

The controller of St. Macarius Hospital is compiling the cost of an asbestos decontamination ARO several years in the future. She is uncertain of the cost, since supplier fees fluctuate considerably. She arrives at an expected weighted average cash flow based on the following probability analysis:

Cash Flow Estimates	Probability Assessment	Expected Cash Flows
$12,500,000	10%	$1,250,000
15,000,000	15%	2,250,000
16,000,000	50%	8,000,000
22,500,000	25%	5,625,000
	Weighted average cash flows	$17,125,000

Follow these steps in calculating the expected present value of an ARO:

1. Estimate the timing and amount of the cash flows associated with the retirement activities.
2. Determine the credit-adjusted risk-free rate.
3. Recognize any period-to-period increase in the carrying amount of the ARO liability as *accretion expense*. To do so, multiply the beginning liability by the credit-adjusted risk-free rate derived when the liability was first measured.
4. Recognize upward liability revisions as a new liability layer, and discount them at the current credit-adjusted risk-free rate.
5. Recognize downward liability revisions by reducing the appropriate liability layer, and discount the reduction at the rate used for the initial recognition of the related liability layer.

When an ARO liability is initially recognized, also capitalize the related asset retirement cost by adding it to the carrying amount of the related fixed asset.

Subsequent Measurement of an Asset Retirement Obligation

It is possible that an ARO liability will not remain static over the life of the related fixed asset. Instead, the liability may change over time. If the liability increases, consider the incremental increase in each period to be an additional layer of liability, in addition to any previous liability layers. The following points will assist in the recognition of these additional layers:

- Initially recognize each layer at its fair value.

EXAMPLE

St. Hallvard Hospital has been operating a facility with known asbestos problems for three years. It initially recognized an ARO of $25 million for the eventual dismantling of the facility after its useful life has ended. In the fifth year, the hospital detects groundwater contamination from a leaking storage tank, and recognizes an additional layer of ARO liability for $4 million to deal with it.

- Systematically allocate the ARO liability to expense over the useful life of the underlying asset.
- Measure changes in the liability due to the passage of time, using the credit-adjusted risk-free rate when each layer of liability was first recognized. Recognize this cost as an increase in the liability. When charged to expense, this is classified as accretion expense (which is not the same as interest expense).
- As the time period shortens before an ARO is realized, the assessment of the timing, amount, and probabilities associated with cash flows will improve. It will likely be necessary to alter the ARO liability based on these changes in estimate. If an upward revision is made in the ARO liability, then discount it using the current credit-adjusted risk-free rate. If a downward revision is made in the ARO liability, discount it using the original credit-adjusted risk-free rate when the liability layer was first recognized. If the liability layer to which the downward adjustment relates cannot be identified, use a weighted-average credit-adjusted risk-free rate to discount it.

Settlement of an Asset Retirement Obligation

An ARO is normally settled only when the underlying fixed asset is retired, though it is possible that some portion of an ARO will be settled prior to asset retirement. If it becomes apparent that no expenses will be required as part of the retirement of an asset, reverse any remaining unamortized ARO to zero.

Tip: If a health care entity cannot fulfill its ARO responsibilities and a third party does so instead, this does not relieve the organization from recording an ARO liability, on the grounds that it may now have an obligation to pay the third party instead.

EXAMPLE

St. Ebba Hospital operates a very old medical facility on a military base, and is legally required by the military to tear down the building and return the grounds to their natural condition in five years. St. Ebba uses the following assumptions about the ARO:

- The tear down and restoration cost is $9 million.
- The risk-free rate is 5%, to which St. Ebba adds 3% to reflect the effect of its credit standing.
- The assumed rate of inflation over the five-year period is four percent.

With an average inflation rate of 4% per year for the next five years, the current tear down and restoration cost of $9 million increases to approximately $11 million by the end of the fifth year. The expected present value of the $11 million payout, using the 8% credit-adjusted risk-free rate, is $7,486,000 (calculated as $11 million × 0.68058 discount rate).

St. Ebba's controller then calculates the amount of annual accretion using the 8% rate, as shown in the following table:

Year	Beginning Liability	8% Accretion	Ending Liability
1	$7,486,000	$599,000	$8,085,000
2	8,085,000	647,000	8,732,000
3	8,732,000	699,000	9,431,000
4	9,431,000	754,000	10,185,000
5	10,185,000	815,000	11,000,000

The controller then combines the accretion expense with the straight-line depreciation expense noted in the following table to show how all components of the ARO are charged to expense over the next five years. Note that the accretion expense is carried forward from the preceding table. The depreciation is based on the $7,486,000 present value of the ARO, spread evenly over five years.

Year	Accretion Expense	Depreciation Expense	Total Expense
1	$599,000	$1,497,200	$2,096,200
2	647,000	1,497,200	2,144,200
3	699,000	1,497,200	2,196,200
4	754,000	1,497,200	2,251,200
5	815,000	1,497,200	2,312,200
			$11,000,000

After the medical facility is closed, St. Ebba commences its tear down and restoration activities. The actual cost is $12 million.

Here is a selection of the journal entries that the controller recorded over the term of the ARO:

	Debit	Credit
Facility decontamination asset	9,000,000	
Asset retirement obligation liability		9,000,000
To record the initial fair value of the asset retirement obligation		

	Debit	Credit
Depreciation expense	1,497,200	
Accumulated depreciation		1,497,200
To record the annual depreciation on the asset retirement obligation		

	Debit	Credit
Accretion expense	As noted in schedule	
Asset retirement obligation liability		As noted in schedule
To record the annual accretion expense on the asset retirement obligation liability		

	Debit	Credit
Loss on ARO settlement	1,000,000	
Remediation expense		1,000,000
To record settlement of the excess asset retirement obligation		

Overview of Environmental Obligations

There are a number of federal laws that impose an obligation on a business to remediate sites that contain environmentally hazardous conditions, as well as to control or prevent pollution. Remediation can include feasibility studies, cleanup costs, legal fees, government oversight costs, and restoration costs.

In general, a liability for an environmental obligation should be accrued if both of the following circumstances are present:

- It is probable that an asset has been impaired or a liability has been incurred. This is based on both of the following criteria:
    - An assertion has been made that the health care entity bears responsibility for a past event; and
    - It is probable that the outcome of the assertion will be unfavorable to the business.
- The amount of the loss or a range of loss can be reasonably estimated.

It is recognized that the liability associated with environmental obligations can change dramatically over time, depending on the number and type of hazardous substances involved, the financial condition of other responsible parties, and other factors. Accordingly, the recorded liability associated with environmental obligations can change. Further, it may not be possible to initially estimate some components of the liability, which does not prevent other components of the liability from being recognized as soon as possible.

EXAMPLE

Arduous Research Labs has been notified by the government that it must conduct a remedial investigation and feasibility study for a Superfund site to which it sent radioactive pellet waste products in the past. There is sufficient information to estimate the cost of the study, for which the controller records an accrued liability. However, there is no way to initially determine the extent of any additional liabilities associated with the site until the study has at least commenced. Accordingly, the controller continually reviews the preliminary findings of the study, and updates the liability for its environmental obligation based on changes in that information.

Once there is information available regarding the extent of an environmental obligation, an organization should record its best estimate of the liability. If it is not possible to create a best estimate, then at least a minimum estimate of the liability should be recorded. The estimate is refined as better information becomes available.

In some cases, it is possible to derive a reasonable estimate of liability quite early in the remediation process, because it is similar to the remediation that has been encountered at other sites. In these instances, the full amount of the liability should be recognized at once.

The costs associated with the treatment of environmental contamination costs should be charged to expense in nearly all cases. The sole exceptions are:

- The costs incurred will increase the capacity of the property, or extend its life, or improve its safety or efficiency
- The costs incurred are needed to prepare a property for sale that is currently classified as held for sale
- The costs improve the property, as well as mitigate or prevent environmental contamination that has yet to occur and that might otherwise arise from future operations

EXAMPLE

St. Kilian Hospital spends $250,000 to construct a concrete pad that is designed to prevent fluid leaks from causing groundwater contamination. Making this investment improves the safety of the property, while also preventing future environmental contamination. Consequently, the controller can capitalize the $250,000 cost of the concrete pad, and should depreciate it over the remaining useful life of the property.

Measurement of Environmental Obligations

In order to determine the extent of the liability associated with an environmental obligation, follow these steps:

1. Identify those parties likely to be considered responsible for the site requiring remediation. These potentially responsible parties may include the following:
    - Participating parties
    - Recalcitrant parties
    - Unproven parties
    - Unknown parties
    - Orphan share parties
2. Determine the likelihood that those parties will pay their share of the liability associated with site remediation, based primarily on their financial condition. There is a presumption that costs will only be allocated among the participating responsible parties, since the other parties are less likely to pay their shares of the liability.
3. Based on the preceding steps, calculate the percentage of the total liability that should be recorded. The sources for this information can include the liability percentages that the responsible parties have agreed to, or which have been assigned by a consultant, or which have been assigned by the Environmental Protection Agency (EPA). If the health care entity chooses to record the liability in a different amount, it should be based on objective, verifiable information, examples of which are:
    - Existing data about the types and amounts of waste at the site
    - Prior experience with liability allocations in comparable situations
    - Reports issued by environmental specialists
    - Internal data that refutes EPA allegations

EXAMPLE

St. Tabitha Hospital has been notified by the EPA that it is a potentially responsible party in a groundwater contamination case. The EPA has identified three organizations as being potentially responsible. The three parties employ an arbitrator to allocate the responsibility for costs among the companies. The arbitrator derives the following allocations:

	Allocation Percentage
St. Tabitha Hospital	40%
Battersea Holdings	20%
Chelsea Pharmaceuticals	20%
	80%
Recalcitrant share (nonparticipating parties)	15%
Orphan share (no party can be identified)	5%
Total	100%

The total estimated remediation cost is estimated to be $5 million. St. Tabitha's direct share of this amount is $2 million (calculated as $5 million total remediation × 40% share). Also, St. Tabitha should record a liability for its share of those amounts allocated to other parties who are not expected to pay their shares, which is $500,000 (calculated as half of the total allocation for responsible parties × the cost allocated to the recalcitrant and orphan shares).

The costs that should be included in an entity's liability for environmental obligations include the following:

- Direct remediation activity costs, such as investigations, risk assessments, remedial actions, activities related to government oversight, and post-remediation monitoring.
- The compensation and related benefit costs for those employees expected to spend a significant amount of their time on remediation activities.

When measuring these costs, do so for the estimated time periods during which activities will occur, which means that an inflation factor should be included for periods further in the future. It may also be possible to include a productivity factor that is caused by gaining experience with remediation efforts over time, and which may reduce mitigation costs. When it is not possible to estimate the costs of inflation, perhaps due to uncertainties about the timing of expenditures, it is acceptable to initially record costs at their current-cost estimates and adjust them later, as more precise information becomes available.

Any costs related to routine environmental compliance activities, as well as any litigation costs associated with potential recoveries, are not considered part of the remediation effort, and so are not included in the environmental obligation liability. These costs are to be charged to expense as incurred.

Changes in the environmental liability are especially likely when there are multiple parties involved, since additional parties may be added over time, or the apportionment of liability between parties may change. Also, estimates of the exact amount of cost incurred will change continually. For these reasons, the amount of liability recorded for environmental obligations will almost certainly not be the exact amount that is eventually incurred, and so will have to be updated at regular intervals. If so, each update is treated as a change in estimate, which means that there is no retroactive change in the liability reported; instead, the change is recorded only on a go-forward basis.

Recoveries Related to Environmental Obligations

It is possible that a firm may contact other entities concerning the recovery of funds expended on environmental remediation, on the grounds that the other entities are liable for the remediation (or are liable because they are insurers).

The recognition of an asset related to the recovery of an environmental obligation should not be made unless recovery of the claimed amount is considered probable and the amount can be reasonably estimated. If a claim is currently the subject of litigation,

it is reasonable to assume that recovery of the claim is not probable, and so should not be recognized.

A recovery can be recorded at its undiscounted amount if the liability is not discounted, and the timing of the recovery is dependent on the timing of the liability payment. This will be the case in most situations, so the recovery will generally be recorded at its undiscounted amount.

Summary

The accounting for an asset retirement obligation can be complex, especially if there are multiple liability layers and changes to those layers occur with some frequency. Because of the additional accounting effort required to track AROs, it makes sense to use every effort to avoid the recognition of an ARO within the boundaries set by GAAP. In many cases, the amount of an ARO will likely be so minimal as to not require recognition.

Environmental obligations can strike any organization, large or small, and can result in a massive liability. The accounting for this liability is not especially difficult. However, given its considerable impact on a health care entity's financial results, it is necessary to thoroughly document the calculation of all recorded environmental liabilities, as well as the justification for *not* recording any additional liabilities.

Chapter 9
Current Liabilities

Introduction

A health care entity can be subject to a large number of liabilities that must be settled within the next year. These liabilities must be paid for with currently-available assets or financing arrangements, and so are tracked with particular care to ensure that there will be no delays in payment. In this chapter, we cover the many types of current liabilities, noting the accounting for each one.

Current Liabilities

A health care entity presents its liabilities on the balance sheet, where the various line items are split into current and noncurrent liabilities. This division is used so that the total amount of current liabilities can be compared to the total amount of current assets, to see if there are sufficient financial resources available from current assets to pay for all current liabilities.

Liabilities should be classified as current if they will be paid within one year of the balance sheet date. Examples of liabilities that are usually classified as current are:

- *Accounts payable*. Also known as trade payables, these are bills presented by suppliers, typically for payment within a relatively short period of time, such as 30 days.
- *Accrued liabilities*. When goods or services have been consumed but there is not yet a supplier invoice to record in the accounts payable account, the liability can instead be accrued. This usually happens only at the end of a reporting period, if a supplier invoice has not yet arrived by the time the books are about to be closed. Accrued liabilities can also involve employees, such as when wages have been earned but not paid.
- *Deferred revenues*. When payments have been received from a patient, resident, or third-party payor, but no corresponding services have yet been provided, the payments are classified as a current liability. After services have been provided, this liability is then reclassified as revenue.
- *Notes payable*. These are debts that are due within one year. A common example is a line of credit, which usually must be paid down to zero at least once a year. Notes payable differ from accounts payable, in that interest must be paid on notes payable.

- *Current maturities of long-term debt.* When any portion of a long-term debt is due for payment within one year of the balance sheet date, that portion is classified as a current liability, separate from the rest of the long-term debt.
- *Commitments, contingencies and guarantees.* A health care entity may have entered into contractual arrangements that obligate it to make payments in the future, depending on whether certain events occur. It may be necessary to record a liability for these items.

Discussions of several issues related to current liabilities are noted in the following sub-sections.

Prepaid Health Care Services

A provider of prepaid health care services may be contractually or legally required to provide services to patients beyond the premium period. If so, the provider must accrue an estimated expense for these additional services.

A health care provider may accept a fixed amount per individual that is paid at regular intervals in exchange for providing health care services. This fixed amount is called a *capitation fee*. When a provider accepts capitation fees, it must recognize a liability for unpaid claims, which includes claims that have not yet been reported. A review of the proportions of claims being reported in later periods, along with their amounts, can be used to estimate the amount of this liability.

Bonus and Risk Retention Plans

Any amounts payable to hospitals, physicians, and other health care providers under the terms of bonus or risk retention plans must be accrued during the contract period for amounts that will be paid in subsequent periods. This accrual may be based on the provider's prior experience with similar payables.

Accounting for Accounts Payable

In this section, we cover the basic journal entries needed to initially process accounts and then pay for accounts payable. We also note the contents of the aged accounts payable report and how early payment discounts are calculated. For more detailed treatment of accounts payable, see the author's *Payables Management* book.

Common Accounts Payable Journal Entries

The day-to-day accounting for accounts payable is relatively simple. Whenever the organization receives an invoice from a supplier, the payables staff enters the vendor number of the supplier into the accounting software, which automatically assigns a default general ledger account number from the vendor master file to the invoice.

If the invoice is for goods or services other than the predetermined general ledger account number, the payables staff can manually enter a different account number, which is only good for that specific invoice – it does not become the new default

account for that supplier. In short, the pre-assignment of account numbers to suppliers greatly simplifies the accounting for payables.

The accounting software should automatically create a credit to the accounts payable account whenever the payables staff records a supplier invoice. Thus, a typical entry might be:

	Debit	Credit
Supplies expense	500	
Accounts payable		500

Later, when the suppliers are paid, the accounting system eliminates the accounts payable balance with the following entry:

	Debit	Credit
Accounts payable	500	
Cash		500

It is possible that small debit or credit residual balances may appear in the accounts payable account. These balances may be caused by any number of issues, such as credit memos issued by suppliers which the company does not plan to use, or amounts that the company had valid cause not to pay. The aged accounts payable report (described in the next sub-section) can be run occasionally to spot these items. Do not use journal entries to clear them out, since this will not be recognized by the report writing software that generates the aged accounts payable report. Instead, always create debit or credit memo transactions that are recognized by the report writer; this will flush the residual balances from the aged accounts payable report.

There is usually a debit memo or credit memo creation option in the accounting software, which automatically generates the necessary debit memo or credit memo. As an example, an organization may have been granted a credit memo by a supplier for $100, to be used to reduce the amount of an outstanding account payable. A payables staff person enters the credit memo screen in the accounting software, enters the name of the supplier and the credit memo amount, and selects the expense account that will be offset. The journal entry that the software automatically generates could be as follows:

	Debit	Credit
Accounts payable	100	
Supplies expense		100

If a supplier offers a discount in exchange for the early payment of an invoice, the organization is not paying the full amount of the invoice. Instead, that portion of the invoice related to the discount is charged to a separate account. If an accounting software package is used, the system automatically allocates the appropriate amount to

this separate account. For example, an entry to take a 2% early payment discount on a supplier invoice might be:

	Debit	Credit
Accounts payable	100	
Cash		98
Discounts taken		2

This entry flushes out the full amount of the original account payable, so that no residual balance remains in the accounting records to be paid. Early payment discounts are covered in a following sub-section.

Aged Accounts Payable Report

The accounts payable aging report categorizes payables to suppliers based on time buckets. The report is typically set up with 30-day time buckets, so that each successive column in the report lists supplier invoices that are:

- 0 to 30 days old
- 31 to 60 days old
- 61 to 90 days old
- Older than 90 days

The intent of the report is to give the user a visual aid in determining which invoices are overdue for payment. However, a key flaw in this report is that it assumes all invoices are due for payment in 30 days. In reality, some invoices may be due on receipt, in 60 days, or almost anywhere in between. Consequently, an invoice listed on the aging report as current might actually be overdue for payment, while an invoice listed in the 31 to 60 days time bucket may not yet actually be payable.

For the report to be effective, it should be periodically cleaned up, so that stray debits and credits are removed from the report. Otherwise, it tends to become cluttered over time, and therefore more difficult to read.

Given the issues noted here, a better solution is to use a report generated by the accounting system, which lists only those supplier invoices that are nearly due or overdue for payment, based on invoice dates and supplier payment terms.

Early Payment Discounts

A key question for the accountant is whether to take early payment terms offered by suppliers. These terms are intended to be sufficiently lucrative for customers to want to pay their invoices early, but not have such egregious terms that the supplier is effectively paying an inordinately high interest rate for access to the funds that it is receiving early.

The term structure used for credit terms is to first state the number of days being given to customers from the invoice date in which to take advantage of the early

payment credit terms. For example, if a customer is supposed to pay within 10 days without a discount, the terms are "net 10 days," whereas if the customer must pay within 10 days to qualify for a 2% discount, the terms are "2/10." Or, if the customer must pay within 10 days to obtain a 2% discount or can make a normal payment in 30 days, then the terms are stated as "2/10 net 30."

The following table shows some of the more common credit terms, explains what they mean, and also notes the effective interest rate being offered to customers with each one.

Early Payment Discounts Table

Credit Terms	Explanation	Effective Interest
Net 10	Pay in 10 days	None
Net 30	Pay in 30 days	None
Net EOM 10	Pay within 10 days of month-end	None
1/10 net 30	Take a 1% discount if pay in 10 days, otherwise pay in 30 days	18.2%
2/10 net 30	Take a 2% discount if pay in 10 days, otherwise pay in 30 days	36.7%
1/10 net 60	Take a 1% discount if pay in 10 days, otherwise pay in 60 days	7.3%
2/10 net 60	Take a 2% discount if pay in 10 days, otherwise pay in 60 days	14.7%

If the terms are different from those shown in the preceding table, it is useful to be aware of the formula for calculating the effective interest rate associated with early payment discount terms. The calculation steps are:

1. Calculate the difference between the payment date for those taking the early payment discount and the date when payment is normally due, and divide it into 360 days. For example, under "2/10 net 30" terms, divide 20 days into 360 to arrive at 18. Use this number to annualize the interest rate calculated in the next step.
2. Subtract the discount percentage from 100% and divide the result into the discount percentage. For example, under "2/10 net 30" terms, divide 2% by 98% to arrive at 0.0204. This is the interest rate being offered through the credit terms.
3. Multiply the result of both calculations together to obtain the annualized interest rate. To conclude the example, multiply 18 by 0.0204 to arrive at an effective annualized interest rate of 36.72%.

Thus, the full calculation for the cost of credit is:

$$(\text{Discount \%} \div (1 - \text{Discount \%})) \times (360 \div (\text{Allowed payment days} - \text{Discount days}))$$

Accounting for Accrued Liabilities

An accrued liability is an obligation that a health care entity has assumed, usually in the absence of a confirming document, such as a supplier invoice. The most common usage of the concept is when an organization has consumed goods or services provided by a supplier, but has not yet received an invoice from the supplier. When the invoice has not arrived by the end of an accounting period, the accounting staff records an accrued liability; this amount is usually based on quantity information in the receiving log and pricing information in the authorizing purchase order. The purpose of an accrued liability entry is to record an expense or obligation in the period when it was incurred.

The journal entry for an accrued liability is typically a debit to an expense account and a credit to an accrued liabilities account. At the beginning of the next accounting period, the entry is reversed. If the associated supplier invoice is received in the next accounting period, the invoice is entered in the accounting system. The effect of these transactions is:

- In the first period, the expense is recorded with a journal entry.
- In the second period, the journal entry is reversed and the supplier invoice is entered, for a net zero entry in the second period.

Thus, the net effect of these transactions is that expense recognition is shifted forward in time.

Most accrued liabilities are created as reversing accruals, so that the accounting software automatically cancels them in the following period. This happens when a supplier invoice is expected to arrive in the next period.

Examples of accrued liabilities are:

- *Accrued interest expense*. A hospital has a loan outstanding, for which it owes interest that has not yet been billed by its lender at the end of an accounting period.
- *Accrued payroll taxes*. An organization incurs a liability to pay several types of payroll taxes when it pays compensation to its employees.
- *Accrued pension liability*. A hospital incurs a liability to pay its employees at some point in the future for benefits earned under a pension plan.
- *Accrued services*. A supplier provides services to a hospital, but has not billed it by the end of an accounting period, because the supplier takes time to compile billings from the time sheets of its employees.
- *Accrued wages*. A hospital owes wages to its hourly employees at the end of an accounting period, for which it is not scheduled to pay them until the next period.

An example of a journal entry for an accrued expense is the common period-end accrual for wages worked but not yet paid. A sample entry to initiate this accrual is:

	Debit	Credit
Wages expense	14,000	
Accrued wages		13,000
Accrued payroll taxes		1,000

In the following period, the accrual entry is reversed, so that it can be replaced by the normal payroll journal entry when employees are paid. The reversing entry that offsets the preceding entry is:

	Debit	Credit
Accrued wages	13,000	
Accrued payroll taxes	1,000	
Wages expense		14,000

An accrued liability may need to be created when an employee is promised a deferred compensation arrangement. This situation is covered in the next section.

Deferred Compensation Arrangements

A health care entity may offer deferred compensation to an employee, where the employee receives compensation in a future period. If such an arrangement is based on employee performance during a specific time period, accrue the cost of the deferred compensation in that performance period. If the deferred compensation is based on both current and future service, only accrue an expense for that portion of the compensation attributable to current service. As of the full eligibility date for the deferred compensation, the employer should have accrued the present value of those benefits expected to be paid in the future. Depending on the terms of the arrangement, it may be necessary to record an accrual based on the life expectancy of the employee, as supported by mortality tables, or on the estimated cost of an annuity contract.

EXAMPLE

St. Dalasina Hospital creates a deferred compensation agreement for its CEO, under which he will become eligible for the benefits stated in the contract after five years have passed. The terms of the agreement indicate that the CEO will render services for five years in order to earn the deferred compensation, so the hospital accrues the cost of the contract over the intervening five years.

Deferred Revenues

A continuing care retirement community may receive advance fees from its residents. These payments are for future services and the use of the community's facilities, so they are treated as deferred revenue, which is a liability. The proper accounting is as follows:

1. Estimate the amount of advance fees expected to be refunded and report them as a liability. This estimate is based on each facility's own experience; if historical records are not available, the estimate can be based on the experience of comparable facilities.
2. Account for the remaining amount of the advance fees as deferred revenue, where they are initially reported as a liability.

A portion of this liability may be presented in the balance sheet as a current liability, depending on when the liability is expected to be settled.

Of the amount recorded in the second step, a portion will be paid to current residents to the extent that proceeds from reoccupancy of a contract holder's unit are accounted for as deferred revenue. When similar amounts are received from new residents that exceed the amount to be paid to previous residents, these amounts are also recorded as deferred revenue.

Deferred revenue from advance fees should be amortized to income on a straight-line basis over the shorter of the estimated life of the resident or the contract term. This amortization period should be adjusted each year based on the actuarial estimate of the remaining lifespan of each individual. If there is a couple in residence, the annual amortization adjustment is instead based on the actuarial estimate of the remaining lifespan of the last survivor of each pair.

There may be cases in which costs are expected to rise at a significantly higher rate than future revenues in the later years of a person's residence. If so, a different amortization method can be used that more closely matches the trend of costs to be incurred. However, the amortized revenue amount should not exceed the amount allowed by management policy, contract provisions, or state regulations.

When a contract with a resident stipulates that some portion or all of the advance fee may be refundable if the contract holder's unit is re-occupied by another party, and the refund amount is limited to the extent of the proceeds from the re-occupancy, the related deferred revenue should be amortized to income based on the remaining useful life of the facility.

When a resident dies or terminates his or her contract with the continuing care retirement community, any unamortized deferred revenue from nonrefundable advance fees can then be recorded as revenue.

Commitments

A continuing care retirement community will provide a variety of nursing services and the use of its facilities to residents over the remainder of their lives under contractual arrangements. The type and amount of these services will depend on many

factors, include a resident's age, health, and sex. The contractual arrangements used by these facilities are of the following types:

- *All-inclusive*. This arrangement includes residential facilities, meals, amenities, and long-term nursing care. The arrangement typically includes little or no increase in periodic fees, other than to offset the cost of inflation.
- *Modified continuing care*. This arrangement includes residential facilities, meals, and amenities, but only a specified amount of long-term nursing care. Beyond the designated nursing care, residents pay additional fees for additional nursing care, which may be at a discounted rate.
- *Fee-for-service*. This arrangement includes residential facilities, meals, amenities, and emergency and infirmary nursing care. Residents have guaranteed access to long-term nursing care, but they will pay for it at full per diem rates.

> **Note:** *Periodic fees* are service charges that are billed to residents, usually on a monthly basis for services provided by a retirement community that are not covered by advance fees. Periodic fees are usually adjusted at intervals to reflect changes in operating costs.

Some elements of these contracts are similar to annuity contracts, in that the continuing care retirement community takes on the risks associated with the cost of providing services and facilities to its residents. Depending on the contract terms, the retirement community may be obligated to provide services even when advance fees and periodic fees prove to be inadequate for meeting the costs of providing those services.

Several different payment methods may be offered to residents in exchange for providing them with services and the use of facilities. The most common payment methods are as follows:

- *Advance fee only*. The resident pays a single up-front fee in exchange for future services and the use of the retirement community's facilities, usually until the person passes away or the contract is terminated. The resident does not receive an ownership interest in the facility.
- *Advance fee plus periodic fees*. The resident pays an up-front fee as well as periodic fees. The periodic fees may be subject to inflationary adjustments.
- *Periodic fees only*. The resident only pays periodic fees, which may be adjustable or fixed.

A resident may meet the requirement for payment of an advance fee by transferring his or her personal assets to the retirement community, or by paying a lump-sum amount in cash.

Depending on the terms of the underlying contract, advance fees associated with the provision of future services may be refunded if a specific event occurs, such as the death or withdrawal from the retirement community of the resident. In some cases, a refund is only paid when a residential unit is re-occupied, so that the money used to

pay the refund comes from the advance fees collected from the next resident to occupy the unit. The amount refunded is based on the terms of the contract. For example, the amount may decline by a fixed amount over a period of time, or it may be based on the resale amount of the unit.

A continuing care retirement community must conduct an annual measurement of its obligation to provide future services and the use of facilities to its residents. The outcome of this analysis may be the recognition of a liability in the financial statements. The liability is derived from an analysis of actuarial assumptions, estimates of future costs and revenues, the historical experience of the entity, and statistical data. The liability should be the amount of costs expected to be incurred that exceeds anticipated revenues from continuing care contracts. The liability related to continuing care contracts is derived from the calculation that appears in the following exhibit.

Calculation of Liability for Continuing Care Contracts

+	Present value of future net cash flows
-	Balance of unamortized deferred revenue
+	Depreciation of facilities to be charged related to the contracts
+	Unamortized costs of acquiring related continuing care contracts
=	Liability related to continuing care contracts

This liability calculation should be made separately for each type of contract. For example, one contract grouping may be for contracts that have limitations on annual fee increases, while another grouping is for contracts that do not have capped fees.

The present value of future net cash flows used in the preceding liability calculation should include all of the following elements:

Cash inflows

- Revenue contractually committed to support the residents
- Monthly fees that include anticipated increases allowed under contract terms
- Payments from third parties
- Committed investment income from services related to retirement community activities
- Contributions pledged by donors to support retirement community activities
- Deferred nonrefundable advance fees

Cash outflows

- Operating expenses, including expected cost increases
- Interest expenses

Note: Cash outflows do not include selling, general and administrative expenses for the purposes of this calculation.

EXAMPLE

The North Wind Retirement Community enters into a standard contractual arrangement with all of its residents, which contains the following provisions:

- Each resident pays an advance fee of $60,000. This fee is refundable minus 1% per month for the first 60 months, after which no part of the advance fee is refundable.
- An additional periodic fee of $3,000 is payable monthly, which will increase by 4% in each year thereafter.

The North Wind facility opened on 1/1/X1. The year ended 12/31/X6 has just concluded. As of the end of 20X6, North Wind has deferred costs of $8,000 related to the acquisition of initial contracts, as well as unamortized deferred revenue of $32,000.

The following table summarizes the present value of the net cash flows being experienced by North Wind.

Resident	Estimated Remaining Life on 12/31/X6 (in years)	Estimated Cash Inflows 20X7	20X8	20X9	20X0
Adams	3	$36,000	$37,440	$38,938	$--
Bridges	2	36,000	37,440	--	--
Carter	3	36,000	37,440	38,938	--
Davidson	4	36,000	37,440	38,938	40,495
		$144,000	$149,760	$116,814	$40,495

Resident	Estimated Remaining Life on 12/31/X6 (in years)	Estimated Cash Outflows 20X7	20X8	20X9	20X0
Adams	3	$35,000	$37,500	$40,500	$--
Bridges	2	39,000	41,000	--	--
Carter	3	38,000	38,500	39,500	--
Davidson	4	28,000	36,000	41,000	43,000
		$140,000	$153,000	$121,000	$43,000

Summary	20X7	20X8	20X9	20X0
Cash inflows	$144,000	$149,760	$116,814	$40,495
Cash outflows	140,000	153,000	121,000	43,000
	$4,000	-$3,240	-$4,186	-$2,505
Present value of net cash flows discounted at 8%				-$4,238

The cost of the facility that can be allocated to residents is $18,000,000, and its estimated useful life is 30 years. On a straight-line basis, this means that North Winds will incur a depreciation charge of $600,000 in each year. The facility houses 300 residents, so this $600,000 annual charge works out to $2,000 of depreciation per year, per resident. This information is used to derive the periodic depreciation charges noted in the following table.

	Estimated Remaining Life on 12/31/X6	Estimated Cash Outflows			
Resident	(in years)	20X7	20X8	20X9	20X0
Adams	3	$2,000	$2,000	$2,000	$--
Bridges	2	2,000	2,000	--	--
Carter	3	2,000	2,000	2,000	--
Davidson	4	2,000	2,000	2,000	2,000
		$8,000	$8,000	$6,000	$2,000
	Total depreciation estimated to be charged to current residents				$24,000

The following table indicates the formulation of North Winds' liability for providing future services to current residents and the use of its facilities by them:

Present value of future net cash outflows	-$4,238
Minus unamortized deferred revenue on 12/31/X6	-32,000
Plus depreciation to be charged to current residents	24,000
Plus unamortized cost to acquire initial contracts	8,000
Liability for providing future services and the use of facilities to current residents as of 12/31/X6	-$4,238

Contingencies

A *contingency* is an uncertain situation that will be resolved in the future, generating a possible gain or loss. A health care entity may be subject to a number of possible contingencies, such as:

- Commitments related to contractual agreements with physicians
- Construction contract commitments
- Litigation losses
- Medical malpractice claims
- Regulatory settlements
- Stop-loss insurance agreements
- Workers' compensation claims

When deciding whether to account for a loss contingency, the basic concept is to only record a loss that is probable, and for which the amount of the loss can be reasonably

estimated. If the best estimate of the amount of the loss is within a range, accrue whichever amount appears to be a better estimate than the other estimates in the range. If there is no "better estimate" in the range, accrue a loss for the minimum amount in the range.

If it is not possible to arrive at a reasonable estimate of the loss associated with an event, only disclose the existence of the contingency in the notes accompanying the financial statements. Or, if it is not probable that a loss will be incurred, even if it is possible to estimate the amount of a loss, only disclose the circumstances of the contingency, without accruing a loss.

In the following two sub-sections, we cover two areas in which a health care entity is more likely to require loss contingencies.

Stop-Loss Insurance Arrangements

A health care provider may enter into a preferred provider arrangement with self-insured employers. Under this arrangement, the provider guarantees that the employer's health care costs will not increase beyond a certain amount or percentage. In effect, the provider has just given stop-loss insurance coverage to the employer, capping the employer's costs and transferring a potentially material risk to the health care provider, which is accounted for as a loss contingency.

When deciding whether to account for a loss contingency, the basic concept is to only record a loss that is probable, and for which the amount of the loss can be reasonably estimated. If the best estimate of the amount of the loss is within a range, accrue whichever amount appears to be a better estimate than the other estimates in the range. If there is no "better estimate" in the range, accrue a loss for the minimum amount in the range.

If it is not possible to arrive at a reasonable estimate of the loss associated with an event, only disclose the existence of the contingency in the notes accompanying the financial statements. Or, if it is not probable that a loss will be incurred, even if it is possible to estimate the amount of a loss, only disclose the circumstances of the contingency, without accruing a loss.

When conducting this evaluation, record losses when it is probable that expected future health care costs and maintenance costs will exceed anticipated future premiums and stop-loss insurance recoveries. Losses can be calculated for logical groupings of contracts, such as for geographical areas or statutory requirements. These groupings should be consistent with the methods used by the provider to establish premium rates.

Medical Malpractice Claims

A health care entity may have significant liabilities related to medical malpractice claims. These liabilities are comprised of the costs to litigate or settle claims, as well as the amount of any eventual settlements. The amount of these liabilities should be accrued when the incidents arise that trigger the claims. To do so, the entity should regularly evaluate its exposure to losses and adjust its claims liability, as appropriate. The loss exposure is based on the best estimate of the final cost of claims, as well as the relationship of past reported incidents to the amount of claims eventually paid.

The cost of probable unreported incidents as of the end of the reporting period should be included in this cost estimation.

Note: The claims liability is based on asserted and unasserted claims, not the amount of any payments made into a medical malpractice trust fund. A medical malpractice trust fund may be established in order to pay medical malpractice claims.

The estimated amount of losses from medical malpractice claims should be reviewed and adjusted as necessary at each reporting date. The amounts of these adjustments should be recognized in the current reporting period as either an expense increase or decrease, with an offsetting current liability.

Guarantees

When a health care entity makes guarantees, it takes on an obligation to perform if certain future triggering events occur. The guarantee involves a payment or action. The guarantor may need to account for and disclose these guarantees. This recognition is likely to occur at the inception of a guarantee, and may require continuing disclosure of the existence of the guarantee until it has expired.

The situations in which guarantees must be recognized are when there is a contingent requirement for the guarantor to make payments based on either a change in an underlying, the failure of another entity to perform, or an indirect guarantee of indebtedness of other parties.

At the inception of a guarantee, recognize a liability for the guarantee, based on its fair value. Once the guarantee period expires, and if a guarantee was not activated during that time, eliminate the associated liability with a credit to earnings.

EXAMPLE

St. Anselm Hospital has recruited a nonemployee physician to move to the hospital's geographic region to establish a practice. St. Anselm has agreed to pay the physician at the end of the current year and the following year if the revenues generated by the new practice do not reach certain targets. This arrangement is a guarantee, where the hospital is the guarantor. The hospital controller will need to disclose this arrangement and, depending on the circumstances, may need to recognize a liability for the guarantee.

Presentation Issues

A health care entity is required to present certain kinds of information in its financial statements, as mandated by the accounting standards. The only liability-related presentation issue relates to malpractice claims. When a health care entity expects to receive insurance recoveries related to a malpractice claim, it should not present the malpractice liability net of the expected recovery. Instead, the liability for the claim and the asset for the insurance recovery are presented separately in the balance sheet.

Disclosures

The following notes related to liabilities should be presented for all types of health care entities:

- *Adjustments and settlements payable*. Explain any estimated adjustment and settlement amounts to be paid by the entity.
- *Prepaid health care liabilities*. If the entity provides prepaid health care services, it must explain the basis for accruing health care costs, also noting significant arrangements with hospitals, physicians and other similar entities.
- *Malpractice claim discounting*. When a health care entity discounts its accrued malpractice claims, state the carrying amount of the discounted claims, as well as the interest rate at which the claims were discounted.

Summary

A health care entity can have an unusually difficult time estimating contingencies and commitments, given the high level of uncertainty regarding its liabilities. For example, the government may levy penalties if a health care entity makes a false or incorrect reimbursement claim. Or, obligations may be incurred under continuing care contracts that are more expensive than the amounts paid by those patients and residents benefiting from the services provided. In these cases, uncertainty arises from the need to create reserves that may not prove to be correct for an extended period of time. Further, it is difficult to make reasonable estimates of liabilities for these reserves. Consequently, the accountant needs to call upon multiple sources of information and may need relatively complex models to arrive at reasonably justifiable reserve estimates.

Chapter 10
Debt Liabilities

Introduction

Health care entities, especially hospitals, have massive investments in assets, which may be funded by obtaining loans or issuing bonds. These liabilities can comprise the bulk of all liabilities reported. In this chapter, we address the accounting for debt, as well as debt modifications and extinguishments. We also note how conduit financing is used to arrange bond issuances through a government entity, and how to account for the premiums or discounts that are likely to be present when a bond is sold at more or less than its face amount, respectively.

Basic Debt Accounting

Debt is defined as an amount owed for funds borrowed. This may take a variety of forms, such as:

- Credit card debt, which can either be paid off each month or carried forward in exchange for a high interest rate.
- A line of credit, which is used to meet short-term needs, and which is usually limited to the amount of collateral that the borrower has available to guarantee repayment.
- A promissory note, which is a fixed sum that a health care entity borrows and then commits to pay back over time, in accordance with a fixed repayment schedule.

There are several issues that the borrower must be aware of when accounting for debt. The initial issue is how to classify the debt in the accounting records. Here are the main areas to be concerned with:

- If the debt is payable within one year, record the debt in a short-term debt account; this is a liability account. The typical line of credit is payable within one year, and so is classified as short-term debt.
- If the debt is payable in more than one year, record the debt in a long-term debt account; this is a liability account.
- If a loan agreement contains a clause stating that the lender can demand payment at any time, classify the debt as a current liability. This is the case even if there is no expectation that the lender will demand payment within the current year.
- If the debt is in the form of a credit card statement, this is typically handled as an account payable, and so is simply recorded through the accounts payable module in the accounting software.

The next debt accounting issue is how to determine the amount of interest expense associated with debt. This is usually quite easy, since the lender includes the amount of the interest expense on its periodic billing statements to the health care entity. In the case of a line of credit, the borrower is probably required to maintain its primary checking account with the lending bank, so the bank simply deducts the interest from the checking account once a month. This amount is usually identified as an interest charge on the monthly bank statement, so the accountant can easily identify it and record it as part of the monthly bank reconciliation adjustments. Alternatively, the lender may provide an amortization schedule to the borrower, which states the proportions of interest expense and loan repayment that will comprise each subsequent payment made to the lender. See the next section for a description of an amortization schedule.

The next issue is how to account for the various debt-related transactions. They are as follows:

- *Initial loan.* When a loan is first taken out, debit the cash account and credit either the short-term debt account or long-term debt account, depending on the nature of the loan. For example, a hospital borrows $1,000,000. The entry is:

	Debit	Credit
Cash	1,000,000	
Long-term debt		1,000,000

- *Interest payment.* If there is no immediate loan repayment, with only interest being paid, then the entry is a debit to the interest expense account and a credit to the cash account. For example, the interest rate on the $1,000,000 just described is 7%, with payments due at the end of each year. After one year, the entry is:

	Debit	Credit
Interest expense	70,000	
Cash		70,000

- *Mixed payment.* If a payment is being made that includes both interest expense and a loan repayment, debit the interest expense account, debit the applicable loan liability account, and credit the cash account. For example, a $5,000 loan payment is comprised of $4,300 of interest expense and $700 of loan repayment. The entry is:

	Debit	Credit
Interest expense	4,300	
Short-term debt	700	
Cash		5,000

- *Final payment.* If there is a final balloon payment where most or all of the debt is repaid, debit the applicable loan liability account and credit the cash account. For example, a borrower has been paying nothing but interest on a $500,000 loan for the past four years, and now repays the entire loan balance. The entry is:

	Debit	Credit
Short-term debt	500,000	
Cash		500,000

The Amortization Schedule

An amortization schedule is a table that states the periodic payments to be made as part of a loan agreement, and which notes the following information on each line of the table:

- Payment number
- Payment due date
- Payment total
- Interest component of payment
- Principal component of payment
- Ending principal balance remaining

Thus, the calculation on each line of the amortization schedule is designed to arrive at the ending principal balance for each period, for which the calculation is:

Beginning principal balance - (Payment total - Interest expense) = Ending principal balance

The amortization schedule is extremely useful for accounting for each payment in a promissory note, since it separates the interest and principal components of each payment. The schedule is also useful for modeling how the remaining loan liability will vary if payments are accelerated, delayed, or altered in size. An amortization schedule

can also encompass balloon payments and even negative amortization situations where the principal balance increases over time.

A sample amortization schedule follows, where a borrower has taken on a $50,000 loan that is to be repaid with five annual payments, using an interest rate of 8%. Note how the proportion of interest expense to the total payment made rapidly declines, until there is almost no interest expense remaining in the final payment. The schedule also notes the total interest expense associated with the loan.

Sample Amortization Schedule

Year	Beginning Loan Balance	Loan Payment	8% Interest	Loan Repayment	Ending Loan Balance
1	$50,000	$12,523	$4,000	$8,523	$41,477
2	41,477	12,523	3,318	9,205	32,272
3	32,272	12,523	2,582	9,941	22,331
4	22,331	12,523	1,786	10,737	11,594
5	11,594	12,522	928	11,594	0
		$62,614	$12,614	$50,000	

* Note: The Year 5 payment was reduced by $1 to offset the effects of rounding.

Reconciling the Debt Account

It is essential for the accountant to periodically compare the remaining loan balance reported by the lender to the balance reported on the books of the borrower. It is entirely possible that there will be a difference, for which there are usually two reasons. They are:

- The loan payments made by the borrower to the lender arrived either earlier or later than the payment due date. This alters the amount of interest expense charged to the borrower.
- The most recent loan payment made by the borrower to the lender is still in transit to the lender, or has not yet been recorded by the lender in its accounting system.

If there is a difference, contact the lender and determine the nature of the difference. If the interest charge recognized by the lender varies from the amount recognized by the borrower, alter the borrower's interest expense to match the amount recognized by the lender. If the difference is due to a payment in transit, no adjustment to the accounting records needs to be made.

The reason why this reconciliation is so necessary is that the health care entity's auditors will contact the lender at the end of the year to confirm with them the amount owed. If the auditors discover a difference, they will require the accounting staff to adjust its loan records.

Debt Modifications and Extinguishments

When a health care entity extinguishes a debt, the difference between the net carrying amount of the debt and the price at which the debt was settled is recorded separately in the current period in income as a gain or loss. The net carrying amount of the debt is considered to be the amount payable at maturity of the debt, netted against any unamortized discounts, premiums, and costs of issuance. If a settlement also involves an exchange of rights or privileges, assign a portion of the consideration received to these rights or privileges.

If debt is extinguished via an exchange of stock (only possible for a for-profit health care entity), calculate the reacquisition cost of the debt at the value of either the stock or the debt, whichever is more clearly discernible.

If there is an exchange or modification of debt that has substantially different terms, treat the exchange as a debt extinguishment. Such an exchange or modification is considered to have occurred when the present value of the cash flows of the new debt instrument vary by at least 10% from the present value of the original debt instrument. When determining present value for this calculation, the discount rate is the effective interest rate used for the original debt instrument.

If the preceding testing concludes that the replacement and old debt instruments are substantially different, account for the replacement instrument at its fair value, which shall also be the basis for calculating any gain or loss on the debt modification.

If a debt modification or extinguishment involves the payment of fees between the debtor and creditor, the related accounting is:

- *If treated as a debt extinguishment.* Associate the fees with the extinguishment of the old debt instrument, so they are included in the calculation of any gains or losses from that extinguishment.
- *If not treated as a debt extinguishment.* Associate the fees with the replacement instrument, and amortize them as an interest expense adjustment over the remaining life of the instrument.

If the health care entity incurs third party costs associated with the debt modification, the related accounting is:

- *If treated as a debt extinguishment.* Associate the third-party costs with the replacement instrument, and amortize them over the remaining life of the instrument.
- *If not treated as a debt extinguishment.* Charge the costs to expense as incurred.

If debt modifications involve a line of credit or a revolving debt arrangement, the debtor should account for the changes using the following decision tree:

1. Compare the maximum borrowing capacity of the old and new borrowing arrangements. Borrowing capacity is defined as the remaining term (in years) multiplied by the commitment amount.

2. If the borrowing capacity of the new arrangement is greater than the old arrangement, defer any unamortized costs associated with the old arrangement and instead amortize them over the term of the new arrangement.
3. If the borrowing capacity of the new arrangement is less than the old arrangement, defer any new fees incurred and amortize them over the term of the new arrangement. Also, write off any unamortized costs associated with the old arrangement in proportion to the reduction in borrowing capacity, and amortize the remaining amount over the term of the new arrangement.

EXAMPLE

St. Fabianus Hospital revises the terms of its line of credit arrangement with Currency Bank. The terms of the original lending arrangement were a remaining term of two years and a $12,000,000 commitment. This results in a borrowing capacity of $24,000,000 (calculated as two years multiplied by $12,000,000).

The terms of the new lending arrangement are a $16,000,000 commitment over a three-year term. This results in a new borrowing capacity of $48,000,000 (calculated as three years multiplied by $16,000,000).

At the time of the conversion to the new line of credit, St. Fabianus has $40,000 of unamortized costs on its books related to the old line of credit. The hospital also incurs new costs of $75,000 related to the new arrangement. St. Fabianus can defer all of these costs and amortize them over the three-year term of the new lending arrangement.

Bond Overview

When a health care entity sells a fixed obligation to investors, this is generally described as a *bond*. The typical bond has a face value of $1,000, which means that the issuer is obligated to pay the investor $1,000 on the maturity date of the bond. If investors feel that the stated interest rate on a bond is too low, they will only agree to buy the bond at a price lower than its stated amount, thereby increasing the effective interest rate that they will earn on the investment. Conversely, a high stated interest rate can lead investors to pay a premium for a bond.

When a bond is registered, the issuer is maintaining a list of which investors own its bonds. The issuer then sends periodic interest payments directly to these investors. When the issuer does not maintain a list of investors who own its bonds, the bonds are considered to be *coupon bonds*. A coupon bond contains attached coupons that investors send to the issuer; these coupons obligate the issuer to issue interest payments to the holders of the bonds. A coupon bond is easier to transfer between investors, but it is also more difficult to establish ownership of the bonds.

There are many types of bonds. The following list represents a sampling of the more common types:

- *Collateral trust bond.* This bond includes the investment holdings of the issuer as collateral.
- *Debenture.* This bond has no collateral associated with it. A variation is the subordinated debenture, which has junior rights to collateral.
- *Deferred interest bond.* This bond offers little or no interest at the start of the bond term, and more interest near the end. The format is useful for entities currently having little cash with which to pay interest.
- *Income bond/revenue bond.* The issuer is only obligated to make interest payments to bond holders if the issuer or a specific project earns a profit or generates revenue. If the bond terms allow for cumulative interest, then the unpaid interest will accumulate until such time as there is sufficient income to pay the amounts owed.
- *Serial bond.* This bond is gradually paid off in each successive year, so the total amount of debt outstanding is gradually reduced.
- *Variable rate bond.* The interest rate paid on this bond varies with a baseline indicator, such as the London Interbank Offered Rate (LIBOR).
- *Zero coupon bond.* No interest is paid on this type of bond. Instead, investors buy the bonds at large discounts to their face values in order to earn an effective interest rate.

Additional features can be added to a bond to make it easier to sell to investors at a higher price. These features can include:

- *Sinking fund.* The issuer creates a sinking fund to which cash is periodically added, and which is used to ensure that bonds are eventually paid off.
- *Guarantees.* The repayment of a bond may be guaranteed by a third party, such as the parent company that owns a hospital.

The following additional bond features favor the issuer, and so may reduce the price at which investors are willing to purchase bonds:

- *Call feature.* The issuer has the right to buy back bonds earlier than the stated maturity date.
- *Subordination.* Bond holders are positioned after more senior debt holders to be paid back from issuer assets in the event of a default.

Municipal Bond Financing

Health care entities are highly capital-intensive, and so must raise substantial amounts of funds. If an entity is classified as a not-for-profit, it can raise debt capital through the municipal securities market. This is done through a qualified governmental agency, such as a health care financing authority. This entity issues securities and then lends the resulting funds to a designated health care entity. This arrangement is called

conduit financing, where a government entity serves as a conduit for the flow of funds to a health care entity. In conduit financing, the issuing government entity has no obligation to repay the debt. Instead, all principal and interest payments are the sole responsibility of the health care entity that has received the funds.

When a health care entity reports bonds received through a conduit and is responsible for payment, it should record the bond proceeds as a liability on its balance sheet. This liability is usually classified as long-term, since the bonds will not be due for payment until many years in the future. However, if there is a due-on-demand feature in the bond agreement that allows bond holders to demand payment at once, then the liability is instead classified as a current liability. The same classification is used when a bond has a *subjective acceleration clause*. This clause is defined as a provision in a debt agreement, stating that the creditor may accelerate the maturity date of the obligation under conditions that cannot be objectively determined. Depending on the circumstances, the existence of this clause may only call for the disclosure of the existence of the clause. If the likelihood of acceleration of bond payment is remote, then it is not even necessary to disclose the existence of the acceleration clause.

The typical municipal bond that is issued on behalf of a health care entity (the obligor) is a revenue bond. Under a revenue bond arrangement, the obligor pledges that its receipts related to a specific revenue stream will be used to pay off the debt.

A tax-exempt bond can be issued to fund health care entity projects when they are being used to finance facilities or services that are for the public good. In this situation, the interest paid to bond holders is exempt from all federal taxes, and may also be exempt from state and local taxes. If the uses to which the proceeds are put is more generic, such as a medical office building, then taxable bonds are issued instead, where the interest paid to bond holders is taxable.

When a health care entity issues municipal bonds through a government financing authority, it prepares an offering statement that provides financial information about itself, the offering, and any guarantors of payment. This offering statement is extensive, requiring the services of auditors, financial advisors, and legal counsel. A preliminary version of this statement is issued to all prospective buyers of the bonds. A bond purchase agreement is then executed by the financing authority, health care entity, and the bond underwriters. The final version of the statement is issued at the effective date of the sale, stating the debt service requirements associated with the bonds. When the closing date of the transaction is reached, the bond sale is finalized, with the proceeds being transferred from the investors buying bonds to the health care entity.

There are Internal Revenue Service (IRS) regulations addressing a situation in which the entity receiving the proceeds from a tax-exempt bond issuance cannot then reinvest the funds at a higher interest rate than it is paying on the bonds. Doing so would mean that the entity is profiting from the tax-exempt status of the bonds. Consequently, the IRS mandates that such an arbitrage profit must be paid to the Department of the Treasury in order for the bonds to maintain their tax-exempt status.

There are three ways in which a health care organization might refund an outstanding bond issuance. The options are:

- *Current refunding.* New debt proceeds are used to repay old bonds. This happens within 90 days of the first call date or the maturity of the old bonds.
- *Advance refunding.* New debt proceeds are held and invested by an escrow agent until a later date, when they are used to repay old bonds.
- *Crossover refunding.* Crossover bonds are issued, where the intent is to pay off existing bonds. The crossover bonds are initially collateralized by investments purchased with the proceeds from the bond issuance, while the bonds to be refunded are still secured by their original collateral or a revenue stream. On the date when the invested funds are used to redeem the original bond issuance, the collateral or revenue stream associated with the original bond issuance is shifted to the replacement bond issuance.

Bond Premiums and Discounts

When a health care entity issues bonds, it is making a commitment to pay the face amount of the bonds on a specific maturity date, as well as interest at certain fixed intervals. The interest paid is usually stated as a percentage of the face value of the bonds, and is typically paid at intervals of six months. The stated interest rate is predetermined, based on expectations for the market rate of interest that investors will demand when the bonds are eventually issued. The rate that investors are willing to pay is based on the credit rating of the borrower, the terms associated with the bond, the taxability of the bonds, the current level of demand in the market for long-term debt, and a number of other factors.

When the bonds are finally offered for sale, investors will likely have a somewhat different view of the interest rate they want to pay. If this is the case, they will either bid more than the face value of the bonds (which results in a lower effective interest rate) or they will bid less than the face value (which results in a higher effective interest rate). For example, an organization offers a $1,000 bond for sale, with a stated interest rate of 6%. An investor buys the bond for $1,080. By doing so, the investor has obtained an effective interest rate of 5.555%, which is calculated as follows:

$60 Annual interest paid ÷ $1,080 Price paid = 5.555%

If the investor had instead paid less than the face value, at a price of $920, then the effective interest rate associated with the purchase would have been 6.522%, which is calculated as follows:

$60 Annual interest paid ÷ $920 Price paid = 6.522%

In the first case, where the investor paid more than the face amount, the journal entry used by the issuing health care entity would be:

	Debit	Credit
Cash	1,080	
Premium on bonds payable		80
Bonds payable		1,000

In the second case, where the investor paid less than the face amount, the journal entry used would be:

	Debit	Credit
Cash	920	
Discount on bonds payable	80	
Bonds payable		1,000

In either case, the entity is taking on a liability to buy back the bond on its maturity date for $1,000, which is why there is a consistent credit of $1,000 to the bonds payable account, irrespective of the presence of a discount or a premium.

When a health care entity records a discount or premium on a bond issuance, it must find a way to gradually charge it off to interest expense over the life of the bond, so that it is completely eliminated by the maturity date of the bond. This charging off process is referred to as the *amortization* of the premium or discount. When a premium is amortized, the periodic charge to interest expense reduces the recorded amount of interest expense. When a discount is amortized, the periodic charge increases the recorded amount of interest expense. By taking this approach, the borrower is recording interest expense at the interest rate at which investors bought the bonds. The concept is illustrated in the following example, which also includes the accounting entries associated with a bond that has been sold at a discount.

EXAMPLE

St. Zenobius Hospital issues a $5,000,000 bond at a stated rate of 5% interest, where similar issuances are being purchased by investors at 8% interest. The bonds pay interest annually, and are to be redeemed in six years.

In order to earn the market rate of 8% interest, investors purchase the St. Zenobius bonds at a discount. The following calculation is used to derive the discount on the bond, which is comprised of the present values of a stream of interest payments and the present value of $5,000,000 payable in six years, with both calculations based on the 8% interest rate:

Present value of 6 payments of $250,000	= $250,000 × 4.62288	$1,155,720
Present value of $5,000,000	= $5,000,000 × 0.63017	3,150,850
	Total of present values	$4,306,570
	Less: Stated bond price	$5,000,000
	Bond discount	$693,430

The initial entry to record the sale of bonds is:

	Debit	Credit
Cash	4,306,570	
Discount on bonds payable	693,430	
Bonds payable		5,000,000

The controller of St. Zenobius creates the following table, which shows the derivation of how much of the discount should be charged to interest expense in each of the following years. In essence, the annual amortization of the discount is added back to the present value of the bond, so that the bond's present value matches its $5,000,000 stated value by the date when the bonds are scheduled for redemption from the bond holders.

Year	Beginning Present Value of Bond	Unamortized Discount	Interest Expense*	Cash Payment**	Discount Reduction***
1	$4,306,570	$693,430	$344,526	$250,000	$94,526
2	4,401,096	598,904	352,088	250,000	102,088
3	4,503,184	496,816	360,255	250,000	110,255
4	4,613,439	386,561	369,075	250,000	119,075
5	4,732,514	267,486	378,601	250,000	128,601
6	4,861,115	138,885	388,885	250,000	138,885
7	$5,000,000	$0			

* Bond present value at the beginning of the period, multiplied by the 8% market rate
** Scheduled annual interest payment for the bond
*** Interest expense, less the cash payment

As an example of the entries that the controller would derive from this table, the entry for the first annual interest payment would be:

	Debit	Credit
Interest expense	344,526	
Discount on bonds payable		94,526
Cash		250,000

The reasoning behind the entry is that St. Zenobius is only obligated to make a cash payment of $250,000 per year, despite the higher 8% implicit interest rate that its investors are earning on the issued bonds. The difference between the actual interest of $344,526 and the cash payment represents an increase in the amount of the bond that the hospital must eventually pay back to its investors. Thus, by the end of the first year, the present value of the hospital's obligation to pay back the bond has increased from $4,306,570 to $4,401,096. By the end of the six-year period, the present value of the amount to be paid back will have increased to $5,000,000.

Tip: GAAP requires that the interest method be used to amortize any discount or premium associated with a note. However, other methods can be used if the results do not differ materially from those of the interest method. Accordingly, we suggest using the simpler straight-line method if the results do not differ materially from those of the interest method.

Summary

The accounting for loans should be relatively straightforward, since the lender provides a schedule, stating the interest component of each payment made. This is not the case for bonds, where the accounting staff must develop its own schedule that states the amount of unamortized discounts or premiums to be recorded in each period. Since this schedule is critical to the proper recordation of a major liability, it can make sense to have it examined by the issuer's auditors, to ensure that they agree with the calculations. Doing so can result in a trouble-free audit examination of the issuer's debt liabilities at year-end.

Chapter 11
Revenue Recognition

Introduction

Revenue recognition in the health care industry has historically been governed by a medley of accounting rules that addressed specific types of health care transactions. Most of these rules were invalidated with the advent of Topic 606 in Generally Accepted Accounting Principles, *Revenue from Contracts with Customers*. This standard establishes a consistent framework for how to address revenue issues, while at the same time eliminating a number of inconsistencies in prior accounting standards relating to revenue. The result should be a higher level of comparability of revenue practices across multiple industries. The trouble is that no formal interpretation of the new standard has yet been released for the health care industry. Consequently, we can only include in this chapter a condensed discussion of Topic 606, along with a few residual accounting standards that still pertain to health care revenue recognition. Hopefully, a detailed interpretation will be released by the time the second edition of this book is released, so that we can provide additional clarity about revenue recognition topics.

Steps in Revenue Recognition

Topic 606 establishes a series of actions that an entity takes to determine the amount and timing of revenue to be recognized. The main steps are:

1. Link the contract with a specific customer.
2. Note the performance obligations required by the contract.
3. Determine the price of the underlying transaction.
4. Match this price to the performance obligations through an allocation process.
5. Recognize revenue as the various obligations are fulfilled.

We will expand upon each of these steps in the following sections.

Step One: Link Contract to Customer

The contract is used as a central aspect of revenue recognition, because revenue recognition is closely associated with it. In many instances, revenue is recognized at multiple points in time over the duration of a contract, so linking contracts with revenue recognition provides a reasonable framework for establishing the timing and amounts of revenue recognition.

A contract only exists if there is an agreement between the parties that establishes enforceable rights and obligations. It is not necessary for an agreement to be in writing

for it to be considered a contract. More specifically, a contract only exists if the following conditions are present:

- *Approval.* All parties to the contract have approved the document and substantially committed to its contents (based on all relevant facts and circumstances). The parties can be considered to be committed to a contract despite occasional lapses, such as not enforcing prompt payment or sometimes shipping late. Approval can be in writing or orally.
- *Rights.* The document clearly identifies the rights of the parties.
- *Payment.* The payment terms are clearly stated. It is acceptable to recognize revenue related to unpriced change orders if the seller expects that the price will be approved and the scope of work has been approved.
- *Substance.* The agreement has commercial substance; that is, the cash flows of the seller will change as a result of the contract, either in terms of their amount, timing, or risk of receipt. Otherwise, organizations could swap goods or services to artificially boost their revenue.
- *Probability.* It is probable that the organization will collect substantially the entire amount stated in the contract in exchange for the goods or services that it commits to provide to the other party. In this context, "probable" means "likely to occur." This evaluation is based on the customer's ability and intention to pay when due. The evaluation can incorporate a consideration of the past practice of the customer in question, or of the class of customers to which that customer belongs.

If these criteria are not initially met, the seller can continue to evaluate the situation to see if the criteria are met at a later date.

EXAMPLE

Oncology Partners has entered into an arrangement to have its blood draws tested by Advanced Monitoring Corporation (AMC). The contract specifies the delivery of daily testing results over the next year. Prior to the start of this service, AMC's collections manager learns through her contacts that Oncology Partners has just conducted a large layoff that was triggered by the discovery of massive fraud losses. It appears that the customer's ability to pay has deteriorated significantly, which calls into question the probability of collecting the amount stated in the contract. In this case, there may no longer be a contract for the purposes of revenue recognition.

There may be instances in which the preceding criteria are not met, and yet the customer is paying consideration to the seller. If so, revenue can be recognized only when one or more of the following events have occurred:

- The contract has been terminated and the consideration received by the seller is not refundable; or
- The seller has no remaining obligations to the customer, substantially all of the consideration has been received, and the payment is not refundable; or

- The seller has transferred control of the goods or services, *and* has stopped transferring goods or services to the customer, *and* has no obligation to transfer additional goods or services, *and* the consideration received cannot be refunded.

These alternatives focus on whether the contract has been concluded in all respects. If so, there is little risk that any revenue recognized will be reversed in a later period, and so is a highly conservative approach to recognizing revenue.

If the seller receives consideration from a customer and the preceding conditions do not exist, then the payment is to be recorded as a liability until such time as the sale criteria have been met.

In certain situations, it can make sense to combine several contracts into one for the purposes of revenue recognition. For example, if there is a portfolio of contracts that have similar characteristics, and the entity expects that treating the portfolio as a single unit will have no appreciable impact on the financial statements, it is acceptable to combine the contracts for accounting purposes.

Step Two: Note Performance Obligations

A performance obligation is essentially the unit of account for the goods or services contractually promised to a customer. The performance obligations in the contract must be clearly identified. This is important in recognizing revenue, since revenue is considered to be recognizable when goods or services are transferred to the customer. Examples of goods and services are noted in the following table, with health care-specific seller examples noted in bold.

Examples of Goods and Services

Item Sold	Example of the Seller
Arranging for another party to transfer goods or services	Travel agent selling airline tickets
Asset construction on behalf of a customer	Building construction company
Grant of a license	Software company issuing licenses to use its software
Grant of options to purchase additional goods or services	Airline granting frequent flier points
Manufactured goods	Manufacturer
Performance of contractually-mandated tasks	**Surgery center**
Readiness to provide goods or services as needed	**Continuing care retirement community**
Resale of merchandise	Retailer
Resale of rights to goods or services	Selling a priority for a new-model car delivery
Rights to future goods or services that can be resold	Wholesaler gives additional services to retailer buying a particular product

If there is no performance obligation, then there is no revenue to be recognized. For example, an organization could continually build up its inventory through ongoing production activities, but just because it has more sellable assets does not mean that it can report an incremental increase in the revenue in its income statement. If such an activity-based revenue recognition model were allowed, organizations could increase their revenues simply by increasing their rate of activity.

If there is more than one good or service to be transferred under the contract terms, only break it out as a separate performance obligation if it is a distinct obligation or there are a series of transfers to the customer of a distinct good or service. In the latter case, a separate performance obligation is assumed if there is a consistent pattern of transfer to the customer.

The "distinct" label can be applied to a good or service only if it meets both of the following criteria:

- *Capable of being distinct.* The customer can benefit from the good or service as delivered, or in combination with other resources that the customer can readily find; and
- *Distinct within the context of the contract.* The promised delivery of the good or service is separately identified within the contract.

Goods or services are more likely to be considered distinct when:

- The seller does not use the goods or services as a component of an integrated bundle of goods or services.
- The items do not significantly modify any other goods or services listed in the contract.
- The items are not highly interrelated with other goods or services listed in the contract.

The intent of these evaluative factors is to place a focus on how to determine whether goods or services are truly distinct within a contract. There is no need to assess the customer's intended use of any goods or services when making this determination.

To reduce the cost of noting performance obligations, it is not necessary to assess whether promised goods or services are performance obligations if they are immaterial in the context of the contract with the customer.

EXAMPLE

Willow Retirement Community receives payments from its residents for services that include residence in the facility, as well as medical care as needed. The residence service and medical care service are linked, since only residents are given medical care – that is, the two services are an integrated bundle. These two elements should therefore be treated as a single performance obligation. Willow also offers various activities for an additional fee, such as transport to local museums. This service is a separate performance obligation, since it is not highly interrelated with the other services being provided.

In the event that a good or service is not classified as distinct, aggregate it with other goods or services promised in the contract, until such time as a cluster of goods or services have been accumulated that can be considered distinct.

Step Three: Determine Prices

This step involves the determination of the transaction price built into the contract. The transaction price is the amount of consideration to be paid by the customer in exchange for its receipt of goods or services. The transaction price does not include any amounts collected on behalf of third parties (such as sales taxes).

EXAMPLE

Evanston Hospital generates $400,000 of sales from its gift shop, of which $8,000 was sales taxes collected on behalf of local governments. Since the $8,000 was collected on behalf of third parties, it cannot be recognized as revenue.

The transaction price may be difficult to determine, since it involves consideration of the effects noted in the following subsections.

Variable Consideration

The terms of some contracts may result in a price that can vary, depending on the circumstances. For example, there may be discounts, rebates, penalties, or performance bonuses in the contract. Or, the customer may have a reasonable expectation that the seller will offer a price concession, based on the seller's customary business practices, policies, or statements. Another example is when the seller intends to accept lower prices from a new customer in order to develop a strong customer relationship. If so, set the transaction price based on either the most likely amount or the probability-weighted expected value, using whichever method yields that amount of consideration most likely to be paid. In more detail, these methods are:

- *Most likely.* The seller develops a range of possible payment amounts, and selects the amount most likely to be paid. This approach works best when there are only two possible amounts that will be paid.
- *Expected value.* The seller develops a range of possible payment amounts, and assigns a probability to each one. The sum of these probability-weighted amounts is the expected value of the variable consideration. This approach works best when there are a large number of possible payment amounts. However, the outcome may be an expected value that does not exactly align with any amount that could actually be paid.

EXAMPLE

Riverwalk Physicians has entered into an agreement with a local group of hospitals to provide radiology services. Payments to be made under the contract are both volume and service-based. The accounting staff reviews the contract and concludes that it could have four possible outcomes, which are noted in the following expected value table:

Price Scenario	Transaction Price	Probability	Probability-Weighted Price
1	$1,500,000	20%	$300,000
2	1,700,000	35%	595,000
3	2,000,000	40%	800,000
4	2,400,000	5%	120,000
		Expected Value	$1,815,000

The expected value derived from the four possible pricing outcomes is $1,815,000, even though this amount does not match any one of the four pricing outcomes.

Whichever method is chosen, be sure to use it consistently throughout the contract, as well as for similar contracts. However, it is not necessary to use the same measurement method to measure each uncertainty contained within a contract; different methods can be applied to different uncertainties.

Also, review the circumstances of each contract at the end of each reporting period, and update the estimated transaction price to reflect any changes in the circumstances.

Possibility of Reversal

Do not include in the transaction price an estimate of variable consideration if, when the uncertainty associated with the variable amount is settled, it is probable that there will be a significant reversal of cumulative revenue recognized. The assessment of a possible reversal of revenue could include the following factors, all of which might increase the probability of a revenue reversal:

- *Beyond seller's influence.* The amount of consideration paid is strongly influenced by factors outside of the control of the seller. For example, goods sold may be subject to obsolescence (as is common in the technology industry), or weather conditions could impede the availability of goods (as is common in the production of farm products).
- *Historical practice.* The seller has a history of accepting a broad range of price concessions, or of changing the terms of similar contracts.
- *Inherent range of outcomes.* The terms of the contract contain a broad range of possible consideration amounts that might be paid.

- *Limited experience*. The seller does not have much experience with the type of contract in question. Alternatively, the seller's prior experience cannot be translated into a prediction of the amount of consideration paid.
- *Long duration*. A significant period of time may have to pass before the uncertainty can be resolved.

Note: The probability of a significant reversal of cumulative revenue recognized places a conservative bias on the recognition of revenue, rather than a neutral bias, so there will be a tendency for recognized revenue levels to initially be too low. However, this approach is reasonable when considering that revenue information is more relevant when it is not subject to future reversals.

If management expects that a retroactive discount will be applied to sales transactions, the seller should recognize a refund liability as part of the revenue recognition when each performance obligation is satisfied. For example, if the seller is currently selling services for $1,000 but expects that a 20% volume discount will be retroactively applied at the end of the year, the resulting entry should be:

	Debit	Credit
Accounts receivable	1,000	
Revenue		800
Refund liability		200

EXAMPLE

Medusa Medical sells a well-known snake oil therapy through a number of retail store customers. In the most recent month, Medusa sells $100,000 of its potent Copperhead Plus combination healing balm and sunscreen lotion. The therapy is most effective within one month of manufacture and then degrades rapidly, so that Medusa must accept increasingly large price concessions in order to ensure that the goods are sold. Historically, this means that the range of price concessions varies from zero (in the first month) to 80% (after four months). Of this range of outcomes, Medusa estimates that the expected value of the transactions is likely to be revenue of $65,000. However, since the risk of obsolescence is so high, Medusa cannot conclude that it is probable that there will not be a significant reversal in the amount of cumulative revenue recognized. Accordingly, management concludes that the price point at which it is probable that there will not be a significant reversal in the cumulative amount of revenue recognized is actually closer to $45,000 (representing a 55% price concession). Based on this conclusion, the controller initially recognizes $45,000 of revenue when the goods are shipped to retailers, and continues to monitor the situation at the end of each reporting period, to see if the recognized amount should be adjusted.

EXAMPLE

International Medical Supplies (IMS) enters into a contract with Diamond Surgery Center to provide Diamond with $250,000 of medical supplies per year. If Diamond purchases more than this amount within one calendar year, then a 12% retroactive price reduction will be applied to all of its purchases for the year.

IMS has dealt with Diamond for a number of years, and knows that Diamond has never attained the $250,000 level of purchases. Accordingly, through the first half of the year, IMS records its sales to Diamond at their full price, totaling $80,000.

In July, Diamond acquires Front Range Surgery, along with its four surgery centers. With a much larger need for medical supplies, Diamond now places several large orders that make it quite clear that passing the $250,000 threshold will be no problem at all. Accordingly, IMS' controller records a cumulative revenue reversal of $9,600 to account for Diamond's probable attainment of the volume purchase discount.

Time Value of Money

If the transaction price is to be paid over a period of time, this implies that the seller is including a financing component in the contract. If this financing component is a significant financing benefit for the customer and provides financing for more than one year, adjust the transaction price for the time value of money. In cases where there is a financing component to a contract, the seller will earn interest income over the term of the contract.

A contract may contain a financing component, even if there is no explicit reference to it in the contract. When adjusting the transaction price for the time value of money, consider the following factors:

- *Standalone price.* The amount of revenue recognized should reflect the price that a customer would have paid if it had paid in cash.
- *Significance.* In order to be recognized, the financing component should be significant. This means evaluating the amount of the difference between the consideration to be paid and the cash selling price. Also note the combined effect of prevailing interest rates and the time difference between when delivery is made and when the customer pays.

If it is necessary to adjust the compensation paid for the time value of money, use as a discount rate the rate that would be employed in a separate financing transaction between the parties as of the beginning date of the contract. The rate used should reflect the credit characteristics of the customer, including the presence of any collateral provided. This discount rate is not to be updated after the commencement of the contract, irrespective of any changes in the credit markets or in the credit standing of the customer.

EXAMPLE

An uninsured patient cannot pay for a major surgery, so Diamond Surgery Center offers the patient long-term financing, where he can pay the full amount of the $34,347 receivable in 24 months. The cash price of the surgery is $30,000. The contract contains an implicit interest rate of 7.0%, which is the interest rate that discounts the purchase price from $34,347 down to the cash selling price over the two year period. Diamond's controller examines this rate and concludes that it approximates the rate that the two parties would use if there had been a separate financing transaction between them as of the contract inception date. Consequently, Diamond recognizes interest income during the two-year period prior to the payment due date, using the following calculation:

Year	Beginning Balance	Interest (at 7.0% Rate)	Ending Balance
1	$30,000	$2,100	$32,100
2	32,100	2,247	$34,347

As of the surgery date, Diamond records the following entry:

	Debit	Credit
Loan receivable	30,000	
Revenue		30,000

At the end of the first year, Diamond recognizes the interest associated with the transaction for the first year, using the following entry:

	Debit	Credit
Loan receivable	2,100	
Interest income		2,100

At the end of the second year, Diamond recognizes the interest associated with the transaction for the second year, using the following entry:

	Debit	Credit
Loan receivable	2,247	
Interest income		2,247

These entries increase the size of the loan receivable until it reaches the original sale price of $34,347. The patient then pays the full amount of the receivable, at which point Diamond records the following final entry:

	Debit	Credit
Cash	34,347	
Loan receivable		34,347

Step Four: Allocate Prices to Obligations

Once the performance obligations and transaction prices associated with a contract have been identified, the next step is to allocate the transaction prices to the obligations. The basic rule is to allocate that price to a performance obligation that best reflects that amount of consideration to which the seller expects to be entitled when it satisfies each performance obligation. To determine this allocation, it is first necessary to estimate the standalone selling price of those distinct goods or services as of the inception date of the contract. If it is not possible to derive a standalone selling price, the seller must estimate it. This estimation should involve all relevant information that is reasonably available, such as:

- Competitive pressure on prices
- Costs incurred to manufacture or provide the item
- Item profit margins
- Pricing of other items in the same contract
- Standalone selling price of the item
- Supply and demand for the items in the market
- The seller's pricing strategy and practices
- The type of customer, distribution channel, or geographic region
- Third-party pricing

The following three approaches are acceptable ways in which to estimate a standalone selling price:

- *Adjusted market assessment.* This involves reviewing the market to estimate the price at which a customer in that market would be willing to pay for the goods and services in question. This can involve an examination of the prices of competitors for similar items and adjusting them to incorporate the seller's costs and margins.
- *Expected cost plus a margin.* This requires the seller to estimate the costs required to fulfill a performance obligation, and then add a margin to it to derive the estimated price.
- *Residual approach.* This involves subtracting all of the observable standalone selling prices from the total transaction price to arrive at the residual price remaining for allocation to any non-observable selling prices. This method can only be used if one of the following situations applies:
    - The seller sells the good or service to other customers for a wide range of prices; or
    - No price has yet been established for that item, and it has not yet been sold on a standalone basis.

The residual approach can be difficult to use when there are several goods or services with uncertain standalone selling prices. If so, it may be necessary to use a

combination of methods to derive standalone selling prices, which should be used in the following order:

1. Estimate the aggregate amount of the standalone selling prices for all items having uncertain standalone selling prices, using the residual method.
2. Use another method to develop standalone selling prices for each item in this group, to allocate the aggregate amount of the standalone selling prices.

Once all standalone selling prices have been determined, allocate the transaction price amongst these distinct goods or services based on their relative standalone selling prices.

Once the seller derives an approach for estimating a standalone selling price, it should consistently apply that method to the derivation of the standalone selling prices for other goods or services with similar characteristics.

EXAMPLE

Luminescence Corporation manufactures a wide range of surgical light bulbs, and mostly sells into the wholesaler market. The company receives an order from the military for 2,000 high-output incandescent surgical bulbs, as well as for 500 units of a new bulb that operates outdoors at very low temperatures. Luminescence has not yet sold these new bulbs to anyone. The total price of the order is $700,000. Luminescence assigns $600,000 of the total price to the high-output surgical bulbs, based on its own sales of comparable orders. This leaves $100,000 of the total price that is allocable to the low temperature bulbs. Since Luminescence has not yet established a price for these bulbs and has not sold them on a standalone basis, it is acceptable to allocate $100,000 to the low temperature bulbs under the residual approach.

If there is a subsequent change in the transaction price, allocate that change amongst the distinct goods or services based on the original allocation that was used at the inception of the contract. If this subsequent allocation is to a performance obligation that has already been completed and for which revenue has already been recognized, the result can be an increase or reduction in the amount of revenue recognized. This change in recognition should occur as soon as the subsequent change in the transaction price occurs.

Allocation of Price Discounts

It is assumed that a customer has received a discount on a bundled purchase of goods or services when the sum of the standalone prices for these items is greater than the consideration to be paid under the terms of a contract. The discount can be allocated to a specific item within the bundled purchase, if there is observable evidence that the discount was intended for that item. In order to do so, all of the following criteria must apply:

1. Each distinct item in the bundle is regularly sold on a standalone basis;
2. A bundle of some of these distinct items is regularly sold at a discount to their standalone selling prices; and

3. The discount noted in the second point is essentially the same as the discount in the contract, and there is observable evidence linking the entire contract discount to that bundle of distinct items.

If this allocation system is used, the seller must employ it before using the residual approach noted earlier in this section. Doing so ensures that the discount is not applied to the other performance obligations in the contract to which prices have not yet been allocated.

In all other cases, the discount is to be allocated amongst all of the items in the bundle. In this latter situation, the allocation is to be made based on the standalone selling prices of all of the performance obligations in the contract.

EXAMPLE

The Aspen Post-Op Recovery Center sells ancillary products to patients that can assist with their recovery. Aspen regularly sells the following three products:

Product		Standalone Selling Price
Walker		$120
Portable knee brace		100
Knee ice pack compression		80
	Total	$300

Aspen routinely sells the knee brace and ice pack compression products as a bundle for $120.

Aspen enters into a contract with the Knee Recovery website to sell Knee Recovery the set of three products for $240, which is a 20% discount from the standard price. Deliveries of these products to Knee Recovery will be at different times, so the related performance obligations will be settled on different dates.

The $60 discount would normally be apportioned among all three products based on their standalone selling prices. However, because Aspen routinely sells the knee brace/ice pack bundle for a $60 discount, it is evident that the entire discount should be allocated to these two products.

If Aspen later delivers the knee brace and knee ice pack products to Knee Recovery on different dates, it should allocate the $60 discount between the two products based on their standalone selling prices. Thus, $33.33 should be allocated to the portable knee brace and $26.67 to the knee ice pack compression product. The allocation calculation is:

Product	Allocation
Portable knee brace	($100 individual product price ÷ $180 combined price) × $60 discount = $33.33
Knee ice pack	($80 individual product price ÷ $180 combined price) × $60 discount = $26.67

If the two products are instead delivered at the same time, there is no need to conduct the preceding allocation. Instead, the discount can be assigned to them both as part of a single performance obligation.

Subsequent Price Changes

There are a number of reasons why the transaction price could change after a contract has begun, such as the resolution of uncertain events that were in need of clarification at the contract inception date. When there is a price change, the amount of the change is to be allocated to the performance obligations on the same basis used for the original price allocation at the inception of the contract. This has the following ramifications:

- Do not re-allocate prices based on subsequent changes in the standalone selling prices of goods or services.
- When there is a price change and that price is allocated, the result may be the recognition of additional or reduced revenue that is to be recognized in the period when the transaction price changes.
- When there has been a contract modification prior to a price change, the price allocation is conducted in two steps. First, allocate the price change to those performance obligations identified prior to the modification if the price change is associated with variable consideration promised before modification. In all other cases, allocate the price change to those performance obligations still remaining to be settled as of the modification date.

The result should be a reported level of cumulative revenue that matches the amount of revenue an organization would have recognized if it had the most recent information at the inception date of the contract.

Step Five: Recognize Revenue

Revenue is to be recognized as goods or services are transferred to the customer. This transference is considered to occur when the customer gains control over the good or service. Indicators of this date include the following:

- When the seller has the right to receive payment.
- When the customer has legal title to the transferred asset. This can still be the case even when the seller retains title to protect it against the customer's failure to pay.
- When physical possession of the asset has been transferred by the seller.
- When the customer has taken on the significant risks and rewards of ownership related to the asset transferred by the seller. For example, the customer can now sell, pledge, or exchange the asset.
- When the customer accepts the asset.
- When the customer can prevent other entities from using or obtaining benefits from the asset.

It is possible that a performance obligation will be transferred over time, rather than as of a specific point in time. If so, revenue recognition occurs when any one of the following criteria are met:

- *Immediate use*. The customer both receives and consumes the benefit provided by the seller as performance occurs. This situation arises if another entity would not need to re-perform work completed to date if the other entity were to take over the remaining performance obligation. Routine and recurring services typically fall into this classification.

EXAMPLE

Maid Marian is a nationwide hospital cleaning service run by friars within the Franciscan Order. Its customers both receive and simultaneously consume the cleaning services provided by its staff. Consequently, the services provided by Maid Marian are considered to be performance obligations satisfied over time.

- *Immediate enhancement*. The seller creates or enhances an asset controlled by the customer as performance occurs. This asset can be tangible or intangible.
- *No alternative use*. The seller's performance does not create an asset for which there is an alternative use to the seller (such as selling it to a different customer). In addition, the contract gives the seller an enforceable right to payment for the performance that has been completed to date. A lack of alternative use happens when a contract restricts the seller from directing the asset to another use, or when there are practical limitations on doing so, such as the incurrence of significant economic losses to direct the asset elsewhere. The determination of whether an asset has an alternative use is made at the

inception of the contract, and cannot be subsequently altered unless both parties to the contract approve a modification that results in a substantive change in the performance obligation.

EXAMPLE

A hospital installs a pacemaker in a patient who has an irregular heartbeat. Following surgery, the pacemaker is clearly in the possession of the patient, since it has been implanted in his body. This is a strong indicator that the sale transaction related to the pacemaker can now be recognized by the hospital.

EXAMPLE

Harcourt Hospital is in talks with a potential acquirer. The acquirer insists that Harcourt have soil tests conducted in the area around the hospital, to see if there has been any leakage of hazardous materials. Harcourt engages Wilson Environmental to conduct these tests, which is a three-month process. The contract includes a clause that Wilson will be paid for its costs plus a 20% profit if Harcourt cancels the contract. The acquisition talks break off after two months, so Harcourt notifies Wilson that it no longer needs the environmental report. Since Wilson cannot possibly sell the information it has collected to a different customer, there is no alternative use. Also, since Wilson has an enforceable right to payment for all work completed to date, the company can recognize revenue over time by measuring its progress toward satisfying the performance obligation.

Measurement of Progress Completion

When a performance obligation is being completed over a period of time, the seller recognizes revenue through the application of a progress completion method. The goal of this method is to determine the progress of the seller in achieving complete satisfaction of its performance obligation. This method is to be consistently applied over time, and shall be re-measured at the end of each reporting period.

Both output methods and input methods are considered acceptable for determining progress completion. The method chosen should incorporate due consideration of the nature of the goods or services being provided to the customer. The following subsections address the use of output and input methods.

Output Methods

An output method recognizes revenue based on a comparison of the value to the customer of goods and services transferred to date to the remaining goods and services not yet transferred. There are numerous ways to measure output, including:

- Surveys of performance to date
- Milestones reached
- The passage of time
- The number of units delivered
- The number of units produced

Another output method that may be acceptable is the amount of consideration that the seller has the right to invoice, such as billable hours. This approach works when the seller has a right to invoice an amount that matches the amount of performance completed to date.

The method picked should closely adhere to the concept of matching the seller's progress toward satisfying the performance obligation. It is not always possible to use an output method, since the cost of collecting the necessary information can be prohibitive, or progress may not be directly observable.

EXAMPLE

24/7 Joint Recovery runs a regional chain of post-surgical joint rehabilitation centers. Participants pay a $600 quarterly fee, which gives then access to all of the centers in the chain without an appointment. In effect, 24/7's performance obligation is to keep its facilities open for use by participants, irrespective of whether they actually use the facilities. Clearly, this situation calls for measurement of progress completion based on the passage of time. Accordingly, 24/7 recognizes revenue from its annual customer payments at the rate of $200 per participant per month.

Input Methods

An input method derives the amount of revenue to be recognized based on the to-date effort required by the seller to satisfy a performance obligation relative to the total estimated amount of effort required. Examples of possible inputs are costs incurred, labor hours expended, and machine hours used. If there are situations where the effort expended does not directly relate to the transfer of goods or services to a customer, do not use that input. The following are situations where the input used could lead to incorrect revenue recognition:

- The costs incurred are higher than expected, due to seller inefficiencies.
- The costs incurred are not in proportion to the progress of the seller toward satisfying the performance obligation.

Tip: If the effort expended to satisfy performance obligations occur evenly through the performance period, consider recognizing revenue on the straight-line basis through the performance period.

EXAMPLE

A surgical center implants an artificial knee in a patient for a total billing of $50,000. The arrangement calls for the initial surgery, plus a total of 30 patient visits over the following three months. The costs associated with the procedure are expected to be as follows:

Artificial knee cost	$22,000
Surgical staff labor	8,000
Post-operative care labor	5,000
Total costs	$35,000

The surgical center intends to use an input method to derive the amount of revenue, using costs incurred. Since the bulk of the costs are incurred up-front (roughly 86% of the total cost), 86% of the $50,000 billing is recognized as revenue immediately, with the residual amount recognized over the following three months to match the distribution of costs associated with post-operative care labor.

The situation described in the preceding example is quite common, since materials are typically procured at the inception of a contract, rather than being purchased in equal quantities over the duration of the contract. Consequently, the accountant should be particularly mindful of this issue and incorporate it into any revenue recognition calculations based on an input method.

A method based on output is preferred, since it most faithfully depicts the performance of the seller under the terms of a contract. However, an input-based method is certainly allowable if using it would be less costly for the seller, while still providing a reasonable proxy for the ongoing measurement of progress.

Change in Estimate

Whichever method is used, be sure to update it over time to reflect changes in the seller's performance to date. If there is a change in the measurement of progress, treat the change as a change in accounting estimate.

A change in accounting estimate occurs when there is an adjustment to the carrying amount of an asset or liability, or the subsequent accounting for it. Changes in accounting estimate occur relatively frequently, and so would require a major effort to make an ongoing series of retroactive changes to prior financial statements. Instead, GAAP only requires that changes in accounting estimate be accounted for in the period of change and thereafter. Thus, no retrospective change is required or allowed.

Progress Measurement

It is only possible to recognize the revenue associated with progress completion if it is possible for the seller to measure the seller's progress. If the seller lacks reliable progress information, it will not be possible to recognize the revenue associated with a contract over time. There may be cases where the measurement of progress

completion is more difficult during the early stages of a contract. If so, it is allowable for the seller to instead recognize just enough revenue to recover its costs in satisfying its performance obligations, thereby deferring the recognition of other revenue until such time as the measurement system yields more accurate results.

Consistency

The preceding five steps must be applied consistently to all customer contracts that have similar characteristics, and under similar circumstances. The intent is to create a system of revenue recognition that can be relied upon to yield consistent results.

Entitlement to Payment

At all points over the duration of a contract, the seller should have the right to payment for the performance completed to date, if the customer were to cancel the contract for reasons other than the seller's failure to perform. The amount of this payment should approximate the selling price of the goods or services transferred to the customer to date; this means that costs are recovered, plus a reasonable profit margin. This reasonable profit margin should be one of the following:

- A reasonable proportion of the expected profit margin, based on the extent of the total performance completed prior to contract termination; or
- A reasonable return on the cost of capital that the seller has experienced on its cost of capital for similar contracts, if the margin on this particular contract is higher than the return the seller typically generates from this type of contract.

An entitlement to payment depends on contractual factors, such as only being paid when certain milestones are reached or when the customer is completely satisfied with a deliverable. There may not be an entitlement to payment if one of these contractual factors is present. Further, there may be legal precedents or legislation that may interfere with or bolster an entitlement to payment. For example:

- There may be a legal precedent that gives the seller the right to payment for all performance to date, even though this right is not clarified within the contract terms.
- Legal precedent may reveal that other sellers having similar rights to payment in their contracts have not succeeded in obtaining payment.
- The seller may not have attempted to enforce its right to payment in the past, which may have rendered its rights legally unenforceable.

Conversely, the terms of a contract may not legally allow a customer to terminate a contract. If so, and the customer still attempts to terminate the contract, the seller may be entitled to continue to provide goods or services to the customer, and require the customer to pay the amounts stated in the contract. In this type of situation, the seller has an enforceable right to payment.

An enforceable right to payment may not match the payment schedule stated in a contract. The payment schedule does not necessarily sync with the seller's right to payment for performance. For example, the customer could have insisted upon delayed payment dates in the payment schedule in order to more closely match its ability to make payments to the seller.

EXAMPLE

A customer of Hodgson Pharmaceutical Design pays a $500,000 nonrefundable upfront payment to Hodgson at the inception of a contract to explore the chemical composition of a new drug. The customer does not like Hodgson's initial results, and cancels the contract. On the cancellation date, Hodgson's billable hours on the project sum to $650,000. Hodgson has an enforceable right to retain the $500,000 it has already been paid. The right to be paid for the remaining $150,000 depends on the contract terms and legal precedents.

Thus far, we have covered the generic revenue recognition requirements stated in Topic 606, with examples inserted that relate to various aspects of the health care industry. In the following sections, we summarize the few remaining revenue recognition topics in the accounting standards that specifically address the health care industry.

The Health Care Revenue Environment

A health care entity can derive revenue in a number of ways, including fees charged for patient care (capitation fees), a flat fee for each patient covered, and service revenue for residents.

> **Note:** A capitation fee is a fixed amount per person that is paid at regular intervals to a health care provider as compensation for providing health care services during a period of time.

A health care entity may also derive revenue from other sources that are unrelated to the provision of services. These sources include the following:

- Interest and dividend income from investments
- Changes in the fair value of marketable securities
- Educational program fees
- Health care facility rentals
- Sales of medical and pharmaceutical supplies
- Transcript fees for attorneys and insurance entities
- Sales of meals in the cafeteria
- Sales of incidentals, such as vending machines and parking fees

The generation of revenue may involve multiple parties that are involved in the provision of and payment for services rendered. For example, the following parties are typically involved in the provision of services:

- The patient receiving care
- The physician ordering services on behalf of the patient
- The hospital in which the service takes place
- The third-party payor that pays the hospital on behalf of the patient

The third-party payor noted in the preceding list is involved in the payment for services to varying extents, depending on the situation. They tend to make the majority of payments to hospitals, home health companies, and rehabilitation facilities, but patients directly make payments to most nursing homes and continuing care retirement communities.

When a patient has insurance, a health care provider's bill is typically submitted by it to the patient's insurance company for payment. The insurance company then adjusts the charges stated on the bill, based on its negotiated rates with the provider, and pays the adjusted bill. Receipt of payment from the insurer (sometimes months later) settles the billing.

Revenue recognition is unusually complex in the health care environment, because there are so many uncertainties and complicated billing situations. The following are examples of the issues that may arise:

- *Price negotiations*. There may be pricing negotiations with third-party payors that may extend well past the point when services were rendered to patients, and where the pricing outcome is uncertain.
- *Retrospective pricing*. Revenue amounts are especially uncertain when retrospective rate setting is used; under this approach, an interim payment rate is used until the end of the applicable rate period, after which a final settlement is made. Although the amount of this final settlement will not be definitive until it is approved by both parties, the health care entity is expected to record a reasonable estimate of what this amount is expected to be. The amounts expected to be paid to or received from third-party payors may be stated in two balance sheet line items, which are:
    - Settlements due to third-party payors
    - Settlements due from third-party payors
- *Billing arguments*. Billing issues can also result in a significant amount of give-and-take over such issues as billing denials and coding changes. In some cases where the insurer wants the health care provider to correct a mistake on a billing, such as a patient's identification number, and the patient cannot be contacted for the correction, a bill may never be paid.
- *Audits*. An audit by one of the federal agencies associated with medical payments may take issue with a reimbursed expense, resulting in a payment back to the federal government.

- *Medical necessity.* There may be arguments over whether a medical procedure was actually necessary, which may result in a payor rejecting the billing associated with the procedure.
- *Improper referrals.* If a service is provided based on an improper referral, a payor may refuse to provide compensation for it.
- *Low-income compensation.* A health care entity may be eligible for additional payments if it serves a disproportionately large percentage of low-income patients.

Consequently, an initial assessment of the amount of revenue that should be recognized may turn out to be materially incorrect from the amount that is eventually realized.

In the following sub-sections, we cover several additional topics related to health care revenue recognition.

Charity Care

A health care entity cannot recognize revenue that is based on the provision of charity care (where services are provided to those who cannot pay). The determination of whether services rendered should be classified as charity care does not need to be made when a person is admitted, but must be made within a reasonable period of time.

Charity care is distinctly different from care provided for a fee, which is later written off as a bad debt. In the latter case, the initial expectation is that a patient will pay for the services provided.

Naming Opportunities

A health care entity may provide a naming opportunity for a resource provider, such as an individual donor, a corporation, or a foundation. A naming opportunity is essentially a public acknowledgment of a gift that advertises the resource provider. For example, a health care entity could name a building after an especially generous donor, or give a donor the chance to sponsor an event in exchange for having its logo prominently displayed during the event. Another variation is a fund raising campaign in which increased levels of sponsorship lead to the transfer of increasingly valuable benefits to the donor.

If the naming rights given are of nominal value, then donations should be accounted for as contributions. However, there are circumstances in which the granting of naming rights can be considered an exchange transaction, where the transaction generates revenue. For example, naming an oncology building after a person probably conveys little actual value to the recipient. However, if the donor is a producer of oncology products, and the building name will be prominently displayed next to a busy highway, then a case can be made that the donor has obtained something of real value. The following table provides indicators that can assist in determining whether naming rights would cause a donation to be treated as a contribution or an exchange transaction.

Naming Right Indicators for the Treatment of a Donor Payment

Indicator	Treatment as Contribution	Treatment as Exchange Transaction
Value of public recognition	The donor receives nominal value	The donor receives significant value
Duration of naming rights	Rights are for a short time, or the health care entity can change the name	Rights are for a long time, and the health care entity cannot change the name
Control over name usage	The donor cannot change the displayed name	The donor can change the displayed name

Patient Payments

Patients are typically held responsible for the portion of a health care billing that is not paid by a third-party payor. This patient-specific portion is comprised of insurance co-pays and deductibles, services provided to uninsured patients, and services that are not covered by insurance. A common practice for recognizing revenue associated with self-paying patients is to recognize revenue at the entity's established billing rates, net of any discounts provided. Then, any nonpayment of this figure is included in the bad debt allowance.

Use Fees

A continuing care retirement community may charge use fees to its residents, based on their personal use of selected services, such as covered parking, salon services, extra meals, and so forth. These fees are usually accumulated and then charged to residents on a monthly basis. Since the related services have already been provided, use fees can generally be recognized as revenue as soon as they are billed.

Presentation

A health care entity records gross service revenue as services are rendered, using its established rates, even if the entity does not expect to collect the full amount of this revenue. When there is a difference between the established rates for the services provided and the amounts that will be paid by third-party payors, the unpaid difference is accounted for as a contractual adjustment. This contractual adjustment is recorded in the same period when the services were provided, so that only a net figure appears in the financial statements. Further, if the entity offers a discount to its patients, the discount is recorded in the same period in which the related services were performed. By taking this approach, the financial statements in any period always reflect both gross revenues and all adjustments and discounts expected to be applied to the gross revenue figure.

Disclosures

When a continuing care retirement community is requiring the payment of advance fees, disclose in the notes to the financial statements the method used to account for these fees, the related refund policy, and the method of calculating the obligation to provide future services and the use of facilities. Also note the gross amount of contractual refund obligations under existing contracts.

Summary

A health care entity can be paid in many ways by a number of third-party payors, and is continually placed in situations where it will be paid significantly less than its standard billing rates. The result is a high degree of uncertainty in revenue recognition, where the accounting staff is continually altering its estimates of bad debts and retrospective pricing adjustments. This is less of an issue for organizations that are paid directly by residents or patients, such as nursing homes and continuing care retirement communities. Conversely, it is a major problem for those entities that rely heavily on third-party payors, such as hospitals and surgery centers. Consequently, the effort required to recognize revenue will vary significantly, depending on the type of health care entity.

Chapter 12
Payroll Accounting

Introduction

One of the primary responsibilities of the accountant in a health care entity is to process payroll, since the organization may employ a large number of people. This chapter contains the essentials of payroll accounting activities, covering the following topics:

- Gross pay calculations
- Types of payroll taxes
- Income tax withholdings
- Benefits and other deductions
- Net pay
- Remitting payroll taxes
- Payments to employees
- The payroll register
- Payroll journal entries

The ordering of these topics approximates the flow of transactions for the processing of payroll, from the initial collection of time worked information, through the determination of gross pay, and concluding with net pay, payments to employees, and the recordation of payroll.

Related Podcast Episodes: Episodes 126-129 of the Accounting Best Practices Podcast discuss the payroll system. They are available at: **accountingtools.com/podcasts** or **iTunes**

Gross Pay Calculations

Gross pay is the amount of compensation to be paid to an employee before any deductions are withheld from the pay. Though not especially difficult to calculate, there are some issues to consider when deriving gross pay, which are dealt with in the following sub-sections.

Hourly Rate Plan

The simplest and most commonly-used method for determining the compensation of an hourly employee is the hourly rate plan, under which hours worked are multiplied by an employee's hourly rate. This method can be more complicated if there is a shift

differential or overtime. A shift differential is extra pay earned by employees who work a less than desirable shift, such as the evening, night, or weekend shifts.

EXAMPLE

Arlo Montaigne works the night shift as a janitor at St. Livinus Hospital. He earns a base wage of $13.50 per hour, plus a $0.50 shift differential. In the most recent work week, he logs 39 hours of work. The calculation of his wages earned under the hourly rate plan is:

($13.50 base wage + $0.50 shift differential) × 39 hours = $546.00

If there is a shift differential, add it to the base wage prior to calculating overtime.

What if an employee works a fraction of an hour? A computerized payroll system automatically converts this to a fraction of an hour. However, an accountant that manually calculates wages may use a variety of simplification methods, such as rounding up to the nearest quarter-hour.

EXAMPLE

St. Livinus Hospital's accounting staff calculates wages for its employees by hand. In the most recent week, Mortimer Davis worked 39 hours and 41 minutes. The hospital's accountant could use a calculator to determine that 41 minutes is 0.6833 hours (calculated as 41 minutes ÷ 60 minutes) and pay the employee on that basis. However, prior calculation errors have led to a policy of rounding up to the next quarter hour. Accordingly, the accountant rounds the 41 minutes up to 45 minutes, and therefore records 39 ¾ hours for Mr. Davis.

Overtime

Overtime is a 50% multiplier that is added to an employee's base wage for hours worked over 40 hours in a work week. This calculation is subject to some variation by state, so review local regulations to see if there is an overriding overtime calculation in place. Here are two rules to consider when calculating overtime pay:

- Do not include in the 40 base hours such special hours as holidays, jury duty, sick time, or vacations.
- Add the shift differential (the extra amount paid to someone working a late shift) to the base wage and then calculate overtime based on this combined figure.

EXAMPLE

Alfredo Montoya works the evening shift at a hospital, which adds $1 of shift differential per hour to his base wage of $15 per hour. In the most recent work week, he worked 50 hours. The overtime premium he will be paid is based on the combined $16 wage that includes his shift differential. Thus, his overtime rate is $8 per hour. The calculation of his total compensation for that week is:

50 hours × aggregate base pay of $16/hour	=	$800
10 hours × overtime premium of $8/hour	=	80
Total compensation	=	$880

EXAMPLE

Alfredo Montoya works 35 hours during a week that includes Memorial Day. His employer will pay him for a 43-hour work week, which adds the eight hours of the federal holiday to his hours worked. However, this will not include any overtime pay, since only 35 hours were actually worked.

There may be situations where an employee is paid different rates at different times during the work period. This situation may arise when the individual works on different jobs that have differing rates of pay associated with them. In these cases, there are three possible options for calculating overtime, which are:

- Base the overtime rate on the highest wage rate paid during the period
- Base the overtime rate on the average wage rate paid during the period
- Base the overtime rate on the wage rate paid after the 40th hour

The last alternative for calculating overtime requires the prior approval of the affected employee.

EXAMPLE

Marcel Moheko worked on two maintenance tasks in a hospital's cooling plant during the past work week. He worked on Job A for 30 hours and was paid $20.00 per hour while working on that job. He worked 15 hours on Job B and was paid $25.00 per hour for that job. The last job on which he worked was Job A. The calculation of his overtime pay under the three calculation methods is:

	Based on Highest Rate	Based on Average Rate	Based on Last Rate
Job A pay rate	$20.00	$20.00	$20.00
Job B pay rate	$25.00	$25.00	$25.00
Weighted average pay rate*	$21.25	$21.25	$21.25
Overtime rate	$12.50	$10.63	$10.00
Overtime hours	5	5	5
Total overtime paid	$62.50	$53.15	$50.00

* Calculated as ($20.00 × 75%) + ($25.00 × 25%)

Types of Payroll Taxes

The government requires employers to pay three types of taxes related to payroll, which are social security, Medicare, and unemployment taxes. In the following subsections, we address the nature, amount, and calculation of each tax.

Social Security Tax

The social security tax began with the passage of the Social Security Act in 1935, which established Old Age and Survivor's Insurance. The insurance was to be funded by compulsory deductions from the pay of wage earners. Initially, these deductions were set at 1% of gross wages, were to be paid by both the employer and the employee, and would continue until retirement age, which was set at 65. By 1948, the amount of these deductions had increased to 3%. Employers have been and continue to be responsible for withholding the social security tax from employee pay.

The tax rate for social security is now governed by the Federal Insurance Contributions Act (FICA). Because of this association, social security taxes are now closely associated with the acronym "FICA".

This tax has increased in size over time, along with the maximum wage cap (also known as the *wage base limit*) to which it applies. The social security tax rate is only applied to a person's wages up to the amount of the wage base cap. Do not apply the tax to any wages earned above the wage cap. For example, on earnings of $250,000 in 2023, the amount of employer tax paid would be $9,932.40, which is calculated as follows:

6.2% Tax rate × $160,200 Wage cap = $9,932.40

The following table shows the history of the social security tax for the past few years.

Tax Year	FICA Tax Rate	Wage Cap
2023	6.2%	$160,200
2022	6.2%	147,000
2021	6.2%	142,800

Note that social security is matched by the employee, so the total tax amount paid to the government by the employer is 12.4%.

EXAMPLE

Benjamin Mayhew earned $200,000 in 2023. Based on the $160,200 wage cap in place that year, his employer must deduct $9,932.40 from his gross pay and match it with another $9,932.40 for a total payment of $19,864.80.

Medicare Tax

Medicare is a health insurance program that is administered by the United States government, and which is primarily available to those 65 years old or older, as well as to those with certain disabilities. It is funded through the Medicare tax, though participants must also pay a portion of all health insurance costs incurred. The program has been in existence since 1965.

Since 1986, the Medicare tax rate that is paid by an employee has been 1.45% (plus matching of the same amount by the employer). There is no cap on the Medicare tax for employed and self-employed people; thus, everyone must pay it, irrespective of the amount of money that they earn.

As of 2014, an additional Medicare tax of 0.9% was imposed, which applies to all wages earned in excess of $250,000 for married filers and in excess of $200,000 for single and head of household filers.

EXAMPLE

St. Rambert Hospital employs Mr. Smith, who earns $5,000 of gross pay in the most recent pay period. The hospital withholds $72.50 ($5,000 × .0145) from the pay of Mr. Smith, matches the $72.50 from its own funds, and forwards $145.00 to the government.

Unemployment Taxes

The federal and state governments of the United States provide unemployment compensation to workers who have lost their jobs. This compensation is paid for primarily by employers, who pay both federal and state unemployment taxes.

The FUTA tax rate is 6.0%. Calculate the FUTA tax based on only the first $7,000 paid to each employee in the form of wages during the year (i.e., there is no FUTA tax on wages higher than $7,000 in each calendar year). Then subtract a credit from the FUTA tax for the amount of tax paid into the state unemployment tax fund. The maximum (and most common) amount of this credit is 5.4%, which means that the actual amount of FUTA tax is only 0.6%.

EXAMPLE

Paisley Helicopter Nursing employs 100 highly skilled flight nurses, all of whom earn more than $100,000 per year. Thus, they all earn more than the $7,000 FUTA wage cap in the first quarter of the year. Within the first quarter, Paisley has $700,000 of wages eligible for the FUTA tax (calculated as 100 employees × $7,000). Its FUTA tax liability is the 6.0% federal rate minus the 5.4% state rate, multiplied by the $700,000 of eligible wages. Paisley's FUTA tax liability is therefore $4,200 (calculated as $700,000 eligible wages × 0.6%).

FUTA taxes are remitted on a quarterly basis. If the total amount of tax payable is less than $500 in any quarter, the employer can opt to carry the liability forward to the

next quarter. The liability can continue to roll forward through additional quarters if the liability remains less than $500.

Each state has its own unemployment insurance program, which evaluates unemployment claims and administers the payment of benefits to individuals. Each of the states has its own rules regarding who is eligible for unemployment benefits, the amounts to be paid, and the duration of those payments, within guidelines set by the federal government.

State governments impose a state-level unemployment tax on employers that can be quite high – even more than the 5.4% credit allowed under FUTA, as noted earlier. A state typically assigns a relatively high default tax rate to a new business and then subsequently adjusts that rate based on the history of unemployment claims made by employees of the business (known as the *experience rating*). If an organization rarely lays off its staff, it will eventually be assigned a lower tax rate, with the reverse being true for a firm with an uneven employment record.

States mail unemployment rate notices for the upcoming year to businesses near the end of the current calendar year. Include the tax rate noted on the form in the entity's payroll calculations for all of the following year.

Income Tax Withholdings

If an individual is classified as an employee, the employer is responsible for withholding income taxes from that person's gross wages. A key input to the calculation of income tax withholdings is the amount of withholdings claimed by an individual on his or her Form W-4. An example of a completed Form W-4 is provided. The amounts specified in the form are the responsibility of the employee, not the company.

Tip: Encourage employees to use the Withholding Calculator located at www.irs.gov/W4App to assist in determining the appropriate withholding amount that they should claim on a Form W-4. It is especially useful for cases in which employees only expect to work part of the year, have self-employment income, are subject to additional taxes, or prefer the most accurate withholding for multiple job situations.

If an employee fails to furnish a Form W-4, then the employer should treat the individual as if he or she had checked the box for "Single or Married filing separately" in Step 1(c) and made no entries in Step 2, Step 3, or Step 4 of the Form W-4.

Form W-4, Employee's Withholding Allowance Certificate

Form **W-4**

Department of the Treasury
Internal Revenue Service

Employee's Withholding Certificate

Complete Form W-4 so that your employer can withhold the correct federal income tax from your pay.
Give Form W-4 to your employer.
Your withholding is subject to review by the IRS.

OMB No. 1545-0074

2023

Step 1: Enter Personal Information

(a) First name and middle initial	Last name	(b) Social security number
Harry D.	Smith	012-34-5678
Address: 123 Main Street		**Does your name match the name on your social security card?** If not, to ensure you get credit for your earnings, contact SSA at 800-772-1213 or go to *www.ssa.gov*.
City or town, state, and ZIP code: Denver, CO 80202		

(c) ☑ **Single** or **Married filing separately**
☐ **Married filing jointly** or **Qualifying surviving spouse**
☐ **Head of household** (Check only if you're unmarried and pay more than half the costs of keeping up a home for yourself and a qualifying individual.)

Complete Steps 2–4 ONLY if they apply to you; otherwise, skip to Step 5. See page 2 for more information on each step, who can claim exemption from withholding, other details, and privacy.

Step 2: Multiple Jobs or Spouse Works

Complete this step if you (1) hold more than one job at a time, or (2) are married filing jointly and your spouse also works. The correct amount of withholding depends on income earned from all of these jobs.

Do **only one** of the following.

(a) Reserved for future use.

(b) Use the Multiple Jobs Worksheet on page 3 and enter the result in Step 4(c) below; **or**

(c) If there are only two jobs total, you may check this box. Do the same on Form W-4 for the other job. This option is generally more accurate than (b) if pay at the lower paying job is more than half of the pay at the higher paying job. Otherwise, (b) is more accurate . . . . ☐

TIP: If you have self-employment income, see page 2.

Complete Steps 3–4(b) on Form W-4 for only ONE of these jobs. Leave those steps blank for the other jobs. (Your withholding will be most accurate if you complete Steps 3–4(b) on the Form W-4 for the highest paying job.)

Step 3: Claim Dependent and Other Credits

If your total income will be $200,000 or less ($400,000 or less if married filing jointly):

Multiply the number of qualifying children under age 17 by $2,000 $ 2000

Multiply the number of other dependents by $500 . . . . . $ 500

Add the amounts above for qualifying children and other dependents. You may add to this the amount of any other credits. Enter the total here . . . . **3** $ 2500

Step 4 (optional): Other Adjustments

(a) Other income (not from jobs). If you want tax withheld for other income you expect this year that won't have withholding, enter the amount of other income here. This may include interest, dividends, and retirement income . . . . **4(a)** $

(b) Deductions. If you expect to claim deductions other than the standard deduction and want to reduce your withholding, use the Deductions Worksheet on page 3 and enter the result here . . . . **4(b)** $

(c) Extra withholding. Enter any additional tax you want withheld each **pay period** . . **4(c)** $ 200

Step 5: Sign Here

Under penalties of perjury, I declare that this certificate, to the best of my knowledge and belief, is true, correct, and complete.

Employee's signature (This form is not valid unless you sign it.) **Date**

Employers Only	Employer's name and address	First date of employment	Employer identification number (EIN)
	St. Bercharius Hospital		84-1234567

For Privacy Act and Paperwork Reduction Act Notice, see page 3. Cat. No. 10220Q Form **W-4** (2023)

The IRS provides a set of wage bracket tables for income tax withholdings in its Publication 15-T, Federal Income Tax Withholding Methods. This publication is available as a PDF download on the www.irs.gov website. The IRS recommends that, if a business is computing its payroll manually, it should use the following worksheet as the basis for determining federal income taxes payable for each employee.

Worksheet 2. Employer's Withholding Worksheet for Wage Bracket Method Tables for Manual Payroll Systems With Forms W-4 From 2020 or Later

Keep for Your Records

Table 5	Monthly	Semimonthly	Biweekly	Weekly	Daily
	12	24	26	52	260

Step 1. Adjust the employee's wage amount

1a	Enter the employee's total taxable wages this payroll period	1a	$
1b	Enter the number of pay periods you have per year (see Table 5)	1b	
1c	Enter the amount from Step 4(a) of the employee's Form W-4	1c	$
1d	Divide the amount on line 1c by the number of pay periods on line 1b	1d	$
1e	Add lines 1a and 1d	1e	$
1f	Enter the amount from Step 4(b) of the employee's Form W-4	1f	$
1g	Divide the amount on line 1f by the number of pay periods on line 1b	1g	$
1h	Subtract line 1g from line 1e. If zero or less, enter -0-. This is the **Adjusted Wage Amount**	1h	$

Step 2. Figure the Tentative Withholding Amount

2a	Use the amount on line 1h to look up the tentative amount to withhold in the appropriate Wage Bracket Method table in this section for your pay frequency, given the employee's filing status and whether the employee has checked the box in Step 2 of Form W-4. This is the **Tentative Withholding Amount**	2a	$

Step 3. Account for tax credits

3a	Enter the amount from Step 3 of the employee's Form W-4	3a	$
3b	Divide the amount on line 3a by the number of pay periods on line 1b	3b	$
3c	Subtract line 3b from line 2a. If zero or less, enter -0-	3c	$

Step 4. Figure the final amount to withhold

4a	Enter the additional amount to withhold from Step 4(c) of the employee's Form W-4	4a	$
4b	Add lines 3c and 4a. **This is the amount to withhold from the employee's wages this pay period**	4b	$

The wage bracket tables are designed to be an easy way to derive the correct amount of income tax withholding for people at lower wage levels (up to $100,000 per year). Each table calculates the proper amount of withholding under a different set of scenarios. An extract from a wage bracket table is shown in the following exhibit, which is taken from the 2023 version of Publication 15-T. The table lists the amount of income tax withholding for someone being paid on a weekly basis, and states the proper withholding for three types of taxpayer – married filing jointly, head of household, and single or married filing separately. The actual full-length table presents information for a much larger range of income.

2023 Wage Bracket Method Tables for Manual Payroll Systems with Forms W-4 From 2020 or Later
WEEKLY Payroll Period

If the Adjusted Wage Amount (line 1h) is		Married Filing Jointly		Head of Household		Single or Married Filing Separately	
At least	But less than	Standard withholding	Form W-4, Step 2, Checkbox withholding	Standard withholding	Form W-4, Step 2, Checkbox withholding	Standard withholding	Form W-4, Step 2, Checkbox withholding
		The Tentative Withholding Amount is:					
$765	$775	$24	$56	$38	$65	$56	$95
$775	$785	$25	$57	$40	$67	$57	$97
$785	$795	$26	$59	$41	$69	$59	$99
$795	$805	$27	$60	$42	$71	$60	$102
$805	$815	$28	$61	$43	$74	$61	$104
$815	$825	$29	$62	$44	$76	$62	$106
$825	$835	$30	$63	$46	$78	$63	$108
$835	$845	$31	$65	$47	$80	$65	$110
$845	$855	$32	$66	$48	$82	$66	$113
$855	$865	$33	$67	$49	$85	$67	$115
$865	$875	$34	$68	$50	$87	$68	$117
$875	$885	$35	$69	$52	$89	$69	$119
$885	$895	$36	$71	$53	$91	$71	$121
$895	$905	$37	$72	$54	$93	$72	$124
$905	$915	$38	$73	$55	$96	$73	$126
$915	$925	$39	$74	$56	$98	$74	$128
$925	$935	$40	$75	$58	$100	$75	$130
$935	$945	$41	$77	$59	$102	$77	$132
$945	$955	$42	$78	$60	$104	$78	$135
$955	$965	$43	$79	$61	$107	$79	$137
$965	$975	$44	$80	$62	$109	$80	$139
$975	$985	$45	$81	$64	$111	$81	$141
$985	$995	$46	$83	$65	$113	$83	$143
$995	$1,005	$48	$84	$66	$115	$84	$146
$1,005	$1,015	$49	$85	$67	$118	$85	$148

To use the wage bracket method, go to the table that corresponds to the company's payroll. Within that table, go to the adjusted wage amount that applies to the employee in question, and then go across the table to find the correct taxpayer type for that employee. The amount in this cell is the amount of income tax to withhold.

EXAMPLE

Albert Montaigne works for Facial Surgery Associates. Mr. Montaigne is an hourly production employee of the company, which pays its staff on a weekly basis. Mr. Montaigne earned $780 during the most recent weekly period. He stated on his Form W-4 that he is filing as a head of household. According to the preceding extract from the IRS wage bracket table, the company should deduct a total of $40 from his wages to cover his income tax withholdings.

Benefits and Other Deductions

Thus far, we have described a set of mandatory deductions from gross pay related to taxes. In addition, there are a number of other deductions that may be taken from gross pay. The essential information related to these deductions is described in the following bullet points:

- *Benefits deductions.* A health care entity that wants to retain its employees over the long term may offer them a benefits package that could include medical, dental, vision, life, short-term and long-term disability insurance. The amount deducted from employee pay is typically the residual amount owed after the employer pays for a portion of the underlying expense.

- *Charitable contributions*. Many employers encourage their employees to make contributions to local or national charities, and may also match these contributions to some extent. Under such an arrangement, an employee signs a pledge card, which authorizes the employer to deduct certain contribution amounts from their pay on an ongoing basis. The employer then periodically forwards the sum total of all contributions deducted to the targeted charities, along with any matching amount that the employer is paying.
- *Garnishments*. Some people resist fulfilling their legal obligations to other parties, or they do not have the financial resources to do so. If an organization employs such a person, it is quite possible that the accountant will receive a garnishment order, under which the entity must withhold specified amounts from an employee's pay and forward it to a third party. A garnishment order usually relates to child support, unpaid taxes, or unpaid student loans.
- *Union dues*. If a health care entity has entered into a collective bargaining agreement with a labor union, the terms of the agreement usually stipulate that the organization withhold union dues from employee pay and forward it to the union.
- *Deductions for financing repayments*. An organization may issue advances or loans to its employees. If so, deductions from future paychecks will be needed to reduce the balances of these outstanding amounts.

Net Pay

Net pay is the amount paid to employees after all of the deductions described in the previous sections are deducted from gross pay. The entire net pay calculation may be included in a remittance advice that is forwarded to employees along with their paychecks. A typical calculation format that may be given to an employee is as follows:

Gross pay (40 hours × $30.00/hour)	$1,200.00
Deductions:	
Social security	74.40
Medicare	17.40
Income tax withholding	225.00
Medical insurance	160.00
Union dues	15.00
Garnishments	100.00
Net pay	$608.20

Remitting Payroll Taxes

An employer has a legal obligation to forward to the government all income taxes that it has withheld from employee pay, as well as social security and Medicare taxes.

These remittances must be forwarded to the government in accordance with a specific payment schedule and method that is described in the following sub-sections. In this section, we review when tax deposits should be made, how to remit funds, and related reporting requirements.

If an employer were to miss a timely remittance, or pay an insufficient amount, the related penalty would be severe. For this reason alone, it is important to have a detailed understanding of tax remittances.

Types of Tax Deposit Schedules

There are two deposit schedules, known as the *monthly deposit schedule* and the *semiweekly deposit schedule* that state when to deposit payroll taxes. The accountant must determine which of these deposit schedules will be followed before the beginning of each calendar year. The selection of a deposit schedule is based entirely on the tax liability reported during a *lookback period.*

The deposit schedule is based on the total taxes (i.e., federal income taxes withheld, social security taxes, and Medicare taxes) reported in line 8 of the Forms 941 in a four-quarter lookback period. The lookback period begins on July 1 and ends on June 30. The decision tree for selecting a deposit period is:

- If the business reported $50,000 or less of taxes during the lookback period, use the monthly deposit schedule.
- If the business reported more than $50,000 of taxes during the lookback period, use the semiweekly deposit schedule.

EXAMPLE

Growing Hospital had used the monthly deposit schedule in previous years, but its payroll expanded considerably in the past year, which may place it in the semiweekly deposit schedule. Growing's accountant calculates the amount of taxes paid during its lookback period to see if the semiweekly deposit schedule now applies. The calculation is:

Lookback Period		Taxes Paid
July 1 – September 30, 2022		$8,250
October 1 – December 31, 2022		14,750
January 1 – March 31, 2023		17,500
April 1 – June 30, 2023		19,000
	Total	$59,500

Since the total amount of taxes that Growing paid during the lookback period exceeded $50,000, the hospital must use the semiweekly deposit schedule during the next calendar year.

Tip: A new employer has no lookback period, and so is automatically considered a monthly schedule depositor for its first calendar year of business.

The schedule for depositing state withholding taxes varies by state. Consult with the applicable state government for this deposit schedule. If the business outsources payroll processing, the supplier will handle these deposits on the organization's behalf.

Monthly Deposit Schedule

If an organization qualifies to use the monthly deposit schedule, deposit employment taxes on payments made during a month by the 15th day of the following month.

EXAMPLE

Magdalen House Nursing Home is a monthly schedule depositor that pays its staff on the 15th and last business day of each month. Under the monthly deposit schedule, Magdalen must deposit the combined tax liabilities for all of its payrolls in a month by the 15th day of the following month. The same deposit schedule would apply if Magdalen had instead paid its employees every day, every other week, twice a month, once a month, or on any other payroll schedule.

The total payroll taxes withheld for each of Magdalen's payrolls in September are noted in the following table, along with the amount of its tax liability that will be due for remittance to the government on October 15:

	Federal Income Tax Withheld	Social Security Tax Withheld	Medicare Tax Withheld
Sept. 15 payroll	$1,500.00	$620.00	$145.00
Sept. 30 payroll	1,250.00	558.00	130.50
Sept. total withheld	$2,750.00	$1,178.00	$275.50
Employer tax matching	--	1,178.00	275.50
Tax deposit due Oct. 15	$2,750.00	$2,356.00	$551.00

Magdalen's tax liability to be remitted on October 15 is $5,657.00, which is calculated as the total of all withholdings and employer matches for federal income taxes, social security taxes, and Medicare taxes ($2,750.00 + $2,356.00 + $551.00).

Semiweekly Deposit Schedule

If an employer qualifies to use the semiweekly deposit schedule, remit payroll taxes using the following exhibit.

Semiweekly Deposit Schedule

Payment Date	Corresponding Deposit Date
Wednesday, Thursday, or Friday	Following Wednesday
Saturday, Sunday, Monday, Tuesday	Following Friday

If an employer has more than one pay date during a semiweekly period and the pay dates fall in different calendar quarters, make separate deposits for the liabilities associated with each pay date.

EXAMPLE

Malvern Care Home has a pay date on Wednesday, June 29 (second quarter) and another pay date on Friday, July 1 (third quarter). Malvern must make a separate deposit for the taxes associated with each pay date, even though both dates fall within the same semiweekly period. The organization should pay both deposits on the following Wednesday, July 6.

EXAMPLE

Vicarage Care Nursing Home uses the semiweekly deposit schedule. The organization only pays its employees once a month, on the last day of the month. Although Vicarage is on a semiweekly deposit schedule, it can only make a deposit once a month, since it only pays its employees once a month.

Note that the semiweekly deposit method does not mean that an employer is required to make two tax deposits per week – it is simply the name of the method. Thus, if an employer has one payroll every other week, it would remit taxes only every other week.

The differentiating factor between the monthly and semiweekly deposit schedules is that an employer must remit taxes much more quickly under the semiweekly method. The monthly method uses a simpler and more delayed tax deposit schedule, which is ideal for smaller businesses.

Federal Unemployment Deposit Schedule

The federal unemployment tax is to be deposited on a quarterly basis. The deposit dates are noted in the following exhibit.

Federal Unemployment Deposit Schedule

Relevant Calendar Quarter	Last Possible Deposit Date
First quarter of the calendar year	April 30
Second quarter of the calendar year	July 31
Third quarter of the calendar year	October 31
Fourth quarter of the calendar year	January 31

Remittance Method

All federal tax deposits must be paid by electronic funds transfer. Use the Electronic Federal Tax Payment System (EFTPS) to make these deposits. EFTPS is a free service that is maintained by the Department of Treasury. The system can either be used

directly or through an intermediary, such as the organization's payroll supplier (if the business is outsourcing payroll) to deposit the funds on the employer's behalf. Go to www.eftps.gov to enroll in EFTPS. If the entity is a new employer, it will likely have been pre-enrolled in EFTPS when it applied for an employer identification number (EIN); if so, it will receive a personal identification number for the EFTPS system as part of the initial EIN package of information.

When remitting taxes to the government, the remittance should include the following types of taxes:

- Withheld income taxes
- Withheld and matching employer social security taxes
- Withheld and matching employer Medicare taxes

When a deposit is made, EFTPS will provide a deposit trace number, which can be used as a receipt or to trace the payment.

The Form 941 Quarterly Federal Tax Return

Following each calendar quarter, any employer that pays wages subject to income tax withholding, or social security and Medicare taxes, must file a Form 941, the Employer's Quarterly Federal Tax Return. The Form 941 must be filed by the last day of the month following the calendar quarter to which it applies. The filing dates for the Form 941 are noted in the following exhibit.

Form 941 Quarterly Filing Dates

Quarter Ending	Form 941 Due Date
March 31	April 30
June 30	July 31
September 30	October 31
December 31	January 31

If a Form 941 is not filed in a timely manner (not including filing extensions), the IRS imposes a failure-to-file penalty of 5% of the unpaid tax due with that return, up to a maximum penalty of 25% of the tax due. In addition, for each whole month or part of a month that payment is late, there is an additional failure-to-pay penalty of ½% of the amount of the tax, up to a maximum of 25% of the tax due. If both penalties apply in a month, the failure-to-file penalty is reduced by the amount of the failure-to-pay penalty. The IRS may waive these penalties if a reasonable cause can be presented for failing to file the Form 941 or pay the tax due.

State Tax Remittances

Each state government has its own system for reporting and depositing state-level payroll taxes. The types of taxes can vary from those collected at the federal level and may include the following:

- State income tax
- Unemployment insurance tax
- Disability insurance tax
- Special district taxes (such as for a transportation district)

The forms used to report this information vary by state. The primary reports that may be required are:

- *Reconciliation statement.* Compares the amount of state taxes remitted to the amount withheld from employee pay.
- *Tax withholdings.* Reports wages paid to employees and the state taxes withheld from their pay.

Most state governments provide preprinted tax remittance and reporting forms to those employers registered to do business within their boundaries. If an employer outsources its payroll, the supplier is responsible for completing and submitting these forms.

The required remittance dates also vary by state, as do the modes of payment – either check or electronic payments may be required. In some cases, an employer can choose between modes of payment, though it is customary to require electronic payment for all future payments, once an employer has switched to that type of payment.

Each state government publishes an explanatory guide to its tax structure, in which it describes the state's reporting and remittance system. These guides are usually also available online as PDF documents or web pages.

Payments to Employees

The standard method for paying employees for many years was the check, though it has been largely supplanted by direct deposit. A check is usually accompanied by a *remittance advice* (also known as a *check stub*), on which is listed an employee's gross pay, tax deductions and other withholdings, and net pay. A simplified sample remittance advice for a one-week pay period appears in the following exhibit.

Sample Remittance Advice

Employee Name: Arturo Johansson							[company name]
Ending Pay Date	Hours Worked	Rate	Gross Pay	Federal Inc. Tax	Social Security	Medi-care	Net Pay
5/15/xx	Regular 40 OT 10	$20.00 $30.00	$1,100.00	$197.25	$68.20	$15.95	$818.60

Direct deposit involves the electronic transfer of funds from the employer to the bank accounts of its employees, using the Automated Clearing House (ACH) system. ACH is an electronic network for the processing of both debit and credit transactions within the United States and Canada.

The payment process is to calculate pay in the same manner as for check payments, but to then send the payment information to a direct deposit processing service, which initiates electronic payments to the bank accounts of those employees being paid in this manner. The processing service deducts the funds from an employer bank account in advance of the direct deposits, so cash flow tends to be somewhat more accelerated than is the case if an employer were to issue checks and then wait several days for the amounts on the checks to be withdrawn from its bank account.

Direct deposit is more efficient than payments by check, because it does not require a signature on each payment, there are no checks to be delivered, and employees do not have to waste time depositing them at a bank. Further, employees working off-site can still rely upon having cash paid into their accounts in a timely manner.

Direct deposit can also be more efficient from the perspective of the remittance advice. A number of payroll suppliers offer an option to simply notify employees by e-mail when their pay has been sent to them, after which employees can access a secure website to view their remittance advice information. This approach is better than sending a paper version of a remittance advice, because employees can also access many years of historical pay information on-line, as well as their W-2 forms.

The implementation of direct deposit can cause some initial difficulties, because each person's bank account information must be correctly set up in the direct deposit module of the employer's payroll software (or software provided by the outsourced payroll supplier). This initial setup is remarkably prone to error, and also usually requires a test transaction (the *pre-notification*) that delays implementation by one pay period. Consequently, even if a new employee signs up for direct deposit immediately, the accountant must still print a paycheck for that person's first payroll, after which direct deposit can be used.

Tip: If employees want to be paid by direct deposit, require them to submit a voided check for the checking account into which they want funds to be sent. The routing and account numbers can more reliably be taken directly from such a check, rather than risking a transposition error if an employee copies this information onto a form. Also, do not accept a deposit slip instead of a check – the information on the deposit slip may not match the routing and account number information on the check.

A final issue with direct deposit is being able to do so from an in-house payroll processing function. If the payroll software does not provide for direct deposit, it will be necessary to contract with a third party to make the payments on behalf of the employer. Direct deposit is much easier to implement if the employer is outsourcing payroll, since direct deposit is part of the standard feature set for all payroll suppliers.

The Payroll Register

The primary internal report generated by the payroll system is the payroll register. This document itemizes the calculation of wages, taxes, and deductions for each employee for each payroll. There are multiple uses for the payroll register, including:

- *Investigation.* It is the starting point for the investigation of many issues involving employee pay.
- *Journal entries.* Journal entries are created to record a payroll based on the information in the register.
- *Payments.* If manual check payments are being created, the source document for these payments is the register.
- *Reports.* The information on almost any government or management report related to payroll is drawn from the register.

The format of the payroll register is built into the payroll software and so will vary somewhat by payroll system. If payroll processing is outsourced, the supplier will issue its own version of the payroll register as part of its basic service package. The following exhibit contains a typical payroll register format, with overtime and state and local taxes removed in order to compress the presentation.

Sample Payroll Register

Empl. Nbr.	Employee Name	Hours Worked	Rate/ Hour	Gross Wages	Taxes	Other Deductions	Check Nbr.	Net Pay
100	Johnson, Mark	40	18.12	724.80	55.45	28.00	5403	641.35
105	Olds, Gary	27	36.25	978.75	74.87	42.25	5404	861.63
107	Zeff, Morton	40	24.00	960.00	73.44	83.00	5405	803.56
111	Quill, Davis	40	15.00	600.00	45.90	10.10	5406	544.00
116	Pincus, Joseph	35	27.75	971.25	74.30	37.50	5407	859.45

A comprehensive payroll register will include the following fields:

- *Employee number*. This is a unique identification number for each employee. The preceding report is sorted by employee number.
- *Department number*. In larger organizations, it is an excellent idea to assign a department number to each employee, so that departmental wage information can be more easily aggregated and charged to the correct department.
- *Employee name*. This is usually presented in last name, first name format. The payroll register may be sorted by employee last name, rather than by employee number.
- *Salary/wage indicator*. There may be a flag in the report that indicates whether an employee is paid a fixed salary or an hourly wage.
- *Marriage code*. This is a flag in the report, indicating whether a person is classified as married or single. Marriage status impacts the amount of income taxes withheld.
- *Allowances number*. This is the number of allowances that a person has claimed on his or her Form W-4. The number of allowances is used to calculate the amount of income taxes withheld.
- *Total hours worked*. This is the combined total of regular and overtime hours worked, and should tie back to the hours listed in the timekeeping system.
- *Regular hours worked*. This states the total amount of regular hours worked during the payroll period, and is used to calculate gross pay.
- *Overtime hours worked*. This states the total amount of overtime hours worked during the payroll period, and is used to calculate gross pay.
- *Regular hours pay rate*. This rate is multiplied by regular hours worked to arrive at part of the gross pay figure.
- *Overtime hours pay rate*. This rate is multiplied by overtime hours worked to arrive at part of the gross pay figure.
- *Gross pay*. This combines wages paid from regular and overtime hours worked and is the grand total from which deductions are then made to arrive at net pay.
- *Federal income tax withholding*. This is the federal-level income taxes withheld from employee gross wages.
- *Social security tax*. This is the employee-paid portion of the social security tax. It does not include the employer-matched amount of the tax.
- *Medicare tax*. This is the employee-paid portion of the Medicare tax. It does not include the employer-matched amount of the tax.
- *State income tax withholding*. This is the state income taxes withheld from employee wages.
- *Other deductions*. This can include a broad array of deductions, such as for medical insurance, life insurance, pension plan contributions, and so forth. Identify each type of deduction on the report with a unique code. Thus, deductions for medical insurance could be identified with the MED code, while deductions for life insurance could be identified with the LIFE code.

- *Net pay*. This is the amount of cash paid to each employee after all deductions have been made from gross pay.
- *Check number*. This is the unique identifying number listed on each paycheck issued, and is used by the bank to identify cleared checks (among other uses).
- *Payment type*. This is a code that states whether payment was made with a check, direct deposit, or debit card.

> **Tip:** Do *not* include employee social security numbers in the payroll register, since these reports may end up in the wrong hands, leading to inappropriate dissemination of the social security numbers.

The payroll register should also provide a variety of summary-level information that can be used to record wage and tax information in the general ledger. It should aggregate gross wages, each type of deduction, state-level taxes withheld by individual state, and the total amount of cash paid. If reports are generated at the department level, the payroll register should provide this information not only in total for the entire organization, but also at the department level.

If an employer were to create a payroll register that contained all of the items in the preceding list, it would be an exceptionally crowded report. However, packing information into the payroll register makes it a great source document when researching payroll issues. Consequently, it is better to create a near-comprehensive payroll register format, rather than one containing the minimum amount of information.

Form W-2

Following the end of every calendar year, and no later than January 31, an employer must issue the multi-part Form W-2, on which it itemizes the wages it paid to each employee during the year, as well as the taxes that it withheld from employee pay. It issues this form to anyone who was paid wages by the employer at any time during the year, even if they no longer work for the organization. This information forms the basis for the personal income tax returns completed by all employees for the federal government and the state government in which they reside. An example of the Form W-2 is shown next.

Sample Form W-2

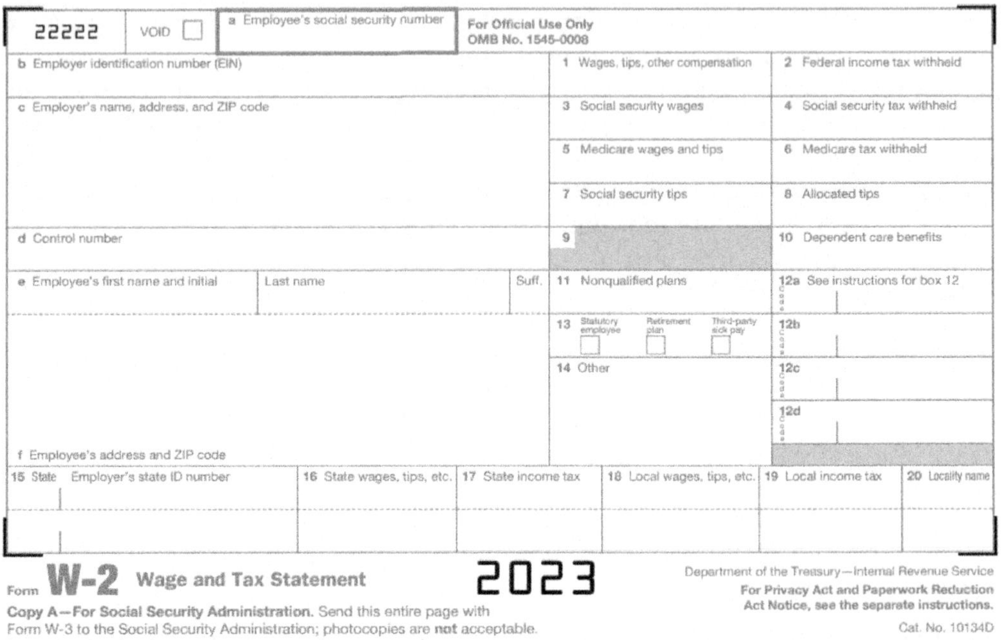
22222 VOID
a Employee's social security number
For Official Use Only
OMB No. 1545-0008
b Employer identification number (EIN)
1 Wages, tips, other compensation
2 Federal income tax withheld
c Employer's name, address, and ZIP code
3 Social security wages
4 Social security tax withheld
5 Medicare wages and tips
6 Medicare tax withheld
7 Social security tips
8 Allocated tips
d Control number
9
10 Dependent care benefits
e Employee's first name and initial
Last name
Suff.
11 Nonqualified plans
12a See instructions for box 12
13 Statutory employee Retirement plan Third-party sick pay
12b
14 Other
12c
12d
f Employee's address and ZIP code
15 State Employer's state ID number
16 State wages, tips, etc.
17 State income tax
18 Local wages, tips, etc.
19 Local income tax
20 Locality name
Form W-2 Wage and Tax Statement
2023
Department of the Treasury—Internal Revenue Service
For Privacy Act and Paperwork Reduction Act Notice, see the separate instructions.
Copy A—For Social Security Administration. Send this entire page with Form W-3 to the Social Security Administration; photocopies are not acceptable.
Cat. No. 10134D

The Form W-2 contains a large number of fields, but many of them are not needed to report the compensation and tax information for a typical employee; many of the fields are only required to report unusual compensation arrangements. The payroll system prints these forms automatically after the end of the calendar year. If the organization is outsourcing payroll, the supplier will issue them on its behalf. Thus, the Form W-2 is usually not an especially difficult document to produce.

Payroll Journal Entries

The payroll system may be entirely separate from an employer's primary system of recording accounting transactions. This is especially true if it has outsourced the payroll function entirely. Thus, the accountant will need a process for transferring the information accumulated in the payroll system to the accounting system. The chief tool for doing so is the journal entry. This section describes where payroll information is stored in an accounting system and the journal entries used to record payroll information in that system.

Note: The accounting system does not contain information about employee-specific wage and benefit information. The payroll system must be accessed to obtain this information.

Types of Payroll Journal Entries

There are several types of journal entries that involve the recordation of compensation. The primary entry is for the initial recordation of a payroll. This entry records the gross wages earned by employees, as well as all withholdings from their pay and any additional taxes owed by the employer. There may also be an accrued wages entry that is recorded at the end of each accounting period, which is intended to record the amount of wages owed to employees but not yet paid. These types of compensation are based on different source documents and require separate calculations and journal entries. There are also a number of other payroll-related journal entries that a payroll staff must deal with on a regular basis. They include:

- Manual paychecks
- Employee advances
- Accrued vacation pay
- Tax deposits

All of these journal entries are described in the following sub-sections.

Primary Payroll Journal Entry

The primary journal entry for payroll is the summary-level entry that is compiled from the payroll register. This entry usually includes debits for wages and the employer's portion of payroll taxes. There will also be credits to a number of other accounts, each one detailing the liability for payroll taxes that have not been paid, as well as for the amount of cash already paid to employees for their net pay. The basic entry (assuming no further breakdown of debits by individual department) is:

	Debit	Credit
Wages expense [expense account]	xxx	
Payroll taxes expense [expense account]	xxx	
Cash [asset account]		xxx
Federal withholding taxes payable [liability account]		xxx
Social security taxes payable [liability account]		xxx
Medicare taxes payable [liability account]		xxx
Federal unemployment taxes payable [liability account]		xxx
State unemployment taxes payable [liability account]		xxx
Garnishments payable [liability account]		xxx

Note: The reason for the payroll taxes expense line item in this journal entry is that the employer incurs the cost of matching the social security and Medicare amounts paid by employees and directly incurs the cost of unemployment insurance. The employee-paid portions of the social security and Medicare taxes are not recorded as expenses; instead, they are liabilities for which the employer has an obligation to remit cash to the taxing government entity.

A key point with this journal entry is that the wages expense contains employee gross pay, while the amount actually paid to employees through the cash account is their net pay. The difference between the two figures (which can be substantial) is the amount of deductions from their pay, such as payroll taxes and withholdings to pay for benefits.

There may be a number of additional employee deductions to include in this journal entry. For example, there may be deductions for 401(k) pension plans, health insurance, life insurance, vision insurance, and for the repayment of advances.

When the employer later pays the withheld taxes and its portion of payroll taxes, use the following entry to reduce the balance in the cash account and eliminate the balances in the liability accounts:

	Debit	Credit
Federal withholding taxes payable [liability account]	xxx	
Social security taxes payable [liability account]	xxx	
Medicare taxes payable [liability account]	xxx	
Federal unemployment taxes payable [liability account]	xxx	
State withholding taxes payable [liability account]	xxx	
State unemployment taxes payable [liability account]	xxx	
Garnishments payable [liability account]	xxx	
Cash [asset account]		xxx

Thus, when an employer initially deducts taxes and other items from an employee's pay, the employer incurs a liability to pay the taxes to a third party. This liability only disappears from the entity's accounting records when it pays the related funds to the party to which they are owed.

Accrued Wages

It is quite common to have some amount of unpaid wages at the end of an accounting period, so accrue this expense (if it is material). The accrual entry, as shown next, is simpler than the comprehensive payroll entry already shown, because all payroll taxes are typically clumped into a single expense account and offsetting liability account. After recording this entry, reverse it at the beginning of the following accounting period, and then record the actual payroll expense whenever it occurs.

	Debit	Credit
Wages expense [expense account]	xxx	
Accrued salaries and wages [liability account]		xxx
Accrued payroll taxes [liability account]		xxx

The information for the wage accrual entry is most easily derived from a spreadsheet that itemizes all employees to whom the calculation applies, the amount of unpaid time, and the standard pay rate for each person. It is not necessary to also calculate the cost of overtime hours earned during an accrual period if the amount of such hours is relatively small. A sample spreadsheet for calculating accrued wages appears in the following exhibit.

Sample Accrued Wages Spreadsheet

Hourly Employees	Unpaid Days	Hourly Rate	Pay Accrual
Anthem, Jill	4	$20.00	$640
Bingley, Adam	4	18.25	584
Chesterton, Elvis	4	17.50	560
Davis, Ethel	4	23.00	736
Ellings, Humphrey	4	21.50	688
Fogarty, Miriam	4	16.00	512
		Total	$3,720

Manual Paycheck Entry

It is all too common to create a manual paycheck, either because an employee was short-paid in a prior payroll or because the employer is laying off or firing an employee and so is obligated to pay that person before the next regularly scheduled payroll. This check may be paid through the corporate accounts payable bank account, rather than its payroll account, so it may be necessary to make this entry through the accounts payable system.

EXAMPLE

Aspen Grove Elder Care lays off Mr. Jones. Aspen Grove owes Mr. Jones $5,000 of wages at the time of the layoff. The accountant calculates that Aspen Grove must withhold $382.50 from Mr. Jones' pay to cover the employee-paid portions of social security and Medicare taxes. Mr. Jones has claimed a large enough number of withholding allowances that there is no income tax withholding. Thus, the employer pays Mr. Jones $4,617.50. The journal entry it uses is:

	Debit	Credit
Wage expense	5,000.00	
Social security taxes payable		310.00
Medicare taxes payable		72.50
Cash		4,617.50

At the next regularly-scheduled payroll, the accountant records this payment as a notation in the payroll system, so that it will properly compile the correct amount of wages for Mr. Jones for his year-end Form W-2. In addition, the payroll system calculates that Aspen Grove must pay a matching amount of social security and Medicare taxes (though no unemployment taxes, since Mr. Jones already exceeded his wage cap for these taxes). Accordingly, an additional liability of $382.50 is recorded in the payroll journal entry for that payroll. Aspen Grove pays these matching amounts as part of its normal tax remittances associated with the payroll.

Employee Advances

When an employee asks for an advance, this is recorded as a current asset in the employer's balance sheet. There may not be a separate account in which to store advances, especially if employee advances are infrequent; possible asset accounts that can be used are:

- Employee advances (for high-volume situations)
- Other assets (probably sufficient for smaller organizations that record few assets other than trade receivables, inventory, and fixed assets)
- Other receivables (useful if the accountant is tracking a number of different types of assets, and wants to segregate receivables in one account)

EXAMPLE

Mnemosyne Memory Care issues a $1,000 advance to employee Wes Smith. Mnemosyne issues advances regularly, and so uses a separate account in which to record advances. It records the transaction as:

	Debit	Credit
Other assets	1,000	
Cash		1,000

One week later, Mr. Smith pays back half the amount of the advance, which is recorded with this entry:

	Debit	Credit
Cash	500	
Other assets		500

No matter what method is later used to repay the employer – a check from the employee, or payroll deductions – the entry will be a credit to whichever asset account was used, until such time as the balance in the account has been paid off.

Employee advances require vigilance by the accountant, because employees who have limited financial resources will tend to use the employer as their personal banks and so will be reluctant to pay back advances unless pressed repeatedly. Thus, it is essential to continually monitor the remaining amount of advances outstanding for every employee.

Accrued Vacation Pay

Accrued vacation pay is the amount of vacation time that an employee has earned as per an employer's employee benefit manual, but which he has not yet used. The calculation of accrued vacation pay for each employee is:

1. Calculate the amount of vacation time earned through the beginning of the accounting period. This should be a roll-forward balance from the preceding period.
2. Add the number of hours earned in the current accounting period.
3. Subtract the number of vacation hours used in the current period.
4. Multiply the ending number of accrued vacation hours by the employee's hourly wage to arrive at the correct accrual that should be on the employer's books.
5. If the amount already accrued for the employee from the preceding period is lower than the correct accrual, record the difference as an addition to the accrued liability. If the amount already accrued from the preceding period is

higher than the correct accrual, record the difference as a reduction of the accrued liability.

A sample spreadsheet appears in the following exhibit that uses the preceding steps, and which can be used to compile accrued vacation pay.

Accrued Vacation Pay Spreadsheet

Name	Vacation Roll-Forward Balance	+ New Hours Earned	- Hours Used	= Net Balance	× Hourly Pay	= Accrued Vacation $
Hilton, David	24.0	10	34.0	0.0	$25.00	$0.00
Idle, John	13.5	10	0.0	23.5	17.50	411.25
Jakes, Jill	120.0	10	80.0	50.0	23.50	1,175.00
Kilo, Steve	114.5	10	14.0	110.5	40.00	4,420.00
Linder, Alice	12.0	10	0.0	22.0	15.75	346.50
Mills, Jeffery	83.5	10	65.00	28.5	19.75	562.88
					Total	$6,915.63

It is not necessary to reverse the vacation pay accrual in each period if the election is made to instead record just incremental changes in the accrual from month to month.

EXAMPLE

There is already an existing accrued balance of 40 hours of unused vacation time for Wes Smith on the books of Mnemosyne Memory Care. In the most recent month that has just ended, Mr. Smith accrued an additional five hours of vacation time (since he is entitled to 60 hours of accrued vacation time per year, and 60 ÷ 12 = five hours per month). He also used three hours of vacation time during the month. This means that, as of the end of the month, Mnemosyne should have accrued a total of 42 hours of vacation time for him (calculated as 40 hours existing balance + 5 hours additional accrual – 3 hours used).

Mr. Smith is paid $30 per hour, so his total vacation accrual should be $1,260 (42 hours × $30/hour), so Mnemosyne accrues an additional $60 of vacation liability.

What if an employee receives a pay raise? Then it will be necessary to increase the amount of his entire vacation accrual by the incremental amount of the pay raise. This is because, if the employee were to leave the employer and be paid all of his unused vacation pay, he would be paid at his most recent rate of pay.

Tax Deposits

When an employer withholds taxes from employee pay, it must deposit these funds with the government at stated intervals. The journal entry for doing so is a debit to the tax liability account being paid and a credit to the cash account, which reduces the

cash balance. For example, if an employer were to pay a state government for unemployment taxes, the entry would be:

	Debit	Credit
State unemployment taxes payable [liability account]	xxx	
Cash [asset account]		xxx

Summary

The payroll function is one of the most crucial accounting operations, since employees are depending on the accountant to correctly determine gross pay, deductions, and net pay – every time. If a health care entity has a continuing problem with payments to employees, this can trigger significant employee dissatisfaction. There are several ways to mitigate payroll errors, which include the following:

- Upgrade the timekeeping system from timecards to an electronic or Internet-based time clock, so that employee hours worked are automatically recorded in the payroll software.
- Outsource payroll processing to a third party. By doing so, a specialist is now being involved in payroll calculations, tax remittances, and payments to employees. This does not completely eliminate errors, since the accountant must still input information into the third party's system – but errors should decline.
- Use formal procedures as part of every payroll processing activity. Doing so reduces the risk that steps will be missed or completed incorrectly. This is especially important when the accountant is new to payroll processing.

Chapter 13
Split-Interest Agreements

Introduction

A donor may decide to contribute funds to a not-for-profit health care entity under an arrangement where both the donor and the not-for-profit retain an interest in the underlying assets and liabilities. These arrangements, known as split-interest agreements, come in many shapes and sizes. Unfortunately, the accounting varies by type of agreement, making this one of the more time-consuming transactions for an accountant to deal with. In this chapter, we discuss the nature and types of split-interest agreements, as well as how they are measured and accounted for.

Split-Interest Agreements

A split-interest agreement is an arrangement under which a not-for-profit splits the benefits of assets with other entities. These other entities are typically *not* not-for-profits. A common example of a split-interest agreement is when a donor gives a not-for-profit the right to receive all interest income from a portfolio of investments held by a bank. Conversely, a donor might want to retain that interest to support her living expenses for the rest of her life, after which the underlying investments become the property of a designated not-for-profit.

A split-interest agreement is comprised of a *lead interest* and a *remainder interest.* The lead interest is the right to receive the benefits of assets during the term of the agreement, while the remainder interest is the right to receive any remaining benefits of the assets after the term of the agreement expires. For example, one beneficiary (the lead interest) may be paid an annuity from the donated funds for the next ten years, after which any funds remaining are paid to another beneficiary (the remainder interest).

EXAMPLE

Ms. Marcy Dawes sets aside $1,000,000 in an investment fund, and stipulates that her favorite hospital, St. Agatha, receives all interest earned on these funds for the earlier of the next ten years or her death. Once either triggering event occurs, the remaining balance in the investment fund will be given to the Advanced Diabetes Care Institute (ADCI). Under the terms of this arrangement, St. Agatha Hospital has the lead interest and ADCI has the remainder interest.

Under a split-interest agreement, funds may be given to an independent third party, such as a bank, that acts as the trustee. The trustee follows the directions of the donor in investing the funds and paying beneficiaries. Alternatively, the funds may be sent straight to a not-for-profit, which takes on the trustee role.

A split-interest agreement may allow a donor to back out of the arrangement under certain circumstances. This is called a *revocable* split-interest agreement. Or, if the donor has no right to cancel the agreement, the arrangement is called an *irrevocable* split-interest agreement.

Types of Split-Interest Agreements

The following are all examples of split-interest agreements:

- *Charitable lead annuity trust.* This is a trust in which a not-for-profit receives a fixed amount of distributions during the term of the arrangement. Once the trust terminates, remaining trust assets are paid to the donor or any stated beneficiaries of the donor.
- *Charitable lead unitrust.* This is a trust in which a not-for-profit receives a fixed percentage of the fair value of the assets in the trust during the term of the trust. Once the trust terminates, remaining trust assets are paid to the donor or any stated beneficiaries of the donor.
- *Charitable remainder annuity trust.* This arrangement is the reverse of a charitable lead annuity trust. Under this arrangement, a not-for-profit receives any assets remaining when a trust is terminated, while the donor or its beneficiaries receive a fixed amount of distributions during the term of the trust.
- *Charitable remainder unitrust.* This arrangement is the reverse of a charitable lead unitrust. Under this arrangement, a not-for-profit receives any assets remaining when a trust is terminated, while the donor or its beneficiaries receive a fixed percentage of the fair value of the assets in the trust during the term of the trust.
- *Charitable gift annuity.* This arrangement calls for a donor to transfer assets to a not-for-profit, after which the not-for-profit is obligated to make certain periodic payments to the donor or its beneficiaries for a period of time. The not-for-profit retains all residual assets.
- *Pooled income fund.* This is a trust arrangement under which donors contribute assets to a pooled fund and are assigned a certain number of units based on the proportion of their contribution to the total size of the pool. The donor is paid the income on these units until the person's death, after which the value of these units is assigned to a not-for-profit.
- *Net income unitrust.* This is a trust arrangement where the donor or a designated beneficiary receives distributions from the trust based on the lower of earned net income or a fixed percentage of the fair value of the assets in the trust. A not-for-profit retains all residual assets.

There are a multitude of variations on the basic split-interest types just noted. For accounting purposes, it is easiest to associate a specific agreement with one of these types, since the accounting standards assign specific accounting treatments to each one. When in doubt about the proper accounting treatment, the accountant should confer with the not-for-profit's auditors.

Accounting for Split-Interest Agreements

The accounting for a split-interest agreement varies, depending on the underlying structure of the arrangement. Here are several possible agreements and their related accounting:

- *Revocable agreement.* This is considered an intention to give, but not a finalized arrangement. When a not-for-profit receives funds under a revocable split-interest agreement, the received funds are recognized as a refundable advance, which is a liability. The advance is then recognized as contribution revenue when the agreement becomes irrevocable, or when the assets are unconditionally distributed to the not-for-profit.
- *Irrevocable agreement – assets held by not-for-profit.* If there are no conditions imposed by a donor, a not-for-profit can recognize contributed assets as contribution revenue as soon as a split-interest agreement is executed. When the arrangement is a charitable gift annuity, charitable lead trust, charitable remainder trust or similar arrangement where the transferred assets are held by the not-for-profit for the benefit of the donor or its beneficiaries, it is also necessary to recognize a liability for the payments due to these other parties. The liability is recorded at its fair value on the initial recognition date.
- *Irrevocable agreement – assets held by third party.* If there are no conditions imposed by a donor but the assets are held by an independent trustee, the not-for-profit recognizes its beneficial interest in the contributed assets as contribution revenue. This recognition relates to the not-for-profit's entitlement to either the lead interest or the remainder interest in the arrangement. Recognition can occur as soon as the not-for-profit is made aware of the existence of the arrangement. However, recognition of contribution revenue is not allowed for as long as the third party has the ability to redirect the assets or their benefits elsewhere.
- *Pooled income fund or net income unitrust.* Under these arrangements, the not-for-profit is given the remainder interest in assets. The not-for-profit recognizes assets as they are received, and recognizes its remainder interest as contribution revenue as those assets are received from the donor. The difference between the assets received and the remainder interest is recorded as deferred revenue (a liability).

EXAMPLE

Mr. Euclid establishes a charitable lead annuity trust agreement. Euclid transfers $150,000 of assets to a bank that acts as the trustee. The agreement authorizes the bank to pay Archimedes Medical Research $8,000 per year until the death of Euclid. The use of these annuity payments is unrestricted. When Euclid eventually dies, the remainder interest shall be transferred back into the estate of Euclid, and will be distributed in accordance with the provisions of his will.

Archimedes estimates that the present value of the annuity payments is $65,000 and so records contribution revenue of $65,000 and a receivable in the same amount. Each year, when Archimedes receives an $8,000 payment, the entry is an increase in cash and an $8,000 reduction of

the receivable. In each year, Archimedes also amortizes the discount on the present value calculation, which increases the value of the split-interest agreement.

EXAMPLE

Newton Hospital receives $200,000 from a donor under a charitable remainder annuity trust agreement. Newton is the designated trustee, as well as the remainder beneficiary. Newton is required to invest the funds and pay a $12,000 annuity back to the donor for the remainder of her life, after which Newton is entitled to all remaining assets.

Newton accounts for this transaction by initially recognizing the contribution portion of the $250,000 as contribution revenue. The amount of revenue is the $250,000 fair value of the trust assets, less the fair value of the estimated annuity payments (which is calculated by an actuary as $172,000). Thus, Newton recognizes $78,000 of contribution revenue, which is classified as a net asset with donor restrictions. Once the donor dies, the annuity restriction is lifted and the net assets are then reclassified as net assets without donor restrictions.

Initial Measurement

The initial measurement of assets received under a revocable split-interest agreement is to do so at the fair value of the assets. The accounting for assets received under an irrevocable agreement has more alternatives, which are as follows:

- *If the assets are held by the not-for-profit.* If the assets are under the control of the not-for-profit or it acts as trustee, assets are initially recognized at their fair value. In addition:
    - If the assets are being held for the benefit of a third party, the fair value of the liability may be measured at the fair value of the future payments to be made to that party.
    - Under a lead interest arrangement, the not-for-profit measures the asset fair value based on the present value of future distributions to be received as the beneficiary.
    - Under a remainder interest arrangement, the not-for-profit measures the asset fair value based on the difference between the fair value of the contributed assets and the fair value of the payments to be made to the beneficiary of the lead interest.
    - Under a pooled income fund or net income unitrust arrangement, the not-for-profit measures assets at their fair value. Fair value can be derived from present value techniques; if so, calculate present value based on the estimated time period until the death of the donor.
- *If assets are held by a third party.* If a not-for-profit is the unconditional beneficiary of a split-interest agreement that is held by a third party, the not-for-profit measures its interest in the assets at their fair value.

Ongoing Measurement

The subsequent measurement of split-interest agreements must be at their fair value if the funds are held by independent trustees. If a split-interest agreement is irrevocable and the assets are held by the not-for-profit, their subsequent measurement is the same as outlined for investments in the Investments chapter. In addition, if assets are held under any split-interest agreement other than a pooled income fund or a net income unitrust, report the following information in the financial statements of the not-for-profit:

- Any income earned on the assets
- Gains and losses on the assets
- Distributions made to other beneficiaries, as per the terms of the agreement

When a not-for-profit holds assets in trust for other beneficiaries, ongoing remeasurement of the liability includes any revisions of expectations regarding future payments to beneficiaries under various actuarial assumptions, as well as the amortization of any present value discount associated with the original contribution (which gradually increases the amount of the liability).

If assets are held by a not-for-profit under a pooled income fund or a net income unitrust, any periodic income associated with these assets is recognized as a change in the liability owed to the beneficiary. Any amortization of the discount associated with future interest is to be recognized as a reduction in the deferred revenue account, as well as a change in the value of the split-interest agreement.

If assets are instead held by a third party under a split-interest agreement and the not-for-profit has an unconditional right to receive funds as a beneficiary, the not-for-profit must measure its beneficial interest in the assets at their fair value. Any change in this fair value is to be recognized in the statement of activities. The fair value valuation method used shall be the same one used to derive the initial value of the assets. Any distribution to the not-for-profit from the trust is to be accounted for as a reduction in the remaining balance of the beneficial interest.

If the assets held by a not-for-profit are revocable under a split-interest agreement, the not-for-profit shall recognize their value in accordance with the guidance noted in the Investments chapter for the subsequent measurement of invested assets.

Termination

When a split-interest agreement is closed out, the asset and liability accounts linked to the agreement are also closed. If there are any residual balances in these accounts at the closing date, they are recognized as changes in the value of the agreement.

Classification of Net Assets

Under GAAP, there are rules for how to classify net assets under split-interest agreements, with different specifications for the initial recognition of net assets, their subsequent measurement, and net asset derecognition.

When net assets are initial recognized under a split-interest agreement, the basic rule is to do so as an increase in net assets with donor restrictions. Or, if a donor gives the not-for-profit an immediate right of use without restrictions, this is classified as an increase in net assets without donor restrictions.

Another initial recognition concept is when assets are received under a charitable gift annuity. Under this arrangement, the not-for-profit makes certain payments back to the donor or its beneficiaries for a period of time, after which the not-for-profit retains all residual assets. The contribution portion of this agreement is treated as unrestricted, if the donor does not restrict use of the assets, and there is no stipulation to invest the assets until the death of the income beneficiary. If these criteria are *not* met, the contribution is classified as a net asset with donor restrictions.

Following the initial recognition of net assets, amounts may be reclassified into net assets without donor restrictions when the underlying restrictions expire.

If assets are made available to a not-for-profit once a split-interest agreement expires, these amounts are then reclassified as net assets without donor restrictions.

Summary

At some point, a not-for-profit health care entity is likely to encounter a donor who proposes a split-interest agreement. The asset amounts underlying these agreements can be quite large, so most not-for-profits will eagerly agree to such an arrangement. However, it makes sense to review the terms of each proposed split-interest agreement to see how the related accounting must be configured, and propose changes to make the accounting more efficient. Where possible, propose a standardized split-interest agreement format to donors, so that the accounting staff can apply a standardized accounting procedure to each one.

Chapter 14
Affiliated Organizations

Introduction

Not-for-profit health care organizations may be related to each other in several ways. For example, their economic interests may be closely aligned, or one entity may exercise a certain degree of control over another organization. Also, since there are a variety of legal forms that a not-for-profit may take, it is possible to have an ownership interest in some not-for-profits. Depending on the type of relationship, it may be necessary to consolidate the financial statements of two or more entities, or at least require additional disclosure of the extent of the relationship. In this chapter, we explore the types of relationships between not-for-profit organizations, and the related accounting rules.

Affiliated Organizations

A not-for-profit may have a number of relationships with other entities. Here are several examples:

- A fund raising organization conducts fundraising events and sends the proceeds to a local hospital.
- A senior citizens support not-for-profit creates a separate legal entity for each of its programs, which deal with providing financial support to the residents of nursing homes.
- A not-for-profit creates a for-profit subsidiary to market a variety of merchandise that bears the logo of the organization.

Under GAAP rules, there is considered to be a relationship with another not-for-profit in any of the following four situations:

- *Ownership.* There is a controlling financial interest caused by either direct or indirect ownership of a majority voting interest or sole corporate membership in the other not-for-profit.
- *Control and economic interest.* There is control of a related not-for-profit via a majority voting interest in the board of directors of the other not-for-profit by some means other than ownership or sole corporate membership; there is also an economic interest in the other entity. An *economic interest* exists in either of the following situations:
    - One not-for-profit has significant resources that must be used for the purposes of the other entity. This use can either be directly for the

other entity, or indirectly by generating income or providing services to the other entity.
    - One not-for-profit is responsible for the liabilities of the other organization.

- *Economic interest and other means of control.* There is an economic interest in the other entity, combined with some other means of control than was described in the last two bullet points.
- *Economic interest or control.* There is an economic interest in or control of the other entity, but not both.

The reporting for interrelated organizations varies, depending upon which of the preceding four conditions exists. The types of reporting are noted in the following exhibit.

Types of Accounting for Affiliated Organizations

Type of Relationship	Reporting Required
Ownership	Consolidate the financial statements of the entities. However, if the majority owner or sole corporate member does not have control, do not consolidate. This can happen when supermajority voting is required to such an extent that control does not exist, or when the other entity is in bankruptcy.
Control and economic interest	Consolidate the financial statements of the entities, unless the holder of the majority voting interest does not have control. A majority voting interest exists when a not-for-profit has the direct or indirect ability to appoint a sufficient number of individuals to constitute a majority of the votes of a board of directors.
Economic interest and other means of control	Consolidation is permitted, but not required. Other means of control include an affiliation agreement. Consolidation is encouraged if doing so would be meaningful.
Economic interest or control	Do not consolidate the financial statements of the entities.

When the required reporting refers to a consolidation, this means that the financial statements of the entities are merged, net of any transactions there may be between the organizations. This usually means that all inter-entity receivables and payables are eliminated from the consolidated financial statements, since an organization cannot be liable to itself for any receivables. Also, if one of the consolidating entities contributes funds to the other entity, the inter-entity contribution revenue and expense must be eliminated in the consolidated financial statements; otherwise, the consolidated statement of activities would be counting revenues that the entity has paid to itself.

Note: Consolidated financial statements should report all asset and net asset restrictions that were reported in the financial statements of the individual entities. Thus, if a subsidiary reports $25,000 of net assets with donor restrictions, this same designation should carry forward into the statement of financial position of the consolidated entity.

Tip: A significant concern for a not-for-profit is whether the financial statements of another entity with which its financial statements are being consolidated have been audited. If not, the not-for-profit's auditors will be unable to render an opinion on the consolidated financial statements, which could be a major issue if those statements are needed for fundraising or grant reporting purposes.

A not-for-profit that is a general partner of a for-profit limited partnership is presumed to control a for-profit limited partnership, irrespective of the extent of that ownership interest, unless the presumption of control is overcome. As such, the not-for-profit should consolidate its results with those of the limited partnership. The presumption of control can be overcome if the limited partners either have substantive kick-out rights or substantive participating rights. The kick-out rights must be exercisable via a simple majority vote of the limited partners.

Special Purpose Entities

A not-for-profit may engage in leasing transactions with a special purpose entity (SPE). An SPE is a legal entity created to fulfill a specific objective, which is usually to separate an organization from a certain type of risk. Thus, a not-for-profit might create an SPE to own a large asset, such as a building, which the not-for-profit then leases from the SPE. When a not-for-profit is engaged in leasing transactions with an SPE, it may be necessary to consolidate the financial statements of the two entities. If all of the following conditions exist, consolidation is mandated:

- *Asset usage.* Substantially all SPE assets are leased to a single entity.
- *Risks.* Expected residual risks and rewards associated with the leased assets, as well as the obligation imposed by the underlying SPE debt reside with the lessee through the lease agreements, residual value guarantees, a guarantee of the SPE's debt, or an option to grant the lessee the right to either purchase leased assets at non-fair value prices or receive sale proceeds over a certain amount.
- *Investment.* The owner of record of the SPE has not made a substantive equity investment that has been at risk during the lease term. If this owner is not an independent third party, the condition is considered to have been met.

The preceding conditions are intended to prove that the not-for-profit and the SPE are essentially the same entity for consolidation purposes. If these conditions are met, consolidation shall aggregate the assets, liabilities, results of operations, and cash flows of the SPE into those of the not-for-profit.

Noncontrolling Interests

When combining the financial statements of a subsidiary with its parent organization, report noncontrolling interests (also known as a minority interest) in the net assets section of the statement of financial position of the consolidated entity. A noncontrolling interest is that portion of net assets in a subsidiary that cannot be attributed to the parent entity. This interest is to be clearly identified and described sufficiently to distinguish it from the ownership interest of the parent entity. An example of the presentation of a noncontrolling interest appears in the following statement of financial position.

St. Flora Hospital
Statement of Financial Position
As of April 30, 20X1

ASSETS		LIABILITIES AND NET ASSETS	
Cash and cash equivalents	$25,000	Accounts payable	$12,000
Accounts and pledges receivable	63,000	Accrued expenses	5,000
Prepaid expenses	5,000	Grants payable	14,000
Investments	10,000	Deferred revenue	8,000
Fixed assets	180,000	Debt	10,000
		Net assets:	
		Net assets without donor restrictions	214,000
		Noncontrolling interests in Subsidiary ABC	20,000
Total assets	$283,000	Total liabilities and net assets	$283,000

Related Parties

A not-for-profit may do business with a variety of parties with which it has a close association, where these parties can exercise control over or at least significantly influence the decisions made by the not-for-profit. These individuals or organizations are known as related parties. Examples of related parties are:

- Affiliates
- Other subsidiaries under common control
- Owners of the business, its managers, and their families
- The parent entity
- Trusts for the benefit of employees

There are many types of transactions that can be conducted between related parties, such as sales, asset transfers, leases, lending arrangements, guarantees, allocations of common costs, and the filing of consolidated tax returns. For example:

- The executive director personally owns office space, and leases it to the entity at a below-market lease rate.

- An affiliate raises money on behalf of the not-for-profit.
- An affiliate shares many of the same members of the not-for-profit's board of directors.

The reimbursement of expenses is not considered a related party transaction. For example, members of the board of directors are routinely reimbursed for the cost of their travel to board meetings. This is not a related party event. Similarly, the payment of compensation to an employee of a not-for-profit is not considered a related party transaction.

Summary

The main point of this chapter was to define those circumstances under which organizations are so closely affiliated that their financial statements should be consolidated. There may be situations in which a not-for-profit has a more modest financial interest in another entity, while exercising some level of control over it. If so, the appropriate accounting may involve use of the equity method, which is described in the Investments chapter.

The concept of related parties is not a minor one, for it is extremely common in the not-for-profit health care arena. It is quite likely that there will be several related parties that interact with a not-for-profit on a regular basis. If so, the accountant must identify these situations and incorporate them into the financial statements.

Chapter 15
Special Accounting Topics

Introduction

There are a number of lesser accounting issues that are specific to health care entities. These topics were too small to warrant treatment within a separate chapter, so they are included here in alphabetical order, with presentation and disclosure issues noted at the end.

Advertising Expenses

A continuing care retirement community may incur significant advertising costs to acquire initial continuing-care contracts. The costs incurred for advertising can be aggregated into two areas, which are the production of advertisements and their dissemination. The accounting for advertising costs is as follows:

- *Production costs*. Charge advertising production costs to expense as incurred or when the related advertising first takes place.
- *Dissemination costs*. Charge advertising costs to expense as used. For example, charge the cost to air a television advertisement to expense as the airtime is used.

This treatment is based on the belief that the beneficial effects of advertising are short-lived, and because it is difficult to determine the number of periods over which the resulting benefits can be measured.

Agency Funds

A health care entity may engage in a number of agency relationships. For example, it may issue billings on behalf of physicians, collect the related receivables, and disburse receipts to the physicians. When collecting assets under these arrangements, the health care entity incurs a matching liability to eventually disburse the assets to the rightful owners. A not-for-profit, business-oriented entity should classify agency funds as unrestricted assets.

Nonreciprocal Transfers

A health care entity may transfer the ownership of its assets to another health care entity without any expectation of payment. This is known as a nonreciprocal transfer. These transfers are classified as contributions.

Prepaid Expenses

If an organization elects to defer the recognition of prepaid costs, it must amortize them over the period benefited. An example of a prepaid cost is the amount paid to physicians for their future services.

Prepaid Health Services

A health care entity may provide prepaid health services, where it agrees to provide health care in exchange for a fixed periodic premium. These entities may reduce their risk under these arrangements by purchasing stop-loss insurance coverage, where the insurer agrees to indemnify a health care provider for costs incurred by the provider's members. In these situations, the health care entity should record both unpaid member premiums and any amounts recoverable from the insurer, along with offsetting reserves for doubtful accounts.

Related Fundraising Entities

A health care foundation may collect funds and then contribute them to an affiliated health care entity. If so, the receiving party reports a contribution from the health care foundation. This treatment is applicable when the foundation can determine to whom the assets will be distributed.

Sale and Leaseback Transactions

Health care entities sometimes enter into leasing arrangements with real estate developers, where the developers construct special-purpose buildings near hospital campuses for their use, such as medical office buildings. If the leasing entity agrees to lease space in these buildings and bears substantially all of the construction period risk, then it is considered to be the owner of the building during the construction period. During this time, the health care entity recognizes a construction in progress asset, as well as a related financing obligation. Once construction is complete and the lease begins, the transaction is essentially a sale and leaseback arrangement. This arrangement occurs when the seller transfers an asset to the buyer, and then leases the asset from the buyer.

General Presentation Issues

The following bullet points note specific items pertaining to the presentation of information in the financial statements for all types of health care entities:

- *Receivables.* Receivables are to be presented net of an allowance for doubtful accounts. Any amounts due from third-party payors for retroactive adjustments (such as appeals or final settlements) are to be reported separately.

- *Refunded advance fees*. When a continuing care retirement community refunds advance fees, these payments are classified in the statement of cash flows as financing activities.
- *Stop-loss insurance premiums*. Premiums paid on stop-loss insurance should be reported within the health care costs section of the financial statements. If there are any insurance recoveries from stop-loss insurance, report them as reductions of related health care costs.
- *Trust funds*. A health care entity may have a trust fund that is to be used to settle malpractice claims. If so, this fund is to be included in the financial statements of the entity. That portion of the fund expected to be liquidated to pay current claims should be classified as a current asset, with the remainder classified as a noncurrent liability. Further, all revenues and administrative expenses incurred by the trust fund should be included in the statement of operations.

Presentation Issues Specific to Not-for-Profit, Business-Oriented Entities

The following bullet points note several items pertaining to the presentation of information in the financial statements that are unique to a not-for-profit, business-oriented entity:

- *Expiration of restrictions*. When a donor has imposed a restriction on a donation, it is recognized in the period in which the restriction expires. However, if the restriction has been placed on long-lived assets, the expiration is recognized when the assets are placed in service, rather than as the assets are depreciated.
- *Interfund items*. Interfund receivables and payables must be eliminated from the financial statements, though they may exist in an organization's internal records.
- *Return on unrestricted investments*. When investments are not restricted, include realized gains and losses, dividends, interest, and similar investment income in the performance indicator. Unrealized gains and losses on debt securities are not included in the performance indicator.
- *Unrestricted net assets*. The entity can include within its unrestricted net assets classification those assets with contractually limited uses. For example, the proceeds of a debt issuance that have been deposited with a trustee and which have a defined use in the accompanying indenture agreement can be classified as unrestricted net assets. Another example is assets limited for use under agreements with outside parties that are not donors, such as assets set aside under a debt agreement.

Disclosures

The following notes should be presented for all types of health care entities:

- *Adjustments and settlements receivable.* Explain the estimated amounts receivable for contractual adjustments and third-party settlements.
- *Concentration of credit risk.* Note the primary geographic sources of patients. This is more of a reporting issue for a standalone hospital, where all of its patients come from the local area. It is less of a reporting issue for a large multi-hospital system that covers many geographical regions.
- *Uncollectible revenue assessment.* Describe the policy used to assess the timing and amount of patient service revenue that cannot be collected, stating any assessment differences by major payor source of revenue.
- *Changes in receivables allowance.* Note significant changes in the allowance for doubtful accounts, pointing out such matters as changes in estimates and assumptions, the amount of third-party payor write-offs, and the amount of patient self-pay write-offs.
- *Medical malpractice coverage.* Disclose the entity's program of medical malpractice insurance coverage.
- *Charity care.* Disclose management's policy for the provision of charity care, as well as the level of such care provided. The level of care provided includes both the direct and indirect costs of charity care. If charity care costs are estimated, then disclose the estimation method. Also note the amount of funds received to offset the cost of charity care.
- *Retrospective premium ratings.* When a health care entity is insured under a retrospectively rated policy, disclose the fact that it is insured under such a policy, and note that premiums are accrued based on the ultimate experience cost.
- *Captive insurance company.* When medical malpractice claims are being insured by a captive insurance company, disclose the existence of the captive provider, and that premiums are accrued based on the captive entity's to-date experience. When a captive insurance entity is used for any purpose, disclose that the health care provider is insured by the entity, its ownership percentage in the entity, and the method of accounting for its investment in the captive entity.
- *Stop-loss insurance.* Disclose the nature and amounts of any significant stop-loss insurance contracts.

The notes that accompany the financial statements of a not-for-profit, business-oriented entity should include the following:

- *Performance indicator.* Describe the nature of the performance indicator that measures the results of operations.
- *Intermediate measure of operations.* If an intermediate measure of operations is reported, describe its nature or the items that have been excluded from the measurement of operations.

- *Tax-exempt status.* When the entity is tax-exempt, disclose this status.

The notes that accompany the financial statements of a continuing care retirement community should include the following:

- *Overview.* Describe the retirement community, as well as the nature of its continuing care contracts.
- *Future service liability.* State the amount of the entity's future service liability related to the provision of future services and facilities, if it has not been separately disclosed in the balance sheet. Also state the interest rate used to discount that liability to its present value.
- *Escrow.* Describe the statutory escrow, or whatever similar requirements apply to the entity.
- *Refund policy.* State the entity's refund policy, as well as the amount of the refund obligation under existing contracts with residents.
- *Trust fund.* If there is a trust fund, disclose its existence and whether it is irrevocable.

Summary

The largest part of the special accounting topics described in this chapter covered the presentation and disclosure of information in the financial statements. We have included a few of these topics in other chapters, but since most of them did not relate to the areas of interest in the various chapters, they have mostly been accumulated here. The discussion of presentation and disclosure items is specific to health care entities. When preparing financial statements, the accountant will need to research the more general disclosures that are frequently included in financial statements, covering such topics as accounting policies, investments, and revenue recognition.

Chapter 16
Management Accounting in Health Care

Introduction

Health care entities are highly complex organizations, which can make it difficult to obtain usable accounting information about them. In this chapter, we discuss a management accounting option that is used to create management reports that highlight how a health care business can be run in a more cost-effective and profitable manner.

Full Costing Analysis

Full costing is used to determine the complete and entire cost of something. In this case, the *something* is the cost of the products being sold to patients. In order to arrive at this figure in a health care environment, we will need to take the following six steps:

1. Define cost objects
2. Determine cost centers
3. Identify the nature of applicable costs
4. Identify allocation bases
5. Select an allocation methodology
6. Link identified costs to cost objects

We will work through each of these activities in the following sub-sections.

Step 1. Define Cost Objects

A *cost object* is an item for which costs are compiled. For example, a cost object might be a laboratory test, which spans the blood draw, cost of the test, posting of the results, and the time spent going over the results with the patient. Or, at a more expansive level, a cost object might be an episode of illness, which would cover the entire time spent in a hospital, starting with the cost of the admission process and running through to the point of discharge, as well as home care costs. In the latter example, hundreds of costs might be assigned to a cost object, spanning such activities as nursing care, laboratory tests, and even laundry services.

Step 2. Determine Cost Centers

A *cost center* is a business unit that is only responsible for the costs that it incurs. Examples are administrative activities, nursing care, housekeeping, and administration. Cost centers are commonly classified within an organization's chart of accounts as separate departments. Each cost center should collect cost information about the cost objects for which it provides services. The sum total of the costs assigned to cost objects come from these cost centers.

In a health care setting, a cost center can be sub-divided further, into a *support center* and a mission center. As the names imply, a *mission center* directly supports the mission of the organization, while a support center assists a firm's mission centers. Examples of support centers are janitorial, housekeeping, and laundry; in essence, these centers provide baseline facility-related services. Examples of mission centers are obstetrics, neurology, and cardiology; these centers provide direct medical care to patients. Since mission centers charge for their activities, they can be considered revenue centers.

EXAMPLE

Middling Hospital is a small facility that services a distinctly rural area. As such, its 70 employees can be broken into the following four cost centers: Administration, Facility (including housekeeping), Medical Services, and Testing. The costs of these cost centers are summarized in the following table:

	Cost Centers				
Costs	Administration	Facility	Medical Services	Testing	Totals
Compensation	$425,000	$850,000	$5,950,000	$1,275,000	$8,500,000
Payroll taxes	50,000	100,000	700,000	150,000	1,000,000
Benefits	25,000	50,000	350,000	75,000	500,000
Supplies	35,000	70,000	490,000	105,000	700,000
Other	115,000	230,000	1,610,000	345,000	2,300,000
Total costs	$650,000	$1,300,000	$9,100,000	$1,950,000	$13,000,000
Total labor hours	10,000	22,000	70,000	18,000	120,000
Cost per hour	$65.00	$59.09	$130.00	$108.33	$108.33

In the table, the unit of service is presumed to be hours of service, though that is not necessarily the case. For example, one test might be significantly more expensive than another, based on the cost of the equipment and supplies used.

An obvious issue in the preceding example is that the administration and facility cost centers do not directly provide services to patients. We will address this issue shortly.

With this information in hand, it is possible to derive the cost of the services provided to a patient by multiplying the units of service by their cost per unit. At this point, the derivation of unit costs is still extremely rough. We will polish the concept in the following sub-sections.

Step 3. Identify the Nature of Applicable Costs

A major refinement in a full costing analysis is determining whether the costs being incurred are direct or indirect. A *direct cost* is totally traceable to a specific cost center, while an *indirect cost* is consumed by multiple cost centers. If there are only a few cost centers in a health care facility, then it is more likely that a cost is classified as a direct cost. Conversely, if you are tracking a large number of cost centers, then it is more likely that certain costs will be associated with multiple cost centers, and so will

be classified as indirect costs. For example, if a supervisor is in charge of both the administration and housekeeping areas, her salary will be classified as indirect, since it must be spread across two cost centers. However, if these two cost centers were to be merged into a single facility cost center (as was the case in the preceding example), then her compensation would be entirely attributable to a single cost center, and so would be classified as a direct cost.

Note: It makes sense to identify all possible direct costs, for they can be applied directly to a cost center. When this is the case, there is no need for the allocation process that we discuss next.

When there is an indirect cost, you will need to allocate it between the applicable cost centers. This can be done by conducting a short cost tracking project, such as by having someone track the hours he spends working for each cost center. For example, if a supervisor earning $100,000 per year works 70% in the medical services cost center and 30% in the testing cost center, it would be reasonable to allocate his compensation, payroll taxes, and benefit costs to these cost centers in the stated proportions. These studies tend to be fairly accurate over the medium-term, and so can be relied on for allocations into the future, with occasionally recurring tracking projects over time to ensure that the allocations are still reasonable.

This type of analysis will need to be conducted for all identified indirect costs, so that they can be applied to the various cost centers in a reasonable and defensible manner.

Step 4. Identify Allocation Bases

As noted earlier, support centers do not provide any services directly to patients. Instead, they provide services to the mission centers, as well as to each other. Therefore, a proper assignment of costs will require you to find a reasonable basis for allocating all support center costs to the mission centers. An allocation base is one or more metrics for each support center that is a reasonable basis for quantifying the use of its services by other parties.

For example, the facilities cost center pays for the upkeep of an entire medical facility, which includes repairs and maintenance on the structure, utilities, depreciation on the building, and the compensation costs of all facilities employees. For this support center, a reasonable allocation base is the amount of square footage[3] used by the consuming cost center. For example, if the total costs incurred by the facilities cost center totals $1,300,000 and the facility has usable square footage of 30,000 square feet, then the annual charge to all consuming cost centers would be $43.33 for each square foot of space that they occupy. Thus, if the testing cost center occupies 5,000

---

[3] Square footage is not the only option for allocating costs. Other options are (for example) the number of visits, the number of personnel, pounds of laundry processed, and compensation dollars. Cost allocations can be based on anything that has a justifiable cause-and-effect relationship with how the resources of a support center are being used.

square feet, then it will be allocated $216,650 of the costs incurred by the facilities cost center.

The use of support center cost allocations means that some support center costs will be allocated to other support centers, such as Administration. In these cases, pick an allocation sequence, such as allocating facilities costs first, and then administration costs. By doing so, some allocated facility costs are now included in the administration support center – which are then allocated out to the various mission centers. We will show several variations on the allocation concept in Step 5.

EXAMPLE

A facilities cost center has incurred $100,000 of costs in its most recent month, which will be allocated out to consuming cost centers at a rate of $6 per square foot of occupied space. This results in $3,000 of facilities costs being allocated to the administration cost center, resulting in a total administration cost of $30,000 for the month.

The administration cost center then allocates out its costs to the mission centers using headcount as its allocation base (on the grounds that much of its costs relate to human resources). In the current month, this allocation is $320 per person (which includes the facilities cost allocated to administration). The testing cost center has 15 staff, so it is allocated $4,800 of the costs incurred by the administration cost center.

A variation on the allocation concept in the preceding example is to allocate administration costs based on dollars of compensation charged to expense within each mission center. This approach tends to burden those mission centers with higher compensation expenses. For example, if the allocation is $0.14 per dollar of compensation expense, and the receiving department has $100,000 of compensation expense, then its allocation of administration cost center charges will be $14,000.

Note: Allocations of the costs of support centers are based on the allocation base in the cost center being charged, not the allocation base in the cost center doing the charging.

Once the allocation process has been completed, all of the costs in the support centers should have been shifted into the mission centers. This means that the total costs in a mission center are comprised of the costs directly incurred by it, as well as the costs allocated to it by the support centers.

Note: A best practice relating to allocation bases is to use ones that are easy to track. The ideal allocation base is one for which the underlying data are already being tracked, so there is no need to create a new data collection system for it. However, ease of data collection must be balanced against how well the resulting allocation base reflects how costs are incurred. In many cases, a lack of available funds will dictate the type of allocation base that can be used.

Step 5. Select an Allocation Methodology

There are several ways to allocate the costs in a support center to a mission center. They are as follows:

- *Direct allocation.* The simplest allocation method is to allocate the costs of a support center only to mission centers. We referred to this option in the preceding sub-section. It is the least expensive approach in terms of accounting resources, but is also the least accurate, since it does not address any possible allocations of costs between support centers.
- *Step allocation.* This approach is used to allocate the cost of the services provided by one support center to another support center. It is more accurate than the direct allocation method, but also requires more accounting resources to complete. The essential steps in this process are as follows:
    1. The support center that provides service to the largest number of other support centers or which has the largest percentage of its costs consumed by other support centers allocates its costs to them first. It also allocates its other costs to the mission centers.
    2. The support center that provides service to the next-largest number of other support centers or which has the second-largest percentage of its costs consumed by other support centers allocates its costs. Again, its other costs are allocated to the mission centers at this time.
    3. The process continues until the support center that provides service to the smallest number of other support centers or has the smallest percentage of its costs consumed by other support centers has allocated its costs. Once these allocations have been completed, the process stops.
- *Reciprocal allocation.* This approach is the most complex way to allocate the cost of services. The reciprocal method uses simultaneous equations to allocate the costs incurred by service centers to other service centers, while also making allocations to mission centers. Since support centers can both issue and receive cost allocations, it is the most accurate of the three methods. Since the calculations can be difficult when there are many support centers, this approach is best implemented with a computer program.

Given the difficulty of using a reciprocal allocation, most health care providers find that the step allocation approach provides a reasonable balance between accuracy and resource consumption.

Step 6. Link Identified Costs to Cost Objects

The final step in the full costing process is to assign the costs apportioned to a mission center to the cost objects produced by it. If the cost objects are all standardized (such as a blood test lab that produces several thousand test results per day), then the easier calculation is to divide the total number of outputs into the total costs of the mission

center. For example, if a blood test lab costs $500,000 to operate each month, and it produces 10,000 tests results during that time, then the cost assigned to each test is $50.

The situation is more involved when a mission center produces a variety of cost object outcomes. For example, a surgery center specializing in joint replacements might deal with hip, knee, shoulder, wrist, or elbow replacements – each of which consumes different costs. In these situations, costs must be accumulated for each individual procedure, which will include a standard hourly rate for the staff involved, which is derived from the total costs assigned to the mission center.

Uses for Full Costing

There are several ways in which a full costing analysis can be used. One is certainly in setting prices. If management wants to set prices based on a markup of costs incurred, then this is a good way to arrive at the baseline cost. In many cases, a health care provider does not have much influence over the prices it is paid by an insurer, but can still use this information to decide whether it is incurring a loss on the services provided. If that is the case, management might decide not to offer the services that result in losses, and instead shift into other services that result in more reasonable insurer payments.

Full costing is also useful for price negotiations for bundles of services to be offered to a managed care plan. In these bundled pricing situations, it might be accepted that some services are loss leaders, but are necessary in order to provide other services that generate profits. If so, a well-designed full costing system will be able to provide a reasonable level of accuracy about the amounts of profits and losses associated with each of the services that the organization offers.

Summary

Health care organizations can be startlingly complex, which (unfortunately) means that a relatively complex method is needed to tease out useful information from the masses of cost data stored in the accounting database. With a full costing system in place, managers can discern the true nature of the costs assigned to cost objects, which gives them more control over price setting and whether to offer some services at all.

Glossary

A

Account. A separate, detailed record about a specific item.

Accounting equation. The concept that the total of all assets equals the total of all liabilities and shareholders' equity.

Accretion expense. An expense arising from an increase in the carrying amount of the liability associated with an asset retirement obligation.

Accrual. A journal entry that is used to recognize revenues and expenses that have been earned or consumed, respectively, and for which the related source documents have not yet been received or generated.

Accrual basis of accounting. The concept of recording revenues when earned and expenses as incurred.

Accumulated depreciation. The sum total of all depreciation expense recognized to date on a depreciable fixed asset.

Allowance for doubtful accounts. A reserve that offsets accounts receivable, containing management's best estimate of the amount of bad debts contained within the current receivable balance.

Amortization. The charging of an intangible asset to expense over time.

Amortization table. A table that states the periodic payments to be made as part of a loan agreement.

Asset retirement obligation. A liability associated with the retirement of a fixed asset.

B

Bank balance. The ending cash balance in an account, as reported by the bank.

Bank reconciliation. An examination of the differences between the ending cash balances reported for a bank account by the bank and the customer.

Blending. When the balances and transactions of a component unit are reported in a manner similar to the balances and transactions of a primary government.

Bond. A fixed obligation to pay that is sold to investors.

Business combination. A transaction in which an acquirer gains control of an acquiree.

C

Capitalization limit. A monetary threshold below which expenditures are charged to expense and above which they are capitalized.

Capitation fee. A fixed amount per person that is paid at regular intervals to a health care provider as compensation for providing health care services during a period of time.

Carrying amount. The original recorded cost of an asset, adjusted for any subsequent depreciation or amortization charges, as well as any impairment write-downs.

Cash basis of accounting. The practice of only recording revenue when cash is received, and recording expenses only when cash has been paid out.

Change in accounting estimate. A change that adjusts the carrying amount of an asset or liability, or the subsequent accounting for it.

Charity care. Health care services provided to a patient who is unable to pay.

Conduit debt security. A bond or similar instrument issued by a government entity in order to provide financing to a third party that is not part of the issuing government. The funding recipient is responsible for any future financial reporting requirements.

Conduit financing. An arrangement in which a government entity serves as a conduit for the flow of funds to a health care entity.

Contingency. An uncertain situation that will be resolved in the future, generating a possible gain or loss.

Contract. An agreement between at least two parties that creates enforceable obligations and rights.

Contribution. An unconditional and voluntary, nonreciprocal transfer of assets by a party that is not the owner.

Control. The ability to directly or indirectly determine the direction of another entity.

Control account. The account in the general ledger where summarized information from a subsidiary ledger is stored.

Cost center. A business unit that is only responsible for the costs that it incurs.

Cost object. Any item for which costs are compiled.

Coupon bond. A bond with interest coupons, which the bond holder sends to the issuing entity or its paying agent on the dates when interest payments are due.

Current liability. An obligation that must be settled within one year.

D

Debt. An amount owed for funds borrowed.

Depreciation. The gradual charging to expense of an asset's cost over its expected useful life.

Diagnosis-related group. A classification system for patients that groups patients who are related medically in regard to their diagnosis, age, or other criteria.

Direct cost. A cost that is totally traceable to a specific cost center.

Direct write-off method. When bad debts are charged to expense only when individual invoices are clearly identifiable as not being collectible.

Double entry accounting. A record keeping system in which every transaction is recorded in at least two accounts.

E

Economic resources measurement focus. An accounting approach focusing on whether a fund is economically better off because of transactions occurring within the fiscal period being reported.

Employee. A person who provides services to an employer in accordance with the legal definition of an employee.

Employer. A person or entity that retains the services of individuals.

Enterprise fund. A fund that is used to account for any activity for which external users are charged a fee for goods and services.

Equity transaction. A shifting of resources from one not-for-profit entity to another, with the issuing entity receiving an ongoing economic interest in the assets held by the recipient.

Equity transfer. A shifting of resources from one not-for-profit entity to another with no expectation of repayment, where one entity controls the other or both entities are under common control.

Expenditure. A payment or the incurrence of a liability by an entity.

Experience rating. A method used by an insurer to determine the pricing of insurance for a business, based on the history of prior claims made by the business.

F

FICA tax. A tax paid by employees and matched by the employer up to a certain wage limit, which is used to fund the federal social security system.

First in, first out. A method of inventory valuation that assumes that the first goods purchased are the first ones sold.

Fixed asset. An expenditure that generates economic benefits over a long period of time. Also known as property, plant, and equipment.

Full costing. A cost accounting technique that considers all the costs of producing a single unit of a product.

Fund. An accounting entity with a self-balancing set of accounts that is used to record financial resources and liabilities, as well as operating activities.

G

Garnishment. The withholding of a specified amount from a person's wages in order to satisfy a legal claim or an obligation to a creditor.

General ledger. The master set of all accounts, in which are stored all of the business transactions that have been entered into the accounts.

Gross earnings. The total amount of an employee's earnings, including regular and overtime pay, and before any deductions.

Gross profit method. A method used to estimate the amount of ending inventory, based on the cost of goods available for sale, the expected gross profit percentage, and the sales in the period.

H

Health maintenance organization. A medical care entity that provides defined health care services to its members in exchange for fixed, periodic premiums that are paid in advance.

I

Impairment. When the carrying amount of a fixed asset exceeds its fair value. The amount of the impairment is the difference between the two values.

Indirect cost. A cost that is consumed by multiple cost centers.

Inherent contribution. A contribution resulting from a voluntary transfer of assets or the performance of services in exchange for either no assets or assets of substantially lower value.

Intangible asset. An identifiable, non-monetary asset that has no physical substance.

J

Journal entry. A formal accounting entry used to identify a business transaction. The entry itemizes accounts that are debited and credited, and should include a description of the reason for the entry.

L

Last in, first out. A method of inventory valuation that assumes that the last goods purchased are the first ones sold.

Lead interest. The right to receive the benefit of assets during the term of a split-interest agreement.

Ledger. A book or database in which double entry accounting transactions are stored or summarized.

Lockbox network. A number of bank lockboxes that channel payor payments into a single bank account.

M

Mission center. An area of responsibility that directly supports the mission of an organization.

N

Net pay. The amount that an employee is paid after all taxes and other deductions have been withheld from his or her pay.

Net position. The difference between all elements in a statement of financial position.

Nonreciprocal transfer. The transfer of asset ownership without any expectation of payment.

Not-for-profit entity. An organization that receives significant contributions, does not intend to generate profits, and which does not have ownership interests.

O

Overtime. A premium wage paid that is calculated as 1 ½ times the regular wage rate, multiplied by those hours classified as overtime.

P

Payroll register. A report that shows the earnings, deductions, taxes, and net pay of each employee during a pay period.

Performance indicator. A measure that reports the results of operations for a not-for-profit health care entity. It is analogous to the income from continuing operations for a for-profit entity.

Performance obligation. A contractual obligation to transfer a good or service to a customer.

Periodic fees. Service charges that are billed to residents, usually on a monthly basis for services provided by a retirement community that are not covered by advance fees.

Periodic inventory system. An inventory tracking system that only updates the ending inventory balance when there is a physical inventory count.

Perpetual inventory system. An inventory tracking system that continually updates the ending inventory balance.

Pledge. A promise to give a not-for-profit entity a contribution in the future.

Posting. The aggregation of financial transactions from where they are stored in subsidiary ledgers, and the transfer of this information into the general ledger.

Prepaid health care plan. A plan in which the provider receives prepayments based on either a per-enrollee amount or a fixed sum. Examples of these plans are eye care plans, dental care plans, and health maintenance organizations. In this situation, the provider takes on the financial risk of delivering health care.

Prospective rate setting. The use of pre-set payment rates prior to the delivery of health care services, with rates usually being set for a one-year period.

R

Remainder interest. The right to receive any remaining benefits of the assets in a split-interest agreement after the term of the agreement expires.

Remittance advice. A document that accompanies a payment, and which gives the details of the payment being made.

Remote deposit capture. A combination of a check scanner and software that routes check images to a depository institution.

Retrospective rate setting. The use of an interim payment rate during a rate period, followed by a final settlement that is based on regulations or contractual agreements.

Revenue. An asset enhancement or liability settlement caused by the delivery of goods or services that comprise an entity's central operations.

S

Sale and leaseback. An arrangement in which a seller transfers an asset to a buyer and then leases the asset back.

Salvage value. The estimated amount that an organization would currently obtain upon the disposal of a fixed asset at the end of its estimated useful life. Also known as *residual value.*

Shift differential. Extra pay earned by employees who work a less than desirable shift, such as the evening, night, or weekend shifts.

Special purpose entity. A legal entity created to fulfill a specific objective.

Statement of net position. A balance sheet used by a government or not-for-profit entity.

Step allocation. A cost allocation method that allocates the cost of services provided by one support center to another.

Stock split. A situation in which more than 20% to 25% of the current shares outstanding are issued to existing shareholders.

Stop-loss insurance. An arrangement in which an insurer agrees to indemnify a health care provider for costs incurred by the provider's members.

Subjective acceleration clause. A provision in a debt agreement, stating that the creditor may accelerate the maturity date of the obligation under conditions that cannot be objectively determined.

Subsidiary ledger. A ledger designed for the storage of specific types of accounting transactions.

Support center. An area of responsibility that supports an organization's mission centers.

T

Tax deposit. Tax payments made by an employer to the government.

Transaction. A business event that has a monetary impact.

Trial balance. A report containing the ending balances of all accounts in the general ledger.

U

Unrestricted net assets. That part of the net assets of a not-for-profit entity that are not restricted by donor-imposed stipulations.

Useful life. The estimated lifespan of a depreciable fixed asset, during which it can be expected to contribute to company operations.

W

Withholding. A portion of an employee's wages that an employer holds back and then forwards to the government as partial payment for the taxes owed by the employee.

Index

Printed in Great Britain
by Amazon

41772205R00139